Praise for
I Loved You More

∽✑∾

"Hats off to Regina Rossi Valentine! Coparenting is a tough undertaking, even when your compatriot is a healthy, well-adjusted human. Coparenting with a narcissist is a horse of a different color. A heartfelt, fierce, and formidable endeavor, Regina Rossi Valentine shares her raw and beautiful exposé with a boldly elegant voice. *I Loved You More* captures the essence of the suffering and the sturdiness that lies at the heart of the parent-child connection, offering the reader an empathically resonant appreciation of a mother's abiding love as she navigates the craggy terrain of narcissistic abuse with heartache, courage, and commitment. This book is a must-have for your resource library!"

—Wendy Behary, Author/Expert
Disarming the Narcissist

"Regina, thank you for sharing your story with me. I'm so blown away by your bravery and resilience. I'm so grateful you are willing to share this story as I know without a doubt it will encourage so many people on this journey. It is so full of hope! Big hugs and congratulations on this amazing undertaking. This book shows so many ways that narcissism presents itself in both covert and overt ways. You highlighted *gaslighting*, which is something that can be very nuanced at times, and you highlighted the *red flags*. I hope this will encourage other people to discern and listen to their instincts and avoid all that you had to go through. I especially loved the letters you wrote to your son. This is something I encourage my clients to do when they are in similar situations. He is so lucky that he has this documentation and words of love from you to him.

"This is a must-read if you or anyone you love has been impacted by a partner with narcissistic features. It cannot be overstated that this is one of the most difficult personality disorders to treat in terms of someone truly changing. This book is a cautionary tale of what it can look like to be in a relationship with someone like this. Regina's willingness to be raw, honest, and open about the struggle that she and her son went through is beyond brave. As a marriage and family therapist, I want my clients going through this to have this book in their hands to give them hope, to be patient, to trust the process, and that the self-sacrifice will be well worth it.

"This book should be in every marriage and family therapist's office. Clients need to have a book of hope in their hands because currently there is nothing like this on the market."

—Tanya Gore, MA, MFT

"I love what I have read. I can feel your pain. I see many parents who have walked in your shoes. Your book is especially insightful to me because the majority of my law practice is guardian ad litem work. I think this book is a must read for any GAL. It provides your perspective of what it is like to deal with a narcissist parent. There is no co-parenting with someone like that.

"Your book is also a must read for any parent fighting against a narcissistic parent for custody of their child. Your book is inspirational in that, with perseverance, parents can eventually save their children. Your book allowed me to feel your struggle to save your son. I will be much more careful as a GAL to try and really get to know the underlying currents of a family dynamic when I am presented with your type of situation in the future. Congratulations! Well done!"

—Lisa Broccoletti, Attorney, Guardian Ad Litem

"I am certain that this adventure has been a roller-coaster ride. Your raw emotion emanates from each page. At times I felt sad and angry, and I have no doubt your words painted images that evoked that feeling. When I used to teach expository writing, one of the strongest vehicles one could use was the 'picture frame model.' The strongest tool of a writer is the ability to paint a picture that causes the reader to feel and act. I think you have done that.

"In all, I have no doubt that this is and has been a cathartic experience. I think my favorite part was when you came out the other side and praised your relationship with Rob. That reassures the reader that there is light at the end of the tunnel. Personally, I'm heartened that your relationship with Gabriel has not only survived but also grown richer and deeper as he saw his own truth. It seems that your sacrifice has been validated as he has elected to nurture that relationship on his own."

—Robert Shirley, Former Supervisor of Secondary English
Curriculum and Instruction

"Your steadfast resolve is impressive. It continues to be important to give voice to the deafening silence of victimization. The book demonstrates the 'long game' required to survive and persevere through the effects of being bound to someone with a personality disorder. A favorite part was learning about how your personal story related to your current circumstances and any points in which that self-reflection was authentic and meaningful. Your courage is exemplified by your willingness to share your story with transparency and detail, laying your soul bare."

—Dr. Anne Michalek,
Old Dominion University, Associate Professor

"You got into the real gut of the reason why you wrote this book from the very first sentence. I immediately felt like I was part of this journey with you. YOU are your child's advocate. Trust your gut. Mother's intuition is real. I have preached this to my own daughters for years. In other words, *Hell no! Not THIS woman!* The letters to Gabriel are a treasure and are your conduit to the readers. Mothers relate to this journaling and writing to your child. Many never get past the first two or three entries. Bravo to you, and how perfect to also create a tangible timeline for you for this project. Great job on the book, but much more important is that you've created an outlet, a pipeline for women who need a roadmap to tapping into their lost confidence."

—Linda Wilder Dyer,
Author, Musician, Non-Profit Administrator

"*I Loved You More* is a true account of what it's like living and raising a child with a narcissistic husband. This story will grab ahold of you. Your heart will sink to your stomach at times but then jump for joy at others. In this book many of Regina's readers will find themselves relating to her in one way or another, which is a great strength as a writer in terms of connecting to her audience. This is a must-read for individuals who have lived through abuse like this or are going through it right now. It eventually becomes a feel-good story for those who have made it through to the other side and a bit of a guide or inspiration for those who are in the fight right now."

—Nena Myers, Master Firefighter/Medic

"This is a beautifully told story—complete with heartfelt journal entries throughout the years—of one mother's journey to raise her son well in spite of seemingly insurmountable hurdles and heartache along the way. With her faith, determination, and perseverance, she navigates the murky waters of divorce, accomplishes her mission, and finds her self-worth, along with new love.

"Although not the intended audience, I would highly recommend this book to singles also. Regina's story might help them detect major red flags while they look past romantic feelings to gain knowledge and use discernment when considering a prospective mate."

—Sandra Holcombe, MFA, MA, Writer/Editor

I loved You More

I Loved You More

Choosing My Child Over My Narcissistic Ex

REGINA ROSSI VALENTINE

Valentine
BOOKS

Copyright © 2021 by Regina Rossi Valentine
All rights reserved.
Published by Valentine Books

No part of this book may be reproduced in any manner without written permission except in the case of brief quotations embodied in critical articles and reviews.

I Loved You More is a work of nonfiction. Some names and identifying details have been changed.

Although the author and publisher have made every effort to ensure that the information in this book was correct at press time, the author and publisher do not assume and hereby disclaim any liability to any party for any loss, damage, or disruption caused by errors or omissions, whether such errors or omissions result from negligence, accident, or any other cause. Forms and agreements are included for your information only.

For information about special discounts for bulk purchases or author interviews, appearances, and speaking engagements please contact:

Web: www.ILovedYouMore.com
Email: info@ILovedYouMore.com

First Edition

Written with the help of; cover, jacket, and book design by Rodney Miles, www.RodneyMiles.com
Edited by Kevin Miller, www.KevinMillerxi.com
Author Photo © Stacey Pryce, Cute E's Photography

*For my son because I always have and
I always will love you more.*

"You may encounter many defeats, but you must not be defeated. In fact, it may be necessary to encounter the defeats, so you can know who you are, what you can rise from, how you can still come out of it."

—*Maya Angelou*

Author's Note

To write this book, I relied on over twenty-two years' worth of notes, journals, letters to my son, and documentation kept for the purpose of fighting my court battles. I also consulted with several of the people mentioned in this book and called upon my own memories of these events and this period of my life. I have changed the names of most but not all individuals in this book, and in some cases modified identifying details to preserve anonymity. There are no composite characters or events in this book. Excerpts from the letters to my son have not been altered in any way except for punctuation and are otherwise exactly as they were written to him.

Contents

Author's Note xiv
Contents xv
Preface xix
Prologue xxiii

PART 1 1
Chapter 1 Colby 2
Chapter 2 Mom & Dad 7
Chapter 3 Newlyweds 14
Chapter 4 Gabriel 19
Chapter 5 Words 25
Chapter 6 Therapy 32
Chapter 7 Letters 39

PART 2 45
Chapter 8 Agreements 46
Chapter 9 Records 53
Chapter 10 Perils 59
Chapter 11 Dark Clouds 68
Chapter 12 Rough Seas 81
Chapter 13 Money 90
Chapter 14 Breaking Heart 93
Chapter 15 SNAFU 101

PART 3 113
Chapter 16 Signs of War 114
Chapter 17 Rene 123
Chapter 18 Throw Me A Rope 131
Chapter 19 Family 137
Chapter 20 Grooming 146
Chapter 21 Football 155

PART 4 167
Chapter 22 Revelations 168
Chapter 23 The Choice 173
Chapter 24 Dreams & Jobs 182
Chapter 25 Cycles 188
Chapter 26 Food & Court 197
Chapter 27 Pre-Trial 209
Chapter 28 October 215

PART 5 231
Chapter 29 Debacles 232
Chapter 30 Precarious 242
Chapter 31 Never Quit 248
Chapter 32 Prepared 258
Chapter 33 Miracles 266
Chapter 34 Beginnings 275
Chapter 35 My Turn 280

PART 6 289
Chapter 36 Fans 290
Chapter 37 Celebrations 296
Chapter 38 College or Bust 301
Chapter 39 Dad.. 304
Chapter 40 Epiphanies 307

Epilogue 313
Acknowledgements 327
About the Author 330

Preface

WHEN WE ARE ATTACKED, our instinct is to fight back. When your five-year-old child looks at you and says, "Mommy, sometimes Daddy says things about you that upset me," you know you're in for the fight of your life.

I decided early on to love my son, Gabriel, more than I hated Colby, Gabe's father and now my ex-husband. With that came a commitment that I would not speak ill of Colby in front of Gabe because it would serve no purpose other than to hurt my son. That proved to be one of the most difficult decisions of my life.

Words have power. They can be weapons or gifts. Good or bad, words impact others, and children are no exception. Our children watch us more than they listen to us, so our actions and reactions make an imprint on their brains that affect their future behavior.

"Hate" is a powerful word. I struggled with using it in the title or even the text of this book. But if we are honest with ourselves, at some point we all experience hate, whether for a bad situation, another human being, or anything at all. After what I've lived through, *hate* is exactly what I felt at times. It was powerful, and it drove me to do anything and everything to protect my precious child from what was happening in our lives. *How dare you so deeply hurt my son—our son—in that way! Our son is not a weapon. He is not to blame. He is innocent, and your shortcomings will not be allowed in his world if I have anything to say about it.* The claws came out. Mother bear was in fight mode. But through it all, my son's well-being was first and foremost, no matter the cost.

With that came the challenge of how I was going to get through a nasty divorce without putting Gabriel in the middle. It meant biting my tongue at every turn and trying to take the high road for his sake. But I did falter, and a few times I lost my cool and directed my frustrations with Colby at my son, immediately feeling horrible. Without hesitation I sincerely apologized, told Gabriel that what I had done was wrong, that I was sorry I had hurt him, and that I would try never to do it again. I asked him to forgive me even though one of those times he was too young to understand fully what forgiveness meant. Later I learned in therapy that we all have our breaking point and doing what I did would teach him that I was human, imperfect, and how to try and recover appropriately from an indiscretion.

Decades later as I started to write this book, I would often stop and pray. I'd ask God to direct this journey and bless it with honesty, so our story would encourage other parents to choose love for their children over hate for an ex.

Gabe was just one and a half years old when Colby and I split. I initiated the separation and ultimately the divorce for many reasons. First of all, what we shared was not love, and it certainly was not what I wanted my child to grow up thinking love between two people was. At that time I had never heard the term "narcissist," and I didn't really know what a sociopath was. I just knew that how I was being treated was abusive, but I didn't have a name for it. Up until then I didn't have a need to know. At the time the Internet was in its infancy, and self-help talk shows didn't really exist like they do today. But in the first three years of our marriage, I got quite an education in narcissism and sociopathy. In time I also began to question myself and my ability to read people.

I Loved You More

Have you ever ignored the "red flags" in a relationship? Me? Guilty as charged. Many such flags showed up before I walked down the aisle to that union with the man who would become my archenemy. I beat myself up for years for being so wrong about who I chose to marry and have children with. I thought I had a great foundation, having come from a big, solid Christian family. I had lived on my own since I was nineteen, got married at age twenty-seven, and prior to marriage, I had traveled the world in my career, meeting all kinds of people. I was worldly—or so I thought. As it turned out, I was naïve and far too trusting. My sister, ten years my senior, knew this about me, but it took many more years for me to figure it out for myself.

God does not speak to me in an audible voice, but I have had three instances (which I describe in this book) where I had an overwhelming feeling that God wanted me to do something. What I do not mention in the pages to follow is that about four years ago, I had a fourth such experience. I was driving and suddenly felt very strongly that I was supposed to write this book to help other people on their journey to put their children first, love their children more than they hated their ex, and not to put their children in the middle. I just didn't know how it was going to happen. I had never written a book before.

It took me two years to begin this journey. It involved a lot of crying because I had to relive everything I survived. I found an editor to help me, and through our research we found there is nothing quite like this book on the market, taken from such a massive amount of real time documentation. Many books have been written about narcissism and relationships, most of which are written by professionals. Along the way, I've found beta readers, including Wendy Behary, a successful author who wrote the book *Disarming the Narcissist,* and I have had our guardian ad litem, attorneys, and psychologists provide feedback before we released this book because I wanted to make sure we released something useful, something to help other people know there is a light at the end of the tunnel, a source of hope.

Regina Rossi Valentine

Do I regret this journey? No. It has made me who I am today, and today I like and respect the person in the mirror. It has also made Gabriel the awesome man he has become, and he continues to evolve. We are stronger for what we've been through. I can see that with time, Gabriel will continue to gain clarity about all that transpired, all that I desperately tried to protect him from. He has already started to question, resolve, and decide. God willing, if he chooses, he will have a loving family of his own one day, something I could not give him.

Regina Rossi Valentine
April 3, 2018
Salvo, NC

Prologue

WE WERE IN COURT again. And *wow,* what a day it turned out to be. So emotional. So difficult. Constantly praying for wisdom for me, my attorney, Saul Marshall, Judge Wallace, and Mr. Garrison, the guardian ad litem.[1] For years I prayed that Judge Wallace would have the wisdom of Solomon to rule on what only God knew were the true intentions of our hearts when it came to what was right and best for Gabriel. I resolved to trust God and His time, not mine. But it was so darn hard!

We went into court that day knowing full well that Mr. Garrison would recommend that Gabe go live with his dad. It was crushing and terrifying to think my son might be lost to me forever. Before we entered the courtroom, Mr. Garrison explained to my attorney, Saul, "He is almost thirteen, intelligent, articulate, and knows what he wants. He keeps saying he wants to live with his dad."

I prayed harder than ever. Just before midnight, at 11:45 p.m., the guardian ad litem took the stand and said, "Your Honor, I am about to do something I have never done in my entire career."

The time between that and his next words seemed like an eternity.

---

[1] A guardian ad litem (GAL) is often appointed in cases involving underage children to represent the children's interests in court.

REGINA ROSSI VALENTINE

PART 1

"The only way to make sense out of change is to plunge into it, move with it, and join the dance."

—Alan Watts

Chapter 1

COLBY

1994

IT WAS NEW YEAR'S DAY, and we were getting ready to host our first party as Mr. and Mrs. Colby Baxter, husband and wife. In two hours we would have an apartment filled with about twenty guests. I was twenty-seven years old. Colby was thirty-one and going to law school in Delaware. We had just moved there, and I had moved away from my family and friends in Virginia. Because I had been a performer on cruise ships the last five years, most of my friends were in other places, but my new supervisor and his family were coming from Pennsylvania, and Colby's parents were coming from Maryland, both an hour away.

Colby was so excited. It was his party. He would have his court of people, some friends he had made at law school. But he did nothing to help get ready. We were just six months into our marriage, and we started arguing. I'm tall, but Colby is taller, and he kept blocking me each time I tried to get around—to get away—from him. Then he grabbed my shoulders. He put his face so close to mine that I saw his nostrils flare and felt his hot breath. His eyes bulged and burned at me. He clenched his jaw. He was furious. *He was a stranger.*

He shook me. In the blur, he raised a fist high in the air, and my life flashed before my eyes. I raised my left hand to block his fist and with my right had pushed him away. I leaped for my purse and keys and ran out the door. I did not know where I was going or what I was going to do; I just needed to get away from him.

My hands shaking, I unlocked the car and jumped in. With a glance back at the apartment, the tires chirped, and I roared down the street, shaking and dizzy with fear, the car swerving.

"Oh my God!" I shrieked. "Who or what have I married?" Colby scared the living daylights out of me. I had married someone I did not know.

Still shaking, I finally became aware of my speed and slowed down, pulling over as I tried to regain control of myself and grasp what had just happened.

Cell phones were still new then, but I had one. It rang. I knew it was Colby. I looked at my purse, which held the phone, and then looked away, through the windshield, down the street. Houses, sidewalks, the world around me was quiet, especially when the phone stopped ringing. I heard myself breathing rapidly. The phone buzzed again. And again and again. When it stopped, I savored the quiet while it lasted.

My phone buzzed again. I jerked it out of my purse, turned it off, and put it in my lap. *Dear God, help me. Who is this person I married? He just tried to assault me.*

I was so scared.

What kind of mess have I gotten myself into?

I brought the sunshade down and flipped the mirror on it open and took inventory of myself. I was pale, wide-eyed, and still shaking, but I recognized myself, and that helped. I have green eyes, one of them lazy and legally blind, and massively curly, long, dark hair. I was in great shape, which reassured me. I blinked, took a breath, and composed myself. For whatever reason, when something like this happened to me, I needed to reassure myself that it was all real and that I was still present.

Colby and I had argued before, but he had never gone mad like that, and he had never tried to hit me. During our engagement Colby and I had a huge fight over our wedding registry. He seemed far too controlling in the selections. Colby had been married before, but for me this was my dream come true, to plan my wedding and select the registry items. Traditionally, couples do this together, so we discussed our ideas. My mother also took me shopping and gave me suggestions on things I had not thought of, which was very helpful. But when it came time to choose, Colby started a fight over our sterling-silver pattern, an important part of a registry back then. He wanted things very ornate. The china he liked had a black-and-gold band around the edges and was super expensive, appropriately named, "Opulence." I liked a more subtle, elegant china. I found a set in ivory with a delicate lace pattern around the edges, which happened to be far less expensive. It was like my mother's china—white with a soft Wedgewood Blue band with a delicate lace pattern. Simple, elegant. The sterling silver he liked was called Grand Baroque. To me it was hideous, bulky. But all Colby seemed to care about were appearances, so everything he acquired seemed designed to give the impression that we had money.

We were in his apartment discussing our registry when he blew a gasket.

"I like my mother's sterling silver," I said.

"I'm sick of you talking about what your mother has, of you wanting the same as your mother!" he shouted. "I gave in on the crystal, and I am *not* giving in on the sterling!"

Why was this such a huge issue? I didn't make the connection at the time, but he had issues with my mother, even though she treated him like gold. In fact, a family joke was that she seemed more interested in making dishes Colby liked for family gatherings than what my siblings and I liked. She always seemed to want to impress him, so what was his beef with her? In time I realized they were both controlling, so their personalities didn't mesh very well. I just didn't figure that out until much later, after the wedding.

While arguing over the silver, I got so upset I took off my engagement ring and threw it at him. He began to cry and beg me for forgiveness. I fell for it—hook, line, and sinker. It was many years before I finally realized these were all signs of a narcissistic personality. In the end, we agreed to pick a completely different sterling-silver pattern, one not so ornate and one that was *not* my mother's pattern. We settled on Old Master by Towle. Thankfully, it was a classic pattern and easy to sell even years after the divorce. I should have paid attention to that red flag, but I chose to ignore it. I let his tears and begging suck me right back in. That pattern began to repeat, and get worse.

These thoughts seemed to calm me down, at least a bit. I looked at the phone in my lap and remembered I had turned it off. As it sat there, unmoving and silent in my lap, I remembered something Colby had said to me before. He told me his ex-wife was in an abusive marriage before he met her. *Maybe that was also a lie, and he was the abuser*, I thought. A million things were running through my head, but the thought that I had an apartment full of guests coming over to celebrate the New Year started to block out everything else. What was I going to do? It seemed I had no choice; I had to go back there.

My senses were on fire. I heard the gentle crush of stones as I slowly rolled the car back into the spot I had just screeched out of. I watched the door to the apartment as, keys in hand, I got out of the car and walked back into my new home. Ready for anything and scared for my life, I found Colby in the kitchen, phone to his ear. He looked at me and then hung the phone on the wall. There were a million things in his eyes—fear, anger, doubt, intensity. He opened his mouth to speak, but before he could, I started yelling.

"I swear to God, if you ever lay a fucking hand on me again, I will walk out that door and never come back!"

Such episodes were always followed up with him crying and begging for forgiveness. As he did so there in that kitchen, with me holding him, I thought of the tall, thin, blond-haired, blue-eyed man I had met two years earlier. I thought he was handsome. Then I thought about how I'd since discovered he always chewed his fingernails and had gross, fungus-infected toenails.

My new supervisor, Don, at the mortgage company where I worked, came to our apartment that day, told me later that his first impression of Colby was how he dressed—sunglasses on the top of his head and a cardigan sweater tied around his shoulders. It was very preppy, which was not really Colby but someone trying to be like the other, younger law school students. Don said he did not get a good vibe from Colby at all and that he could tell I wasn't happy. I wish he'd told me.

Colby didn't touch me again. The abuse became emotional, verbal, and psychological. Colby's physical outbursts were redirected to punching holes in walls or busting into the locked bedroom where I was and wrenching off the doorframe to do so. Once again after each of these episodes came the crying and begging for forgiveness. In our new marriage, I was about to cry as well—a lot.

Chapter 2

Mom & Dad

1966–1988

IN HER YOUNGER DAYS, MY MOTHER had strikingly beautiful, movie-star looks, even as short as she was, at around five feet four inches. She had porcelain-white skin, catlike green eyes, and thick, wavy dark brown hair. She was Miss Norfolk and first runner-up in the Miss Virginia pageant, winning the talent competition. She has always been thin. It's no wonder my dad fell for her. She also had a lovely lyric soprano voice back then. My dad was a very handsome guy in his younger days, standing five feet eleven inches tall and slim with jet-black hair. He had kind, gentle, brown eyes and a smile that lit up the room. He also had an amazing tenor voice, was a full opera scholarship student at Julliard and sang with the Buffalo Philharmonic and others.

Mom taught my siblings and I how to cook once we were tall enough to reach the stove. We're all great cooks today, and I believe we all still enjoy cooking. She taught us how to take a recipe and make it our own, tweaking and adding. When it came to nutrition, she was ahead of the game, always making meals that included a salad as well as protein, starch, and a green vegetable. She also taught me the importance of dressing nicely, taking care of my skin, and the value of staying physically active.

While my parents did a lot of entertaining when we were growing up, Mom was not fun to be around during prep, with my siblings and me as her helpers. She wasn't very organized, and she was often stressed out, so she wasn't very pleasant, and she definitely was *not* a clean cook. Pots and pans were everywhere after any given meal, and, of course, my siblings and I had to do the washing and cleaning up. She was like a drill sergeant. As a result, I am super organized and make lists of what to do up to two weeks in advance of a dinner party or family gathering. I like to enjoy the gathering, so I do as much in advance as possible. I also clean as I go because I remember having to dig dirty plates, pots, pans, and utensils out of the sink just so I could fill it with soapy water before adding all those things back in to clean them.

My parents were huge advocates of us being allowed to try anything we showed an interest in, whether it was sports, music, or something else. In that respect, it exposed us to many things. I was a star athlete when I was younger, earning the title of MVP in middle school basketball as a first-string point guard. I ran track, played softball, and tackled synchronized swimming. I felt like I could be a tough, sweaty, taunting athlete on the court or field and then turn around, put on a dress, and sing a beautiful song.

When I was little and would imitate my brother Richard's piano playing (I did it by ear), my mother told me, "It's time for you to get lessons." Money was tight with my brother, Michael, in private college and Richard and I in private Catholic school, so my oldest brother, Danny, offered to pay for my lessons.

Growing up at the oceanfront in Virginia as a young girl, my mother passed on her love of the ocean and swimming to all of us, despite our dad's fear of the water. However, Dad loved surf-cast fishing in the ocean and inspired my love of fishing as a result, but he only went out until he was knee deep. My maternal grandmother taught swimming lessons to most of us—her *forty* grandkids. She had the patience of a saint!

Last year my lifelong girlfriend, Laura, and I were out to lunch celebrating her birthday, and I was telling her about something my mother had recently done to annoy and hurt me.

"Well, your mom has never been nice to you, even when we were growing up," she said.

I was shocked at her remark. "Mom was always on her best behavior around our friends."

"Regina," she replied, "just because you saw it as her best behavior, those of us whose parents didn't treat us that way could see the difference, and she was mean to you."

I'm very protective of my father because anybody you meet, even Laura, will tell you he was a saint. But when I was fifteen, something horrible happened, and it came up in that conversation with her.

"I remember that," she said. "I never knew what happened afterwards, but I remember that. Regina, your dad had to know."

"Laura," I said, "I'm the fifth child, and I was fifteen years old. Of course he knew something *by then*, which is why he did what he did in that situation. I just don't think he knew the magnitude of how bad it was with my mom."

In 1981 when I was fifteen, there was a thespian meeting after school. Back then there were no cell phones, of course, just a payphone at school, and I called my mom.

"Who's giving you a ride home?" she asked.

"Barbara," I said. She was Laura's sister. "Barbara's driving me home."

"OK. Well, if Barbara can't take you home, call me, and I'll come pick you up."

"OK," I replied.

I went to the meeting. It turned out Barbara didn't go to the meeting, but another girl who was an approved person for me to ride with, Kim, was there. Not wanting to bother my mom, I figured Kim could take me home. She had to go right by my house anyway.

When I got home, my mother wasn't there. After a while, when she arrived home, she was displaying very intimidating body language, glaring at me. "So, who drove you home today?" she asked snidely.

Fear shot through my body, and my heart began to race. *Oh shit,* I thought. *I'm going to get in trouble for not calling her.* Even though I had ridden home with somebody who was OK, fear caused me to back away from her—and lie. "Barbara," I said as calmly as I could.

"You're lying," Mom said, "and I've been waiting to catch you in a lie. Wait till your father gets home!"

Decades later I told my brother, Michael, about this. "Oh my God!" he said. "She set you up. She went to the school. That's how she knew. She drove to the school to see who drove you home. She was spying on you!"

I was a good kid. I didn't do anything—I didn't drink, smoke, or curse. I got teased all the time in eighth grade for being "square" and a "Miss Goody Two Shoes." I wasn't a bad kid, but my mother made me feel like I was, and that put the fear of God in me.

When my dad came home, he executed my punishment, even though I cried and begged him not to do it.

"Please, Dad, don't!" I sobbed as the bar of soap scraped across my teeth.

It was the first and only time in my life that my dad ever disciplined me that way, whereas Mom did that all the time. What he did wasn't anything compared to what I endured from my mom, so it was more of an emotional devastation for me. I adored my dad. My mother was verbally, emotionally, and physically abusive to us. She came from a generation where corporal punishment was commonplace. So, my siblings and I were raised with corporal punishment executed by her. When I was very young, I decided I will never do that to my children. I was going to break the cycle.

The abuse was bad. My siblings and I have talked about how she did it when our dad wasn't home. She did a lot of things when he wasn't home, so I believed he didn't really know. When she would beat us with a belt, she would chase us, and we would run from her.

I vividly remember running up the stairs to get away from her and lock myself in the bathroom, but she grabbed my ankle and dragged me back down the stairs. If I did lock myself in the bathroom, she would threaten me and scream. "If you don't come out, it'll be twice as bad!" One time she even broke a wooden spoon on my buttocks while hitting me with it. It was horrible. Sometimes the beatings would yield welts that lasted for days. The irony is, I'm the youngest of five children. The oldest three are close in age, being a year or so apart. Three years went by before they had my fourth sibling and older brother, Richard. Then after four years they had me. I used to hear all the time from my oldest three siblings how I had it easy, how I was the spoiled baby. *Holy shit!* I'd think. *If I had it easy, what the hell did they go through?*

For most of my teenage years and into my early twenties, I had a horrific recurring nightmare. Our house was on fire, and I was at the top of the stairs trying to get down. My father was at the bottom of the stairs trying to help me, but in between us were two Dobermans, fiercely snarling at me with such ferocity that I froze, unable to move. I was crying hysterically, begging my dad to help me, but I couldn't get to him. I never knew why I kept having that nightmare until the subject recently came up while watching a TV drama, and I shared the nightmare with Rob, my husband. Of course, that prompted me to Google it. I learned that recurring nightmares are common after an accident, injury, physical abuse, or other traumatic events.

"That was about your mom," Rob said when I told him what I had learned. "She was the Dobermans."

It wasn't until about four years ago that my siblings and I started swapping stories about a year before our sister passed away. I was having lunch one day with my brother, Michael, the middle child, who has his PhD in education administration and a master's degree in English.

"Michael, Mom used to say some of the most hateful things to me until I was twenty-two years old," I said. "I thought something was mentally wrong with me. When she would get angry with me—like I did something bad or wrong or got in trouble—she would yell at me and she would tell me I had the devil in me. She said that to me repeatedly for many years."

"She often told me I was pathetic and would never amount to anything," Michael replied, "as well as many other horrible things. She also lied to Dad once and accused me of hitting her, so she could keep me from going out that night with my friends. I would never hit my mother. What mother does that?"

My mother had a way of always reducing me to tears. Then she would psychologically and emotionally abuse me with that and sneer. "Look at you," she'd say. "You're such a baby. You cry at everything. You're so sensitive." She did it in such a nasty way all the time that I can still hear it in my head to this day. I really thought something was wrong with me when I would get upset and cry so easily.

I have never had a loving, close relationship with my mother, and yet I yearned for it my whole life—until I no longer did. I came to accept that it would never happen. Thankfully I have friends who have wonderful relationships with their moms, so I live vicariously through them. Sadly, I just can't relate.

I Loved You More

"You never know what someone is dealing with behind closed doors. You only know what you see or what you think you see."
—Mackenzie Phillips

Chapter 3

NEWLYWEDS

1991–1994

IN THE SUMMER OF 1994, about a year into our marriage, it was a gorgeous, balmy evening, and we were at the Baltimore Inner Harbor at a restaurant called the Rusty Scupper with a group of Colby's friends. The sun sparkled on the water, and beautiful boats were all around us as introductions were made, and I met a group of Colby's friends for the first time. Everyone was getting along, reminiscing about the good old days as they toasted one another. We were finishing up our entrees and considering dessert. While almost everyone was having a grand time, Colby was complaining about the service throughout the meal, making us all uncomfortable. When my dessert coffee showed up with something floating in it (probably a coffee ground), Colby made a scene.

"There's a foreign object in my wife's coffee that could make her sick!" he shouted. He demanded to speak to the manager, posthaste. When the manager came to the table, he immediately apologized and said they would get me a fresh cup of coffee, which the waiter had already offered to do.

Colby stood up and got in the manager's face and barked, "Not good enough! Since no one knows what's in her coffee, and it could be some kind of bug carrying an infectious disease, everyone's dinner needs to be comped!"

Oh dear God. My heart began to race, and I wanted to crawl under the table and hide. Only now this was my *husband*, not my fiancé. These were his friends, not mine. I couldn't imagine how they felt as I looked around the table at them. *Was this how he behaved when they knew him growing up, or did he become this person along the way as an adult?* I wanted to run for the door. *Who was this person I married?*

As I sat there, cringing inside, I remembered it had happened before. One night about a year earlier while we were still engaged, we went out to dinner with a group of my friends at a Japanese steakhouse called Shogun. We were having a great time, eating and laughing and being entertained by the hibachi chef, who did amazing tricks while preparing our food. Then, out of nowhere, Colby was rude and condescending to the wait staff. He complained during the rest of the meal and asked for the manager in the end, just like he was doing now. Everyone else, me included, felt the meal and the service were fine, but Colby demanded the manager comp the meal. I was mortified.

Afterwards I hurried out to our car with his friends following and thinking I could not get out of there fast enough. How I left the restaurant and let that slide that night, I'll never know, but because of his tirade, the manager discounted our bill.

When I first met Colby, I was so blinded by his charm and ability to spin things that I ignored such red flags. The initial one appeared during our first phone call together, back in 1991. Colby and I met through the personal ads in the local paper, so talking on the phone came first. And boy, did we talk! We talked for hours during that first call.

"Ever been married before?" I asked as I lay on my couch.

"No," he said, and I believed him. There was no reason not to, but it was the first of many lies.

I was brought up to give people the benefit of the doubt, so I trusted people, at least until given a reason not to. Talk about the wrong approach! Even Dr. Phil says it's insane to give someone the benefit of the doubt. He says to keep your eyes open, collect data, make informed decisions, and be careful of who you let get close—words I live by now.

We kept talking on the phone. When we met in person at the beach a few days later, Colby confessed, "I have been married before."

"Why did you lie, then?" I asked, perplexed.

"I could tell by our conversation that your Catholic faith was important to you, and I didn't want you to pre-judge me."

As I listened to the waves crash in the background, I allowed myself to accept his excuse. So began our courtship. About seven months later we were engaged.

My dad had been a church choir director for as long as I could remember, and I loved singing in the choir, especially when I had the opportunity to sing with my father. It was during my engagement to Colby that I told my dad that between work, planning the wedding, and other things, I could not be in the choir that year. Colby was with us when I broke the news, and he essentially threw me under the bus by telling my dad that *he* would be happy to sing in the choir! That pressured me to do the same, and I hated him for that because I was overwhelmed at the time.

Colby would also go to morning mass before work because my parents were very devout and attended daily, but for him it was all for show. He bought a little rosary, a finger rosary, and he prayed with it, or so he claimed.

Red flag.

Sitting there mortified at that restaurant, I remembered more red flags. For example, during our engagement he said, "I really hope that you never gain a lot of weight."

I was a singer/dancer. I was thin and in great shape, but he planted that seed, and when I got pregnant I gained seventy pounds. His comment triggered the childhood abuse I endured at the hands and mouth of my mother. "I love what you're wearing today. You really should dress like that more often," she'd say, as if I didn't always try to look nice, or "Why does your hair look greasy?" It wasn't. I probably have the driest hair on the planet. During our humid, sticky summers, it was usually so hot that while singing in church, I would slick my hair back in a French twist while it was wet to keep me cool. It looked really nice, until she handed out those backhanded compliments, laced with criticism.

That's exactly what Colby did.

Gradually, it became my new normal. It doesn't mean that "new normal" is good or healthy or okay but I didn't know that then. Later, I realized this happens to many women in my situation. The good news is, all it takes is one conversation somewhere along the way to help somebody escape that trap and see what's actually going on. The bad news is, victims of narcissists are so rarely told what others see. It took me years to understand and break free of that.

Recently, when I was talking to my dental hygienist about some of the information that's in this book, she was surprised. "Wow, I'm really shocked. I never would have known because you're always so happy, upbeat, and positive."

"Because that's who I am," I said. "I choose to see the joy in life. The dark part of my life is behind me now, and I'm not going to live that every day. I want something better for me."

Through those more than seventeen years of battle, a black cloud hung over our lives, my son's and mine. I feel like we missed out on so much potential joy in his life because while in the darkness, I felt like I was doing battle with Satan himself on a daily basis. It felt like it was ever present even though my faith was always there as the underlying support system for me.

It still is.

Chapter 4

GABRIEL

1993–1995

"LET ME READ THIS TO YOU!" Colby said a few days before our wedding reception. "It's going to make everyone cry. This is good!" He was as giddy as a schoolboy, all smiles and excitement as if he had some amazing news to share. He wanted to read what he wrote for his groom's toast to me, but his toast was anything but *for me*. It wasn't even personal. It wasn't full of his love for me, and it wasn't even about me. It was about his performance for our guests and whether he could make them cry. It was full of insincere sentiments, a show about him. I chose to ignore that red flag too.

I had a cousin at the time who was sixteen. Apparently, when Colby and I got married, he said to his dad, my uncle, "Did Aunt Barbara [my mother] pick him for her? Because he seems a little too perfect." A teenager could see it, but I looked past it.

Sometimes we enable behavior by being quiet. Eventually though, about a year into our marriage, I couldn't take it anymore, and I asked Colby if we could go to marriage counseling. "No," he said, and he stuck to that for another two and a half years.

People look past red flags for all sorts of reasons, especially when going into a marriage, hoping all will be well afterwards. That was certainly true for me.

My marriage took place amidst the early days of home computers and the Internet. One night, I walked in on Colby, still a law school student, in his home office and saw porn on his computer screen. I freaked out. So did he.

"Oh!" he said, practically jumping out of his chair. "I accidentally clicked something, and it popped up." He frantically clicked and clicked until the images changed. "I didn't mean to," he said. "I didn't mean to, honey!"

I wanted to believe him, but deep down I didn't. I turned and left the room and then the house in tears and called my sister for support. That too, became a pattern.

To back up a bit, when we got engaged, he was just getting out of the Navy to go to law school, which was in Delaware. So, for the first year of our marriage, we only saw each other about twice a month, and it was always a honeymoon. He was always on his best behavior. Now that we were living together, I faced constant rejection. He would be doing homework. I'd come around behind him and put my arms around him and be loving with him, but he would just keep typing away on the computer, his body rigid. It sucked. Somehow "we got pregnant," but it was definitely planned. So, "it" became scheduled. "Is this a good time?" I'd ask. I even suggested we go for counseling. Instead, Colby had other ideas.

Throughout our marriage, intimacy, and the lack thereof, was an ongoing challenge. Near the end when we briefly tried to save the marriage, Colby had an idea. "Why don't we just get away one weekend?" he suggested. We left Gabriel with Colby's parents and went to a hotel in Baltimore's Inner Harbor. We could see the stadium from our room.

"Do you want to fool around?" I asked gingerly.

"I have another idea, Regina," he said with excitement in his eyes. "Why don't we rent a porn flick? It will help us get in the mood."

I was mortified and deeply hurt that he would need that when I was right there. Needless to say, that killed the mood for me, and nothing happened.

At this point it's important to note that I deeply wanted a child and that my son was conceived in love. I loved and wanted him desperately, but the overall rejection was a surprise, and it messed with my head. *What's wrong with me?* I wondered.

Any advances I made were snubbed with the excuse that he was studying or tired. Sometimes he had no reaction, as if I wasn't even in the room, let alone touching him lovingly. (I discovered two decades later that he most likely had other sexual outlets.) But we wanted a child, and there is only one way to make that happen, so I know when I conceived.

Once I became pregnant, sex between us became even rarer, if that were possible. My advances were usually rebuffed with, "I don't want to hurt the baby." So, I let it go.

During my eighth month of pregnancy, we drove back to Virginia Beach from Delaware for a baby shower with my family and friends. After the shower we were driving with my sister back to my parents' home, where we were staying. On the way we decided to go to Babies R Us. That's when my sister experienced Colby's road rage for the first time.

He was furious—tailgating, getting angry with other cars "in his way," and aggressively changing lanes. Once we were in the store, his road rage spilled over to how he treated the salesclerk. It was embarrassing, to say the least.

Later on, my sister questioned me. "What just happened? Does he do that a lot?"

"I really think things will change once the baby is here," I replied.

"Regina," she said, "the baby is already here, inside you, and he was driving like a maniac with no regard for the safety of *any* of us!" My response was my way of making excuses for him, which I did a lot.

Nonetheless, Colby and I were both overjoyed when my pregnancy was confirmed, if for different reasons. My joy was at becoming a mother and having the gift and responsibility of this new life growing inside me. For Colby I think it was about replacing one trophy for another. When it came time for Gabriel to be born, Colby was more concerned with getting to wear scrubs at the hospital than he was with my labor and helping me through it all.

I suffered through my entire pregnancy with arthritis in my right hip but would never take anything for it other than Tylenol, which was no help at all. I did not want to risk harming my baby from drugs because I could not tolerate some pain. I was in a painful labor for fifteen hours, pushed for another hour, then had an emergency C-section. Along the way I decided, as so many women do, I needed an epidural.

"Wow," Colby said, laughing, "I thought your threshold of pain was higher than that!"

Did he seriously just say that?

He seemed to have no idea what kind of pain I had been through all those months and all of those endless nights with little to no sleep due to my arthritic hip and the weight of this big baby boy growing inside me. I was also commuting well over an hour each way to work during my pregnancy, and all that sitting made my hip pain much worse.

I Loved You More

At birth Gabe weighed eight pounds seven ounces and was twenty-one inches long. He was the most beautiful baby, with his cherubic face. He had liquid blue eyes that had a natural sparkle of joy in them; curly sandy-blond hair that later turned medium brown, exactly like mine; and a heart-stopping smile. People stopped me all the time in public, saying he looked like the Michelin Baby and should be in commercials.

As a toddler and into the first few years of school, he had a slight lisp—cute when he was little but not so much when older, so I immediately got him in with a speech therapist.

None of my friends or family told me at the time, but it's amazing what people will reveal to you *after* a divorce. I was a performer when Colby met me, and apparently, Colby would parade me around on his arm as if I were a trophy wife. Once our son was born, it became clear that I was suddenly in the background of Colby's life, even more than before. Gabriel became all that mattered to him. People also (only later) shared with me that they did not like the way Colby spoke to me or treated me. At times it was those outside the family, like my brother's friends who were visiting, who noticed. "Does he always talk down to her like that?" they asked. My friends told me years later that they thought Colby was always condescending to me. One of my brothers told me I seemed to laugh it off, as if Colby was only kidding, but he wasn't.

What stuns me to this day is that I was oblivious to this, or somehow I chose to ignore it, but why? While it pains me to think I was that stupid, to let someone speak to me like that, I had no idea how bad it would get.

By 1996, I had been asking Colby to go to marriage counseling for two and a half years. It wasn't until the very end, after I had mentally checked out, that he said he would do it. So, I went.

"I'm not going to stay married for the sake of our son because that's the Catholic thing to do," I told the therapist. "This is not love, and I'm not going to teach this to my child."

It came up in counseling that it pissed Colby off when I walked away from arguments, but my idea was, *I'm just going to walk away and calm down before I say something I regret.* And it helped—well, it helped me. Colby wanted to fight. He wanted to control. He wanted to be in a position of power. To this day he still wants that fight.

People like Colby put on their best behavior in front of everyone else. In social settings he was charming and charismatic, with streams of stories to tell, always laughing. He was "on" like an actor. The thing was, on certain occasions when he brought me to tears, he would make me think I was crazy by mocking me and saying, "Oh, you're such an actress, Regina. You can just turn on the tears when it suits you." In reality, that was what he was always doing. I was made by God to be sensitive and emotional, so when the tears came, they were genuine. Nonetheless, Colby would accuse me of doing the very thing he did to manipulate me and then made me question myself.

In short, he was gaslighting me.

Chapter 5

WORDS

1996 & 1988

I WAS SITTING OUTSIDE of a Barnes & Noble in Delaware at a little bistro table under a green umbrella one day in 1996, talking to my sister on the phone. It was pouring rain, and we were talking about my soul-crushing marriage—and our mother.

"Loretta," I said, "I used to pray as a kid that Mom and Dad would get a divorce, so we could go live with Dad. I just didn't want to be around her abuse anymore. I also hated the fact that she would bring out horrible behavior in me that I disliked in myself. She would push me to my limits over and over again, and I would yell and scream back at her like a crazy person."

My mother always looked younger than her age. She took great care of her skin and colored her hair. She remained petite but a force to be reckoned with if we talked back or disobeyed or got in trouble. Her electric green eyes could be fierce and menacing when she was yelling at us, and her singing voice developed a rasp to it from all her years of yelling at us kids. Over the last six months of writing this book, she has been in hospice care. Most of her hair has fallen out, so she wears a wig, and she looks pale, sickly, and frail.

Loretta and my oldest brother, Danny, desperately wanted to move out when they were twenty-one and twenty because of our mom, but my dad laid a guilt trip on them, so they waited because we all would do anything for Dad. A year later, Danny couldn't take it anymore and hightailed it out of there, but Loretta got into too much debt and had to stay longer. As a result, she lived at home until she was twenty-seven. Meanwhile, Michael and Richard purposely found jobs to keep them away at college when there were breaks, and kids would normally go home.

When it was my turn to make the move. I was unhappy and musically unfulfilled in college, and I left after fall semester. My dad had asked me if I was homesick and I quickly reassured him that I was not. Being back home and dealing with my mother again after four months of total freedom catapulted me into maintaining my independence. I searched the newspaper and went apartment shopping. Once I put down a deposit on a two-bedroom/two-bathroom apartment, (with no roommate yet, to speak of) I dropped the bomb on my parents about my move-out date, which was just two weeks away. My mother freaked out and was furious. She did not look at me or speak to me for those two weeks once she made it clear that my moving out was, in her opinion, to be promiscuous. She said when a girl moves out of her parents' home, and it's not for college or marriage, then it is for other reasons and will look bad to others. How hateful. I was a "good girl," and that was a slap in the face, but she would never admit it had anything to do with her. She justified her moving out at nineteen to pursue Broadway by saying she lived in a convent in New York City. While that was true, she was twisting her logic with me to suit her story and to make me look bad.

On moving day my dad brought two antiquated suitcases out of the attic that were so old I could flick them with my finger, and dust went flying in the air.

"Here," he said sweetly, "you can use these to move your clothes."

"Oh, thanks, Dad, but I already borrowed two of your newer suitcases, and I will bring them right back after I unload my clothes at the apartment."

"You did what?" my mother yelled. It was the first words she had said to me in two weeks. "You are not using our suitcases!" She ran upstairs and down the hall to my bedroom. I was right on her heels in hot pursuit to see what she was going to do next. She pushed through the door to my bedroom, flung open the luggage, and dumped my clothes all over the floor.

"You bitch!" came flying out of my mouth before I could stop it. I knew that was a monumental mistake. Instead of slapping me, which I anticipated, she ran to her bathroom and began crying loud enough for my dad to hear. I proceeded to refold all my clothes and put them in the dusty suitcases my dad offered. I packed up my car, and as I was about to head out, she came out onto the porch.

"You leave this house, and you are *never* coming back!" she yelled.

I "happily" waved goodbye, got in my car, and cried the whole way to my new apartment, full of freedom.

Mom continues to decline. Sadly, she has never had a relationship with any of her five children nor any of her six grandchildren. Yet, we were all in her life. My therapist explained that I didn't have to like her, but I needed to respect her position as my mother. So, I always did all the things I was supposed to do as a good daughter. Nonetheless, she still got emotionally abusive with me. She always used emotional blackmail, saying, "If you really loved me . . ." When she'd done something to hurt me, she'd turn around and leave me a message, gaslighting me, saying, "I forgive you." My brothers couldn't believe it.

My brothers agreed I needed to include my (our) abuse at her hands in this book. All five of us went through it, and my mother has also inflicted a degree of psychological abuse on at least two of her grandchildren. My older siblings thought because I was the baby of the family that I had it easy and was spoiled. It has come to light during the last few years that I actually got it the worst, and it pains me to say that has continued to be the case even during Mom's time in hospice.

My therapist once explained to me that when Mom got that way, I should distance myself from her. So, at one point, I put Mom on notice. At one of our meetings, she started with, "If you really loved me . . .," and for the first time I didn't react or get angry.

"Mom," I said, "that doesn't work on me anymore. Stop saying it. It doesn't affect me. It doesn't upset me or hurt me. So, just stop wasting your breath." Then I left!

I didn't talk to her for about a week until she called and left me a message saying she thought I'd like to know she was sick. So, I called her back. I also called the nurses at the assisted-living facility to try and get some things rolling for her, to get her a new doctor and other things.

Then I called my mom. "I want to let you know that I can't afford to be around somebody who's sick right now because I have to sing this Saturday night for four hours," I said. "The good thing is that you have medical staff there, trained nurses who are taking good care of you, and that's great."

"Oh, don't worry," she said. "I didn't expect you to do anything."

Backhanded. That's what I dealt with. That's how she was all the time.

I Loved You More

"I have come to accept that nothing I do for you will ever be good enough," I replied calmly. I told her such things before because they say you don't want to let somebody die without telling them how you feel. I had never been fully, brutally honest with her or discussed all the abuse, but I wrote her letters and said things like, "Mom, I know that in your eyes I'll never measure up, but I know in my heart that I always do my best for you, and I can live with that."

My beautiful sister, Loretta was five feet two inches. From her early twenties on, she was short and very heavy. None of us ever understood why because she didn't eat like somebody who should be heavy like that. Growing up, there were ten years between us.

About a year before Loretta passed away, Richard and I were swapping stories. "Richard," I said, "I used to go to my room and cry because Mom would be so hateful to Loretta. She would pick on her about her weight and how her clothes were too tight and how she couldn't possibly go out of the house dressed like that." Loretta always dressed nice, and it was just horrible how my mom treated her.

"I did the same thing! I used to go to my room and cry too, and I would pray to God to deflect it to me, so Loretta didn't have to feel the pain."

We never talked about it, Richard and I. We lived in the same house, were four years apart and thick as thieves, but we had never discussed it.

"I used to hate coming home from school to Mom's to-do list," he continued. She would have a to-do list for each of us when we came home from school. "Then when I would hear the garage door, and I knew Mom was coming home, I would literally freeze in panic."

"I felt the same way," I told him, "and it was because I knew that when she got home, she wasn't going to praise me for anything I did right. She was going to find something I did wrong on that list. I'd get in trouble for it, and she would use it to keep me from my friends." Throughout our lives, nothing was ever good enough.

If I hadn't made the conscious decision not to beat my son, to parent him with love and encouragement and positive reinforcement, things might have turned out much differently. Today, Gabe will tell you that my constant dialogue with him was, "Follow your dreams. Your dad and I both love you. You should feel free to love us both," even though in the back of my mind I knew that asshole was telling Gabriel that I didn't care, that I didn't support him. And as the years passed, that suspicion was proven. It almost extinguished my relationship with my son. A parent can poison a child in many ways if they choose to or if they're not careful.

"Mom has always been so difficult to deal with," Loretta said on the phone as I sat there in the rain. "She's a glass-half-empty person and I've told her that. If Mom pays you a compliment, it's followed by a backhanded insult." That was the truth. That's how she always was. She would dole out what she often labeled as "constructive criticism," which was often hurtful and insulting. She would upset me, and then she would come back at me with, "Oh, stop being so sensitive!"

Sensitive. That word still stands out for me today, like a jab in the gut. She would say it with such venom that the word felt like a punch. It's stuck with me and made me introverted and question myself about my crying and my own emotions. To this day I can hear her scoff at me, her voice snide and nasty. "You're so sensitive."

Sitting outside Barnes & Noble in the rain, talking with Loretta, I recalled how when I was twenty-two, in 1988, I was working on a Holland America Cruise Line ship on the Alaska run as an entertainer. I met a passenger, John, and we hit it off. We sat in a lounge talking till all hours of the night, long after closing time. I don't know what possessed me to tell him, I don't even remember how the conversation started, but at some point, I told him all the horrible things my mother used to say to me and how I thought something was mentally or emotionally wrong with me.

"Clearly, I'm too sensitive and I just don't know how to control it," I concluded.

He looked at me, and then he said something so profound. "My dear, Regina, there's nothing wrong with you. Being sensitive is a gift, not a curse. It makes you more in tune to other people's feelings. It makes you more empathetic and sympathetic. It really is a blessing."

That conversation changed my life forever.

Chapter 6

Therapy

1996

IN JANUARY of 1996, Colby was admitted to the practice of law in the State of New York as well as Delaware, where we were living. He started making good money, as I understood, but I never knew where some of the money was going. I was still the sales manager of the eastern region of PA for a large bank's mortgage division. It's funny; He wanted me to use Quicken to account for all of our money, so when taxes came due, it would be easy, but he would go to the train station and take out twenty dollars a day and could never account for it. I didn't understand this for the longest time, but years later I learned from other women what he probably spent "our" money on.

Colby's risky behavior scared me. He was never thrifty. He had no problem spending *my* money when I was the only one working while he finished law school and studied for the bar, often picking things off the rack for Gabriel that were designer brands while I focused on the sale racks.

On our first Christmas with Gabriel, when he was barely two months old, and I was still nursing, Colby spent three hundred dollars on a pair of silk lounging pajamas for me from Saks Fifth Avenue. I totally freaked out! Remember, I was the one working so it was my income, while he clerked for a Baltimore judge and studied to pass the bar the following month. Initially, he did not want to tell me the price, and when I dragged it out of him, I felt physically nauseous at the cost. I couldn't even wear them because I was nursing and was worried about ruining them. I made him take them back, and we went to Victoria's Secret to buy fake silk ones at an after-Christmas sale for about seventy dollars. Colby was furious about that, and I mean livid. It pretty much ruined our Christmas morning. But he did such things all the time, overspending on everything while I was coupon and sale shopping, which was like having another job.

He always wanted to impress and look like he was paying big money for things in front of other people. It was like an addiction. Early on in our marriage he told me how he "defined himself." There was an article in the paper by a famous football coach who said he defined his greatest success by the success of his family and his children. Of course, Colby said all that to me, and I was such a sucker because I believed it, even though it wasn't the truth. It was really about, "Oh, I'm on a conference call, and the other attorneys are talking about having a Tag Heuer watch," so he had to go get one. It was all about impressions. "Oh, now I have to learn how to drink Scotch, which I hate, but everybody's drinking it at these functions." It was all a façade.

A few years later when Gabriel was around four years old, Colby bought him a Mercedes kid's electric car because it was, after all, a Mercedes. Gabriel could barely fit into it, so I made Colby take it back, and we got a Power Wheels all-terrain electric car for less than half the price. It was much bigger, and Gabriel could enjoy it for several years.

Colby's need to impress others became one of many behavior patterns that, in time, seriously concerned me. But it was his controlling, aggressive behavior, along with all the rejection that put me over the edge of unhappiness. Looking back, I probably wouldn't have stayed the three and a half years that I did if we didn't have a child. As a matter of fact, sometimes when I watch Dr. Phil, I want to bang my head on the wall because he says, "You knew this about the person, and you still chose to have a child with him." I had this picture of my future, and it included marriage and a family and being a stay-at-home mom, but I realized I never loved Colby. I was in love with the package he presented, but it was all a lie.

It wore on our young marriage, and it wore on me until I was ultimately brought to the point of *goodbye*—but not before giving it one more try.

In late spring/early summer 1996, our marriage was seriously struggling. That's when Colby, in his narcissistic way, began to push his ultimate personal agenda. He spun it in a way that he tried to make it sound like his intentions were for the sake of our marriage and for my personal dreams. He had made it clear for years that he wanted to work and live in New York City while I made it clear that I would never raise my children there. I had already given up my dreams of Broadway in exchange for having a family. In retrospect, what he did was very cunning and manipulative.

"Regina, let's move to New York! You can pursue your dreams of Broadway, after all!" he said with exuberance.

"No, Colby. I've said it a million times that I will not raise my children in the city."

"Then we'll rent a house outside the city limits with a yard for Gabriel. It'll be great!"

"There's more to it than that. You don't understand what a Broadway performer's life is like. If I were cast in a show, I would be at the theater six nights a week plus matinees. It's exhausting.

And to get cast in a show, I would have to spend my life going to auditions and networking. I can't fathom orchestrating all of that around childcare in a city where we know no one."

This went on for months until he finally wore me down, constantly painting the picture of what our life could be like and how the move would "fix things" in our marriage. I didn't realize until years later that I was searching for some type of fulfilment, some essence of happiness that was totally lacking in our marriage, and I was willing to give anything a try at that point.

I began to cave, saying, "The only way I will remotely consider this is if I have validation from an expert in the field as to whether or not I even have a shot at making it on Broadway."

So, we made plans to visit the city, which was only a two-hour drive away. We met with Dick Corrado, a big agent at the time at ICM Artists on West 57th Street in Manhattan. He was senior vice president of operations, managing mostly conductors and instrumentalists. He managed such greats as Doc Severinsen, Skitch Henderson, JoAnn Falletta, the Manhattan Rhythm Kings, the Mormon Tabernacle Choir, and many others, and he was the first to manage Yo-Yo Ma.

Dick was a long-time friend of my father's, who had met Dick when he was just a teenager, and his father was the stage manager at a Broadway theater where my dad was performing. I had great respect for Dick.

"I am not here as my father's daughter," I said, sitting across the desk from him. "I'm here as a prospective client and a professional. I have a VHS demo tape for you that I want you to review and tell me, in your professional opinion, if you think I'm good enough for Broadway. And I want you to be brutally honest with me."

"I'm not going to look at this now," he said, taking the tape from me. "I'll take it home, and Lois and I will review it together. Then I'll get back to you."

Lois was Dick's wife and a well-known opera singer under the name Louise Russel. She had sung with Placido Domingo, Robert Merrill, and Luciano Pavarotti, among other greats.

About a week later, Dick called me, and he sounded serious. "Regina," he said with thoughtful deliberation, "Lois and I have reviewed your demo." He hesitated, so I thought he was trying to break the news to me gently. "I mean this. I would be remiss if I did not encourage you to pursue Broadway." I have to admit it excited me. I had not felt that sense of hopefulness in a long time.

That's all Colby needed to seal the deal with me to move to NYC. He found a job with a prominent law firm in New York that paid for us to be packed up and moved, and we found a house to rent outside the city. His perfect plan was falling into place. Then came moving day.

Colby was sick with only a cold but milking it to the hilt. I was the one orchestrating the movers while dealing with a baby. The day the movers arrived, it was pouring rain. Everything was unloaded, and we were totally exhausted. As I walked through the old, musty house we had rented, I took in the radiators, the creaking old floors, and the damp chill that seemed to discharge from the walls. Inside I began to shiver, but I knew it wasn't from the chill in the air. I felt a huge lump in my throat but said nothing. I had to focus on setting up Gabriel's crib, so he could get to sleep at a decent time. Once he was resting in his crib, I shut the door, leaned against the hallway wall, and slowly slid down it, crying.

"We have made a monumental mistake," I said to Colby in a strangled sob. "We just left a beautiful new home with a wooded backyard in a great neighborhood . . . for this. This is not what I want for Gabe. I don't know what I was thinking."

Colby was shocked.

"I want to move back to our home in Delaware," I added.

The next day I was searching the yellow pages for a moving company that we would now have to pay for the move back. Thankfully, our house in Delaware was not yet sold, so we were able to move back into it. That was the beginning of the end of our marriage.

Colby was verbally abusive, and it got worse because his New York dreams were not playing out as planned. Initially, he commuted via train to New York, but soon he was able to secure a job with a firm in Delaware. He argued with me at every turn. I had been asking for counseling for years—two and a half years out of our three-and-a-half-year marriage—but he just kept saying, "No, we can fix it. We can fix it."

But after three and a half years, realizing it was not love, and realizing it was not going to improve, I finally told Colby that I wanted a separation.

Only then did he agree to therapy. "OK, I'll go," he said begrudgingly, but I had already checked out of the marriage at that point, and I didn't see him changing. I am a Catholic, and I have always believed in "married for life," but that was it for me.

Of course, nobody around me wanted to say anything while I was engaged or married, but when our marriage finally blew up, I began talking with my family about everything. I've always been an open book with them, except with my marital problems. Suddenly, everybody started sharing their concerns with me.

"Well, we didn't say anything to you because you probably wouldn't have listened," they said, which was probably true. When I was younger, I guess you could say I needed a man. I had long-term relationships, but I went from one to the next to the next. When I met Colby, he seemed like everything I thought I was looking for. I realized in 1996 when I came across a journal that I wrote when I was working on cruise ships that my mother had done a good bit of grooming with me, setting me up to husband hunt, essentially. So, when I met Colby, and he figured out I was a devout Catholic and that I wanted a family, he presented all that to me on a silver platter. I bought it all. Over the years in therapy, I have beat myself up with "How the heck did I fall for it? Especially when I considered myself intelligent and worldly?"

My therapist would say it to me repeatedly, until I finally got it, that, "This is not about you. This is who they are. Narcissists. They're so good at what they do, they suck you in, and they do whatever they need to in that moment to serve their purpose."

Eventually, I discovered Colby's purpose was to lure the next woman in to financially support him and then suck her dry.

Chapter 7

LETTERS

1996

BEGINNING WHEN GABRIEL WAS ONE year old, every year around his birthday I wrote him a letter. I sealed it, labeled it, and decorated it. I don't even know what's in them anymore because I never went back and reread them, but I saved them to give to him some day in the future when I felt he was ready. I did this for twenty years, but I wrote an extra one for the day he went to college and another one when he went on a retreat in high school. I've always wondered when I'd give them to him. Would it be when he got married? When he had his first child, if he had a child? As a result of how life turned out, I eventually decided I would give them to him when he turned twenty-five.

Writing them gave me a line of communication with my future son, focused me on my goal of preserving as much of his childhood as possible, and if I'm honest, gave me at least a point of light to hope for, an exhaust vent for my constantly breaking heart. One tiny hedge against my stress, frustration, and angst at all that Colby put me through. I felt robbed of enjoying Gabriel's life as he grew up because I was always doing battle with Colby. And I cried, a lot. It was over two decades of constant stress, all the while trying to do what was best for my son. The things Colby did to us made me angry and stressed and made me cry in the privacy of my home or behind the wheel of my car, and it went on and on and on.

Maybe these letters helped me as much as I hope they help Gabriel understand someday.

October 30, 1996

My Dearest Gabriel,

I am writing this letter to you on your 1st birthday. Just beginning this I am already teary eyed at reflecting back on your first year of life.

You have brought your father and me so much joy and love that words cannot express the way we feel about you and how happy you have made us. So much has happened this year: I don't know where to begin.

When we brought you home from the hospital, you were a whopping 8 lbs. 7 oz. and 21 inches long. Now you are 26 lbs. 14 oz. Whew! What a change. You have also had eight teeth for several months now. You cut your first tooth around 3½ months old. You began walking at a mere 9½ months and now you are at a full run!

My, my, my, what a talker you've become. Your current vocabulary consists of the following words: Mama, Dada, Pooh, Tigger, see, shoes, see you (a chasing game we play thanks to your godmother who taught it to you when she came for your birthday party!), ball, nana (banana), bye-bye, hat, huh, nite-nite, baby, pee pee.

I am so happy at your excitement of music. Anytime we play something with a beat to it, you immediately begin dancing and smiling. You love your Disney Sing-a-Long Songs videos, too!

You love to cuddle with your daddy and me, and you love taking baths. You're not very happy when we take you out of the tub though.

At the age of six weeks, you began sleeping through the night, only to stop that the day I quit working (3 mos. old). It was at this time you began cutting teeth. But now you're a big boy, and sometimes you even sleep till 9:30 in the morning. Wow! Mommy really loves it when you do that!

I love you with all my heart, little one, and I am so very proud of you. You are everything to me and I would give my life for you.

Love,

Mommy XXX OOO

BY THE MIDDLE OF 1997, Colby and I had separated and arranged for visitation of Gabriel. Gabe was one and a half years old when we split. I was late in writing to him that year.

October 30, 1997

2 yrs. Old

To My Darling, Little Gabriel,

. . .

You are so advanced for your age in both your motor skills and your verbal skills. You were talking in complete sentences before you turned two and were saying the whole "Guardian Angel Prayer" by yourself at 21 months! During this past year you also learned to sing "Edelweiss" by yourself, however, you prefer when mommy sings it with you most of the time.

Your excitement over Santa Claus this year was overwhelming! You knew that he was coming down the chimney and was going to bring you lots of toys if you were a good boy. When we put cookies and milk out for Santa on Christmas Eve, you proudly drank some of Santa's milk and said you wanted one of the cookies—you took the biggest one too!

Mommy took you to see Santa two times at the mall. The first time Daddy came too, but both times you were such a good boy, and you didn't even cry. You proudly went up to Santa and gave him a big "squeeze," as you would put it, sat on his lap, and told him you wanted presents. On Christmas morning you saw the easel Santa brought you, and all you wanted to do was color with the chalk on the chalkboard. The other presents could wait as far as you were concerned. Not for long though. When you opened up presents of clothes, just like any child, you quickly moved on to the next box, hoping for another toy. Santa was very good to you, dear, because you really were a very good boy!

Just after your birthday, Mommy checked out a Montessori school for you, and we made plans for you to start after Christmas. Since this letter is late, I can fill you in on your first week, which we just finished. Your first day was a great one! You couldn't wait to go, and when we got there, you jumped right in playing. Mommy was so proud of you. Your second day was show-and-tell, and you brought one of your many fire trucks to class.

Today was your third day and the first one that was hard for Mommy. You kept crying and asking me to pick you up, saying you didn't want to stay. But when I picked you up after school, you were so happy, and the teacher said you were great; you even colored your first picture at school for Mommy to take home. It's on the refrigerator, and I will keep it always since it was your first one from your first school! I love it!

Gabriel, I can't count all the times you simply run up to me and throw your arms around me and say, "I love you, Mommy!" My heart just melts every time I hear that. When we were riding back from Va. Beach after Christmas, you reached over to hold my hand as I was driving and said, "I love you, Mommy, my best friend?" You were asking me that, and I don't know where you heard it—maybe Barney, but you actually made me cry, although I hid my tears from you. How did you get to be so smart and so bright? You seem to know just when I need to hear loving things from you.

My friends are always remarking how polite you are. I'd like to take credit for that, but you deserve credit for listening to me and remembering to say "thank you," "please," and "God bless you," among other polite things. I'm just soooooooo proud of you. You are only two and already have made the connection on so many things of when to say "thank you." WOW!

Gabriel, you have been the light of my life and the one thing that has given me true pleasure and *happiness these past 2+ years. I don't know how I would have survived some of my life's difficulties if it hadn't been for you, my son. You gave me the will to hang in there and realize that we deserve to be happy and loved. Every decision I have made since you came into my life has been influenced by you as I want only the best for you and for me. I won't settle for anything less. I love you, my darling. You have made Mommy very proud and very, very happy!*

My undying love,

Mommy (I love you with my whole heart!)

PART 2

"Sometimes things have to get worse
before they get better."

—Marilyn Ferguson

Chapter 8

AGREEMENTS

January–March 1998

BY 1998, MY DIVORCE from Colby was final, and we had made arrangements regarding the shared mortgage on the house we still owned together and who had Gabriel when. I would not typically call Colby directly. Talking to him always put me on edge; he was always intimidating and controlling. So, when he would call to talk to Gabriel, first I would make sure Gabe wasn't in the room and couldn't hear (for me it was always about protecting him), and then I'd handle "business" with Colby before he spoke with Gabriel. It had to be before he spoke with Gabriel because when they were done talking, Colby would hang up quickly to avoid me.

To start the year off, on New Year's Day we had such a conversation, and I tried to make it brief, as always.

"Hey, Colby. Mortgage check, I don't have it. What's up with that?"

"Oh. Yeah, yeah, I'm so sorry. I'll get that to you." It was a stall tactic, but I had started documenting our interactions. Later, I was very glad I did. "I'll give it to you when I pick up Gabriel."

When he arrived, he said he'd forgotten his checkbook because he drove from New York, where he was now working, to see us in Delaware. Did I mention that two weeks after our divorce was final, he chose to go back to New York to work instead of staying in Delaware where his son was? He was making $80,000 a year at a law firm in Delaware, but a six-figure salary in New York apparently trumped his wanting to live near his son. Money was and still is more important to Colby.

Along with so many others in our ugly divorce situation, the constantly late or shorted child-support checks and late or missed visitations were a regular thing. I can't count the number of times I had to deal with things like that. The entries on this in my records seem endless. Late pickup excuses ranged from the train "broke" to full out canceling his visitation altogether, many times at the very last minute. The stress of these situations created a whole other challenge to deal with and was always playing in the background of all the other ugliness I had to deal with when it came to Colby's issues.

With the late or missed visitations, I could have chosen to make my ex look bad in Gabriel's eyes and place the blame where it honestly belonged, with my ex. Instead I chose to make an excuse that Gabriel could easily process without hurting him. As a parent, you don't want your children to think the other parent's inability to follow through is a reflection on the children or the children's fault because it isn't, and they need to know that and be assured of it. Otherwise, children will always at first consider if such a family problem is their fault. Children start out seeing the world as revolving around them because, after all, at first it does!

An easy deflection or a positively delivered "change of plans" conversation works well with small children. Once they are older and more mature, you can be a little more honest and real without giving them your personal slant about your ex, their other parent.

As they grow, while you still put the children first, you begin to be more honest with them without bad-mouthing your ex. Kids are super smart, and in time they will figure it out on their own. My son did. Remember, they are watching you both *all the time*.

While these situations may inconvenience you, let's be honest, who is more important? Your personal and social time is necessary to recharge and connect with others, and I don't mean to devalue it in the least, but when you signed up to be a parent, sacrifice was in that contract, and it is a regular occurrence in life with children. My current husband told me many times that his ex, who did not want to participate in driving their kids to activities and sports, would tell him, "I'm not a taxi." Well, as a parent, yes you are! That's in the contract too!

On a daily basis I had to discipline myself on how to handle the frustrations with my ex as I determined what was best for Gabriel in the long run. Human nature is to react, to give back as good as you get, and this was always taunting me. After all, I am a survivor, which means I will fight to the finish if I must. But *how* I fought was the key. It truly is a choice to stop, think, and do what is best for your children and not what you want to do in every moment. It is not always easy, not even close. Yet, it is imperative when you sincerely want what is best for your children. It's similar to what an addict has to do every day—wake up and make a conscious decision to do the right thing. It is a journey, and it's not only the choice you make to protect your children and love them more; it is also the foundation of living by example for them and the people they will become one day.

On January 29 I told Colby that the divorce was final, and he was not to short my check each month by the mortgage amount, as he had been doing, claiming he would pay the bank directly for his half. I would write my own check to Summit Mortgage rather than trust him to send it on his own behalf. Yet the very next day, my check from Colby was short by $609, which was his share of the mortgage, and he did not pay the bank his portion, either. On February 3 I had to ask him for the mortgage payment, again. On February 13 his alimony and child-support payments were due but not received. On February 25 he was an hour late to pick up Gabriel, who was now almost two and a half. He wanted to take Gabriel to New York City (Colby was still living in Delaware but commuting to NYC each day for work). He wanted to keep Gabe overnight, so he could work even though I told him ahead of time that Gabriel was sick.

Despite my eventual consent, Colby dropped Gabriel back at the house at 7:30 p.m. I guess he didn't want to deal with a sick child. I had to work that night, so I had to quickly arrange for a last-minute babysitter.

The next weekend was Colby's scheduled weekend with Gabriel, but again at the last minute, he could not take him. Due to my work, Colby's parents ("Mom-Mom" and "Pop-Pop") had to pick Gabriel up and take him an hour away to Baltimore overnight. Hectic! Frustrating!

By the end of the month, Colby was late with alimony and child support once again. In March he was late with his payments, and when they were made, they were $609 light.

Ugh.

The frustrations I experienced are just part of the daily dealings with a parent who does not put their children first and does these things to get under his or her ex's skin. Some, however, are worth sharing because they give you a better glimpse of the person I was dealing with. It's a serious concern when you realize you were married to a habitual liar, a narcissist who will say whatever is needed in a situation to serve his purpose. As a result, you are constantly filtering everything that comes out of the person's mouth, and you never honestly know if your children are safe and secure when they are not with you.

One day in March 1998, Colby was supposed to pick up Gabriel at 3:30 p.m. for his Wednesday visitation. As I mentioned, Colby was living in Delaware, as were Gabe and I, and he was commuting to work in New York City by train. He didn't bother to call me until 4:00 p.m., stating he would be there by 4:30. At

4:45 I called him to see where he was, and he claimed he was still on the train because the train "broke." Yes, he really said that. I called three different Amtrak agents, who each assured me all trains running between New York City and Delaware that afternoon were on time or early; none had broken down.

I had to be at work, so I asked a neighbor to watch Gabriel. She told me later that Colby did not arrive until 5:45 p.m. The train between New York and Newark, Delaware, has a ride time of less than two hours, so clearly Colby lied when we spoke at 4:00 p.m. and he said he would be there by 4:30. He must have left New York at the very time he was supposed to pick up his son and knew he would not be there for another two hours. Gabe was too little to know what was going on so I just told him that it was exciting that he could play at his friend's house until Daddy got there.

Colby pulled something even worse the following Wednesday. Initially, he tried to cancel his visitation, but then he offered a "solution." Gabriel would stay at the NY law firm's affiliated daycare during the day.

"I'm reluctant, Colby," I said. "Gabriel isn't quite two and a half years old yet. That would be a strange place with strangers, and he would be there eight or more hours."

"It's fine, Regina!" he insisted. "It's not going to be a regular thing."

"Well, you absolutely have to check out the daycare in advance and provide me with information and contact numbers, OK?"

"Fine. But it will be better if I pick up Gabriel the night before to make it easier on Gabe to wake up, eat, and go directly with me to New York," he said.

I called Colby the day before and reminded him to have a diaper bag ready with Gabe's things packed as well as a change of clothes. I also reminded him that he agreed to check out the daycare in advance. He agreed and was "thankful."

I Loved You More

Colby was an hour late picking up our son. Then he took him on an evening train to New York City. He had rented an apartment in the city the day before, unbeknownst to me. My baby was going to a strange apartment and then the next day to a daycare with strangers—or so I thought.

At the end of Gabe's full day at the law firm daycare, I called Colby's work, cell, and apartment phone numbers and left a voicemail at each of them for Colby to call me, so I could speak to Gabriel and see how he was doing. An hour later I did the same thing. Still no return call. Before 9:00 p.m. I tried all three numbers again, trying to speak to Gabriel.

No answers, no return calls, nothing. I was worried sick, hoping my baby was OK.

About thirty minutes later, Colby's cell number showed up on my caller ID. He claimed they were back at the Delaware apartment.

The following day I called Colby to request information on the daycare that he promised to provide, so if Gabriel had to go there in the future I would be informed. Only then did Colby admit that Gabe never went to the law firm's daycare, as we agreed. Instead, he kept Gabe in his new apartment with a stranger from some agency in New York. He claimed to have interviewed this person on Monday or Tuesday, but until that moment he maintained the lie that Gabe was going to the law firm's daycare. I asked for the phone number of the agency and the name of the person he dealt with, because I did not believe anything from him at that point. The second we hung up I called the agency and asked to speak to the caregiver, only to find out that Colby was already on the other line with the person, probably getting his story straight.

If his plans changed, why didn't he just tell me? Why lie? Honest communication between parents about children is paramount, whether the parents are divorced or not. I acknowledge that certain people can't make that happen because their ex is incapable of being honest or communicating, as was my case. As a mother, my only concern was Gabriel's well-being. Colby was proving to be inadequate in the parenting department.

A couple of weeks after that fiasco, I overheard Gabriel on the phone with his dad. He mentioned how he "fell down from the fan at Daddy's house and had to go to the doctor for a shot." I asked Gabriel to hand me the phone.

"Colby, what was that about?"

"Gabe climbed up on the radiator, and the sitter told him to get down, or he'd get hurt."

"And," Gabriel added as he listened, "she said I would have to go to the hospital and would never see my mommy or daddy ever again."

I was freaked out to, say the least.

"Colby, that is not OK to tell a toddler!"

"What's the big deal?"

A couple of days later we met to discuss his visitation. "First," I said, "Gabriel is never to be put in that situation again."

"OK, fine," Colby said. Then he told me he realized he could not keep the Wednesday visitations and asked to extend his weekend visits, making them last from Thursday evening to Tuesday morning. This would mean Gabriel missing Montessori preschool on Fridays and Mondays, which was not OK. Of course, when I disagreed with this new arrangement, Colby threatened me with our economic agreement, which was still being hashed out. "You can forget any changes now!" he said. Colby also claimed he could guarantee the same sitter every time with that same agency. I called the agency once again, and they said they could not guarantee the same sitter. Yet another lie on Colby's part.

And so it went . . .

Chapter 9

RECORDS

April–November 1998

COLBY AND I HAD AGREED to file joint tax returns for 1997, which was during our divorce proceedings. I had repeatedly asked him when the returns would be ready because he was preparing them, as he had done in the past. He stalled constantly, and on April 15 I realized why. He had couriered them to me to arrive on that day, assuming I would blindly sign them and stick them in the mail before midnight. I guess he also thought I did not know how to read them. However, having been in the mortgage business for many years, we regularly had to review borrowers' tax returns, and I had a working knowledge of them. I was no CPA by any stretch, but I knew the basics.

While I knew by then that his honesty and integrity were greatly lacking, I did not expect him to defraud the government—and expect me to follow suit. Child support can't be written off, but

Colby claimed the total of child and spousal support as a combined tax deduction. Other write-offs did not add up, either.

I called him to let him know I was not signing the returns. Then I ran around like a crazy person to find tax filing extension forms. I had a performance that night, but there I was, trying to find an extension form just before midnight, after the final curtain of my show. Crazy!

Two decades later I came into possession of multiple documents, including three different 2008 tax bills in his name stating that he owed over $20,000 to the IRS from 1998, 1999, and 2000. He also never filed corporate tax returns for his law practice for 2005, 2006, and 2007. Included in my Internet searches were a laundry list of warrants in debt from numerous creditors, many of which were documented as "guilty in absentia" because Colby rarely, if ever, showed up for those hearings. Thankfully, my not signing the 1997 tax returns helped me dodge a bullet.

Meanwhile, Colby had canceled seeing Gabriel at Easter. The next day I got him on the phone. "Did you move from your apartment in Delaware?" I asked. "I thought you said you'd live there through October."

"Yes."

"OK. Where is Gabriel going to spend the night this Wednesday then?"

"The same place as last week."

"Which was?" I was confused and annoyed by his short answers.

"A hotel."

"OK. I was unaware of that," I replied, trying to maintain my composure.

"And look, Regina, I need to do away with my Wednesday visitations. It's no longer going to work with my schedule." He also canceled taking Gabriel on April 22.

I Loved You More

Over the next nine months, I continued to deal with Colby being grossly late for visitation pickups, cancelled visitations, shorted support payments, and having to constantly ask for his share of the mortgage payment. Then there was the repeated disregard for letting our toddler ride in the front seat of a car all the way from New York City. Months later Colby rented a Grand Marquis, and we argued about how a toddler can't ride in the front seat with an airbag.

Colby was book smart but common-sense-poor, and there were times when he not only made bad parenting decisions, he would then tell me about them! It was also important to Colby to "beat me to the punch" on milestones with Gabriel, so he had to be first to take him to Disney World. Gabe was only three years old when Colby did this, even though Gabe was too young to remember such an important trip. When they returned, Colby told me the park was not "single-parent friendly." He said at "Breakfast with Pooh," which was "packed with people," it was too difficult for him to go through the buffet line with Gabriel, so Colby sat him at a table all by himself, in a crowd of strangers, while he went to the buffet line to get their food. He claims he was watching three-year-old Gabriel the entire time, which I find highly unlikely. The thought of my child potentially getting kidnapped put my stomach in knots.

Over the next few years, that was my worst fear, that Gabriel would be abducted while with his dad on the streets of New York City. I could just see Colby strolling down a Manhattan sidewalk, distracted on a call while someone snatched my son. Gabe was a beautiful baby, with gorgeous blue eyes and light, golden-brown, curly hair. His adorable looks alone would make him a target for abduction, let alone an inattentive parent.

One day while I was working at MBNA in Delaware, a fellow employee sauntered into my cubicle, and we had a small conversation that changed my life forever. In fact, it's the reason this book is in your hands right now. His name was Seth. He had short hair with a receding hairline, hazel eyes, and a big smile. I found him cocky, maybe even a bit arrogant, but very smart. He worked in technology for MBNA. Seth walked into my cubicle and looked me over. "Regina, you OK?" he asked.

"Yeah. I went through a divorce when my son was one and a half," I said. "My ex just seems to always make things difficult. And—" I wasn't sure I could get the words out. I became that *sensitive* person again, but for some reason telling Seth seemed the thing to do. I started to get a bit choked up and emotional. "I think he's poisoning my son against me."

After a quiet pause, which allowed me to calm down a bit, Seth nodded. "Yeah, my parents divorced when I was one and a half too." I looked at him. It seemed something important might follow. I turned in my chair to face him as he folded his arms across his chest and relaxed against my cubicle wall. "My dad was always the fun parent, did this, did that, but my mom was my rock."

In that moment, I decided I wanted my son to think that about me one day.

"Yes," I said, as I leaned in to talk with Seth. "There are times Gabriel will come home and tell me about the things they do, and I feel like I'm not the fun one and that Gabriel may never know all the things his dad is doing to make life unbearable for us." I told him about some of things my ex had been doing, like showing up late or cancelling his visitations, shorting Gabriel's child support checks, or when he did pay, his checks would bounce. "One day, when my son is a man and can think for himself, I want him to look back on his life and see the path I chose was not one that put him in the middle but one that put him first."

Seth thought about that briefly. Then he pointed at me. "You know, you might want to write that down. Just saying." That was all he said. (I found Seth recently to let him know what an impact he had on my life that day. He was surprised.)

I did start journaling. I did it for the purpose of court. And when I say I journaled everything, I journaled *everything*, from every missed child-support payment to every missed visitation to every shitty thing that Colby said to me over the phone or in person and every scene he created in front of my son. I documented it all. Remember, we did not have smartphones back then where I could dictate notes to transfer later or to video bad behavior. Journaling required me to sit down and boot up a desktop computer either late at night or while at work, always when Gabe was not around.

Our court system is so screwed up though, they wouldn't look at anything. I would walk into court with file folders that were six inches thick. One was my copy, and the other was the court copy, but they would never take it. Even so, journaling played a huge role for me. It was a simple yet profound statement that ultimately led to my keeping big binders full of documents, a collection spanning two decades, that included legal documents, emails, you name it. I discovered communicating via email with my ex produced a treasure trove, a paper trail of him sinking his own ship. He would easily spew the hateful, controlling vernacular I experienced in person on the pages of emails, all now in my records.

And so began the "Colby Log."

I always felt like I had to "reprogram" Gabriel from all the negative grooming he was getting from Colby against me and my family. I had to feed in different and positive information. One of the things I would always say to him before he went to bed was, "Sweetie, I love you. Your daddy loves you, and you need to feel free to love us both." I didn't want him burdened with what I assumed he was getting from his dad, who I assumed was badmouthing me all the time. So, I continued to journal because one day I wanted him to see and to know what we went through. I hid my journals in the attic. Gabe didn't know they existed until 2018 when I began this book, nor did he know about my yearly letters. Not yet.

Recently, I was watching an episode of Dr. Phil, and he was talking to a fractured family with two adult children in their early twenties and three other minor children who were not present on the show. He explained that you have two different accounts for your parents. "Loving one of them one hundred percent doesn't affect the value of the other parent's account." I thought that was a brilliant analogy. It was essentially what I told my son all those years ago. Meanwhile, it seemed all Colby did was find new ways to add to my stress, with Gabriel in the middle.

On June 14, 1998, I waited for Colby to bring Gabriel to me at the annual Italian Festival at my church. When Colby drove Gabriel there for his drop-off, I noticed that Gabriel's car seat was in the front seat of Colby's Geo Metro. *Here we go again!* In addition to the safety issue, it was against the law.

However, Colby eventually proved to have total disregard for the law on many levels.

Chapter 10

PERILS

1999

ON MY BIRTHDAY, February 2, 1999, Colby called me in the morning.

"What are you doing around noon today?" he asked.

"Going out for lunch to celebrate my birthday. Why?"

"I have a conference call at work," he said, "and I don't know what to do with Gabe during the call. Can you talk on the phone with Gabriel while he's in my office, so I can go to another floor and take the conference call?"

"Are you crazy?" I asked. "That's not safe. If something happens to Gabe while you're gone, I'll be on the phone *two states away*. Can you ask someone at work, maybe a secretary, to watch him since the call isn't supposed to take long?"

"It would be an insult," he barked at me, "to ask someone at work to watch my son."

Colby later admitted that he locked Gabriel in his office all alone and went to the other floor to take the call. The call lasted over thirty minutes. Yep, he actually told me that, although I imagine it took much longer than what he professed. He claims he ran back up every fifteen minutes to check on Gabe, which is hard to believe. Additionally, no one knew Gabriel was locked in the office alone, so if something happened, they would not have heard, nor could they have helped him. He was three years old. He could have easily fallen off his dad's chair and hit his head on the desk. He could have cut himself with scissors or hurt himself with a stapler. The opportunities for him getting hurt were endless. I thank God, and Him alone, for protecting my child in that and many other situations.

From February through May 1999 I had to ask Colby for the mortgage payment every month because he never paid it voluntarily.

On May 30, Colby took Gabriel to Ocean City, Maryland, for several days. He told me that he took Gabe to the Jolly Roger's Amusement Park and paid extra money at the gate for Gabe to be able to go on additional waterslides and rides because according to their guide at the front, he met the height requirement of forty inches. However, the park had a flume ride where each rider had to ride alone in a tube, and Gabe was too short. Colby said he argued with the attendant, who stupidly obliged and allowed Gabriel on the ride. Gabe was just three and a half years old.

When I asked him, Colby admitted he had not checked the ride out in advance for safety and the level of danger for Gabriel. He told me at one point they went through a dark tunnel where he was unable to see anything, and Gabe got scared. Colby even admitted he was a little scared himself. At the end of the ride, people were dumped into a pool of water.

"Gabriel riding alone was totally unsafe," I said. "He could have drowned."

"Gabe had his water wings on and was totally safe," Colby replied.

I couldn't believe I had to explain to someone with a law degree that water wings are neither a floatation nor a safety device. He was dismissive of my concerns, and once again, I felt lucky that God's hand was protecting my child.

In June, July, August, September 1999, yep, you guessed it, I had to ask Colby for the mortgage payments again.

We argued, of course.

Later that month I penned another letter to my son, decorated it, sealed it, and placed it in the attic with his other letters to be given to him when he was grown.

September 22, 1999

Dear Gabriel,

I am so sorry that no matter how many reminders I gave myself, I never wrote a letter for birthday #3. I have found though, that over the past year so many things happened that I could not possibly remember them all at the end of each year. So, I have decided to try and update my annual letters to you as you do neat things or things I want to share with you when you read these someday as an adult. I will mention some things you did most recently and then try and go back.

A couple of weeks ago, you made me laugh so hard because you found a "googly eye" (a tiny, jiggly, plastic eyeball we use to glue onto things and make faces) and stuck it to the middle of your hand. Then you hid under the kitchen table and put your hand up over the edge and began talking like an alien, a la puppet show! I don't know where you thought up the idea.

You and I have done many little puppet things, but where you got the idea to turn your hand with that one tiny eyeball into an alien blew me away. You were a hoot!

Then a couple of days ago, you took a whistle from your cowboy hat that we got at the rodeo and stood on the driveway blowing the whistle and waving your arms.

When I asked you what you were doing, you said you were a lifeguard on the beach directing the swimmers. How funny!

In the last few months, you have grown up so much. You and I have developed such a special bond. You are so loving, and we kiss and hug ALL THE TIME!!!!!!! I am so very proud of you, my little son.

In October Gabe had a cold all week. I informed Colby in advance that he needed medications for when he was with him. I even suggested that he pick some up on the way to New York City. Instead, Colby left Gabe all alone in his NYC apartment while he walked down the street to get some medicine.

"It's too much trouble to get him dressed and take him out," he said. "I think Gabe has a fever, but I don't have a thermometer."

Regardless, it would have been safer to bundle Gabe up and take him along instead of leaving him alone, again. The weather was mild and in the sixties, so it wasn't a winter blizzard outside.

"I was alone, Mommy," Gabe told me on the phone, "but it was OK because Daddy told me I was a big boy."

It's hard to co-parent and take the high road with an ex who constantly uses threats and intimidation to get his way with you. And when that ex is an attorney and browbeats you to take you back to court and says things like, "I'll see you in court, Regina!"

or "I'll pay you what I think you deserve!" or better yet, "I hope you can pay your legal fees," it's all the worse.

I realized years later that Colby also used those threats and intimidation with Gabe, who in the beginning used to tell me everything without solicitation. Gabe called me from his dad's cellphone while they were on their way to New York once and proudly told me, "Daddy let me ride in the front seat because we were so close to Burger King." It's amazing how a toddler so young knew to justify this "privilege" by saying they were close to Burger King because I was constantly telling him he could not sit in the front seat because of his size and the airbag. He knew it was wrong, but Daddy told him it was OK.

When parents teach right and wrong differently or dishonestly, as was the case with my ex, it confuses children. In time, Gabriel clammed up and stopped sharing things with me when he had spent time with his dad. I knew Colby's nature, so I would refrain from quizzing Gabriel for information. It would have put him in the middle, and that was not fair to him. Did I want to know things? Of course I did! But I was not going to use my son as the direct source of information unless he volunteered something. Ultimately, his dad would find out, and Gabe would be punished for it. And that was not going to happen if I had any say over it.

Yet that is exactly what many parents do. It's so unfortunate because it not only puts the children in the middle, it also skews their understanding of what being honest and telling the truth means. If they are getting yelled at or punished for telling the truth, they learn that truth does not hold value in their life because it yields a negative result. What do you want to teach your children? Do you want them to grow up to be honest citizens with a moral compass? Then remember that every time you open your mouth, they are watching you and listening to you. Everything you say and do is a teaching moment. Think about what you want to teach them.

One time while at his dad's, Gabriel told me over the phone that he was allowed to cross the street all by himself without any grown-ups. "That it is not OK or safe for you to do that," I told him.

"Mommy, there are different rules at different—" Before he was able to finish, Colby grabbed the phone from him for the second time during that call and began yelling at me because he had received papers that day from my attorney. I had no doubt Gabe could hear all of this, so I hung up. Despite my calls back to finish my conversation with Gabriel, Colby didn't answer the phone until I left a message with his service stating that he was interfering in my contact with Gabriel. Only then did he allow Gabe to call me. When he did, Gabe sadly told me his daddy got mad at him.

"You did nothing wrong, sweetheart," I said, "You don't have to worry about it."

A couple of days later, I was eating lunch with Gabriel. "Did you get into trouble the other night for telling me the truth?" I asked.

"Yes," he said, "Daddy got mad at me."

"What did your daddy say to you?"

"Daddy told me not to tell you stuff like that because it's like you're controlling our house."

"Gabriel," I said, "it's never wrong to tell the truth, and Mommy was not mad at you for doing the right thing. You don't need to worry about grown-up stuff like that."

Yes, your children are listening to you—and watching you.

From October 3–10, 1999, I had to ask Colby for that month's mortgage payment four times.

Defeated, when he dropped off Gabriel, I gave him a postage-paid envelope to mail it with the next day.

Later that month, on Gabriel's birthday, I sat down and wrote my son a new letter. The next day I wrote him another.

I Loved You More

October 30th, 1999:

Well, today my big boy is 4 yrs. old, and tomorrow is your big party at Hound's Pound [a kids' play place with pizza, video games, and rides]. Today I am a little sad because although it was my weekend with you, your daddy asked if he could have you for the weekend, and I said yes, as I always try and do. But I have things to do to get ready for your party, so that helps pass the time. I have to pick up your "spooky" (as requested) birthday cake, wrap your new big boy bike with a horn, and wrap the smaller presents I got you. I can't wait for you to come home. I always miss you so much when we are apart.

Tomorrow after your party, we are going trick or treating with Nicholas and Miss Trisha across the street. You are going to be an alien like in Star Wars, and I am dressing up as Princess Jasmine from Aladdin (my blue Kismet costume). Do you remember last year when you were a pirate, and I was a clown? The year before you were a fireman, my hero!

Two days ago we had your party at school, and you and I made two kinds of cookies.

...

You also have a girlfriend, or at least she thinks she is. Samantha is her name, and she follows you around everywhere and clings to you. Sometimes you like it, and sometimes you don't. Like the day she kept kicking over your leaf pile. You would always refer to that day as "not a good day with Samantha, Mommy, because she kicked over my leaf pile."

Regina Rossi Valentine

October 31st

Well, today was your party, and your friends from school were invited and came. You had lots of fun, mostly on the arcade games, and, as usual, you did not eat birthday cake or your pizza, for that matter. I guess it was all the excitement! Daddy and I bought you a new "big boy" bike. It was royal blue w/decals that said "SPEED BLASTER" on it. 16" w/training wheels.

...

Tonight was Halloween, and we went trick or treating together with Miss Trisha and Nicholas, who was Buzz Lightyear from "Toy Story." We had a big day together, my little angel, and I love you more and more with each passing day. I just can't seem to get enough hugs and kisses from you. Your cheeks are always so soft and sweet, and your little arms around my neck are so wonderful and make me feel all warm and snuggly inside. I love you, my big 4 yr. old.

Soon it will be Christmas. I wonder what Santa will bring you this year considering you ask for EVERYTHING you see even if you don't really know what it is or what it does. Hugs and kisses, my sweet little one. My whole heart, soul, and my being love you more than you will ever know, my angel.

Love,

Mommy

On November 4, 1999, I called Colby in the morning. "Just calling to see about the mortgage check for this month, the money you promised me for Gabriel's birthday party, and the money you promised for the doctor's for Gabriel. Any news?"

"Well, yeah, and we should discuss Thanksgiving, Christmas, and summer," he said.

"Summer?"

"Yeah, Regina. I want you to know I'm prepared to take you to court for the full summer visitation."

I fell silent. Panic began to set in as I wondered what was next.

"Kelsey will be taking care of Gabe in the afternoons." Kelsey was his latest girlfriend.

"Do you plan on marrying her?" I asked after a pause.

"I don't know."

"OK . . ."

"Regina, I hope you can afford attorney fees to go to court."

Summer was eight months away.

Chapter 11

Dark Clouds

2000

"Behind every dark cloud is an ever-shining sun.
Just wait. In time the cloud will pass."

—Marianne Williamson

LIFE WAS FULL OF DARK CLOUDS all around me, from dealing with my ex to constant concern for Gabe's safety, not to mention my deepest fears of my son growing to hate me under his father's influence. After the holidays in 1999, I was left to face a new year.

In January we seemed to be doing OK as a divided family. January 7 was my scheduled weekend with Gabriel, but Colby asked to take it, and I acquiesced. So far, so good.

I Loved You More

The next weekend Gabriel was very sick, and I did not want Colby to lose his weekend with him, so I offered for Colby to spend the weekend at the house while I stayed at a friend's place. It went well, but I was a bit uncomfortable about Colby staying there. By the end of the month Colby asked to pick up Gabriel for a long weekend, to which I agreed.

Then through February and March, Colby bounced four checks to me in a row. I incurred $285 in bank fees from my checks not clearing as a result, putting me in bad standing with my bank and several creditors, including my credit union, which serviced my car loan. I also found out that as of that February, Colby was no longer dating his girlfriend, Kelsey, who he planned on having babysit our son during the summer, which was when he said he wanted full summer visitation and about which he had threatened to haul me into court. While he was dismissive of my concerns to plan the summer visitation around someone he was dating back in November, apparently, she ended up being dismissive of him entirely.

In early March we spoke on the phone, going over several issues. "I'm considering continuing to pay you the full amount of spousal support through August.," Colby said. This was in contrast to him trying to previously reduce his support amount by $180. "It's an insignificant amount, decreasing it by $180, and it's important that you stay home and care for Gabriel full time."

OK.

In May, Gabriel came home from his dad's sick with a fever, and Colby gave no medicine to him at all. Gabriel said his throat hurt all day. When I looked at his throat, it was covered in white spots. I paged our doctor, who called in an antibiotic. Since he was still there with us, I asked Colby to pick up the prescription, so I did not have to take Gabriel out.

"Seriously?" he said.

"Yes, please. Gabe's sick!" I replied.

"So, let me get this straight, I'll need to drive around and wait for this prescription to be filled, right?"

"Maybe. I guess so, Colby."

While he waited, Colby repeatedly called me to complain about what "an inconvenience" this was for him. Then he hung up on me. Gabe ended up having strep throat, which I then got from him, and I spent Mother's Day in bed sicker than I had ever been.

In June, Colby asked me to take Gabriel that first weekend because he had other personal plans. I agreed. June 6 was Gabriel's last day of school and his party with the parents. Colby was not there. On June 10 was Gabriel's school's family picnic. Colby did not take him when it fell on his weekend in the past, and he did not attend that year either. I had given him several weeks' notice.

I was relieved because at the end of that month was my weeks' vacation with Gabriel, during which we visited my family in Williamsburg. Enjoy those moments when you can! Our vacation didn't last long that summer. I came back early, so Colby could still have his weekend with Gabriel. He asked to keep him through the Fourth of July holiday, which was my rotation that year, but since I had to work, I said it was fine.

When I saw him, Colby said he forgot his checkbook, so he gave me partial payment for child support in cash and said he had to wait until July 5, when he dropped Gabriel off, to pay the balance.

Every day seemed like a huge challenge dealing with Colby, and that black cloud was ever present. Whether over the phone or via email, something was always an issue. It seemed like every time Gabriel came home from being with his dad, he was exhausted from not enough sleep. Many times he came back sick. Almost always, he came back in clothes that no longer fit him while the outfit I sent him in to his dad's never came back at all. While it took time for me to understand and accept that I had no control over what happened while he was with his dad, when things were brought to my attention that I believed threatened Gabe's safety, I had to speak out about it.

One summer day in 2000 when Gabriel and I were at lunch, he told me, for the second time, that his daddy said he was drinking too much milk, and milk was bad for him. Gabriel knew that I, as his mother, was the one giving him the milk; therefore, Colby was trying to make him think I was a bad mother. Gabriel had no known allergies and no negative reactions to milk, so what was the point of doing that except to cause internal conflict in our son who was not quite five years old?

Gabriel was also expanding his vocabulary under Colby's care. Gabriel was in Montessori preschool for his second year. Shortly after the new year started, we were driving home when he said, "It's bitchin', man!"

"Where did you hear that word?" I asked.

"My daddy."

"It's not OK for you to say that word, Gabriel."

"My daddy said it was OK," he announced proudly.

That was the third time he had used profanity he heard from his dad. In the fall Gabe was sitting next to his dad one day while he was on a phone call, and his dad used the F-bomb, which Gabriel repeated to me a few days later. Another day it was "shit" that he said he heard his dad say.

Colby would cancel or change our arrangements for him to see Gabriel so often that I never really knew what was going to happen. It stressed me out, and storm clouds were not only over my head but at times also my heart. I didn't know on any given weekend when Colby was to have Gabriel, if he'd cancel at the last minute, or conversely, extend the time they were together. I was concerned about Gabriel's safety as much as my sanity.

In late July my bank informed me that Colby's check from July 15 did not clear. When I confronted Colby about this, he insisted it *did* clear. (It was years before I understood what gaslighting was.)

When my bank said again that his check did not clear, Colby finally admitted it.

"Yes, that check bounced," he said. I don't know why, but even this truth felt like a sucker punch. "Look, I'll FedEx another one tomorrow to you." Meanwhile, when Gabriel came home I kept hearing about trips to parks, the beach, new apartments, even vacation plans.

"Colby," I explained, "I'm losing faith that this next check will clear."

"I don't know what to tell you."

"Just please understand, I've had to liquidate my IRA to cover myself financially from all these bounced checks. This leaves me with nothing in my savings or retirement at this point." I was trying to appeal to his better nature, to his empathy, but I found it non-existent. Years later I would learn that narcissists lack empathy altogether. "I know these are small amounts of money, but I didn't have much in savings or retirement. They're *gone*. Please just let me know I can rely on you."

"I don't know what to tell you."

When I hung up, I noticed my hands were shaking.

IN THE SUMMER OF 2000, Colby moved from New York to New Jersey. For the trip he had Gabriel ride in the front seat of his Geo Metro, this time knowing full well that Gabriel could be killed from the airbag should there be an accident. On August 15 I spent the day in New Jersey with Gabriel during his month with his dad. When I picked him up at Colby's new rental house, Colby showed me around, and I noticed he had Gabriel sleeping in the top bunk bed without a bedrail to protect him. I expressed to him my concerns. Colby always treated Gabriel like he was an equal to him, not like the toddler that he was.

"If Gabe did fall out of his bed, he would just fall on the bunkbed below," Colby said, even though it was at a perpendicular angle to the top bunk.

Seriously?

Colby blew it off, and Gabriel told me that he was a big boy. "Mommy," Gabriel, now four years old, said, "I'm not going to fall out, and if I do, I'll fall on the bed below." I was outnumbered.

When I dropped Gabriel off at the end of our day, Colby handed me an envelope with a check for $180. It was supposed to be $1,145. I had to close my eyes and just breathe.

I was being maligned by Colby when I was not around. I bit down on the thought and resisted all those fiery-hot urges to just unload and tell my four-year-old all the shitty things his dad did and was doing to me, to us.

As fall started, and the year wound down, it seemed the more I tried to create civility between us, the more it backfired. On August 27, after I'd put Gabriel to bed, I spoke to Colby about my concerns with the top bunk bed not having a bedrail. I told him I had a bedrail he could use for Gabriel, so he didn't fall out.

"I don't want to talk about it right now," he said, "I'll think about it."

In September it was as hard as usual getting Colby's share of the mortgage from him. I was looking forward to writing my annual letter to Gabriel that year because things had simply deteriorated. I enjoyed the outlet that writing the letters provided. It could pull me back from it all, but sometimes it seemed to push me right into what I was fighting through. Through these years, I cried *a lot*.

Regina Rossi Valentine

October 30, 2000
HAPPY BIRTHDAY, GABRIEL!

My Darling Gabriel,

Once again another year has passed, and there is so much to remember that I don't know where to begin! For starters, you were already beginning to read early reader books back in the spring while you were still in Montessori Preschool. And just the other day you sounded out a hard word that you saw on the computer, "dentist"! Wow! I can't believe just how bright you are.

One of your favorite "big" words to use lately is, "actually," which you use a lot! You've also been using the word, "realize" too, and you just sound so grown up when you speak. You also played team soccer for the first time in the spring and did very well. They said you were a natural goalie, although when the ball was at the opposite end of the field you had a tendency to sit down and wait or play with another teammate at the goalpost. Ha-ha.

There have been lots of changes for the two of us this year. In July I had to go back to full-time work, and that meant daycare for you until school started. But you loved going to Miss Elaine's house because she had a big pool, and you went swimming almost every day! Boy, was I jealous! Then for the first time your dad took you for a one-month summer visit, and you got to spend a lot of time at the beach with him. Your hair got so blond, and you did a lot of growing up over the summer. You learned how to boogie board and ride the waves, and you learned how to "skim" in the *shallow water. You have no fear of the ocean, and that thrills me because I grew up at the beach. Before summer started you took swimming lessons and did so well that by summer you were no longer using water wings to keep you afloat! Gosh, what a big boy and how very fast you are growing up before my eyes! You have also done quite well on your skateboard this summer, learning all kinds of tricks!*

After summer was over, you started all-day preschool with aftercare, which was a huge adjustment for us both. You used to go to half-day preschool and then be with me all the time, so this was a major switch for us. You have such a long day. Initially you were not too happy about it, but within two weeks you adjusted and are doing great! You have become quite the expert scissors cutter with all the work you do at school, and you color so well and stay in the lines like an artist! I am always being told by the aftercare helpers that you are one of the nicest children there. They tell me that even though you hang out with the ornery and wild boys that you are always so nice and polite, and you don't act like them. THAT makes me VERY proud! I guess I am doing something right.

You and I get closer all the time, and your hugs and kisses can turn my day right around! There are times when out of the blue you look at me and say, "Mommy, I love you!", and that just melts my heart. Lately, you have told me how much you miss me when you are at Daddy's. I also know how much you miss him when you are with me. It breaks my heart that you have to be carted back and forth between us, but the most important thing is that we both love you deeply.

. . .

One book that is special to us has a little song in it that the mother would always sing to her son while she would rock him as he slept at night. And when she got old and sick and could no longer sing it to him, he held her, rocked her, and sang it back to her. Any chance you remember this song? It goes:

I'll love you forever. I'll like you for always.

As long as I'm living, my baby you'll be.

I remember the first time I read you that book and I had to fight back the tears, so you wouldn't see me get upset, but what a wonderful story—just like I know it will be with you because you are such a caring, loving boy who I know will grow up to be a caring, loving young man.

So, now you will be 5 years old, and boy, do I have a surprise birthday present for you! I have been working for weeks on it, and you have no idea what it is! I can tell you that I have put a great deal of hard work, sweat, and, most of all, love into it! I have been getting a new "BIG BOY" bedroom ready for you. I've painted outer space from the ceiling to halfway down the walls. It looks as though the night sky is oozing down the walls, and there are glow-in-the-dark stars and planets all over. Plus, I got you a cool, triangle-shaped bedside table that is red and a light that hangs in the middle of the ceiling that looks like a flying saucer. You won't see the room until this Sunday, which is the day before your birthday, so I am very excited for you!

I Loved You More

For your party next week you are having Jungle John come over, and he brings all the live reptiles, like hissing cockroaches, a chameleon, and a giant, yellow python or boa constrictor—I can't remember which. But you and your friends and your family will all be there. I also got you a dinosaur pinata, and all the decorations are from the Disney movie "Dinosaur." Real cool! At school on Monday (30th), you will have your party with your class, and we got you a giant chocolate-chip cookie pie decorated with bats and Halloween stuff, and I made little stuffed pumpkins (orange crepe paper/napkins filled w/treats and toys wrapped up and sealed w/floral tape as stems to look like pumpkins!) for your whole class.

...

I had decided that for your 5th birthday we would begin a responsibility list that you would have to check off and do each week to earn an allowance. But just last week when I had already worked a 40 hr week and then sang for two jobs on the weekend, you surprised me. I woke up on Saturday morning, and you had made your bed all by yourself without me asking (which I never had asked you to do yet for the most part). It looked perfect. Then you did it again on Sunday morning—both times before I woke up. So, I gave you your first allowance ($.50 for each time), and you bought two little toys at the party supply store with it. I kept the receipt, which is in this envelope as a memory of your first official purchase with your own money. I am truly proud you are my son!

Well, my little buddy, I love you so much. I always tell you that I love you to the moon and back—and then some! But I love you much, much more than that.

I can't express it. I walk in your room in the mornings to wake you for school, and sometimes I just look at your sweet, little face, and I can't believe you are my little dear one. You are turning out to be such a sweet, loving, caring little person who makes me so proud. I love you, my darling, and you must know that everything I do is for you. You are my life, my world, and I could not imagine my existence without you!

I really love you, my darling little boy,

Mommy

I had an unspoken rule back then that during dinner time, phones were off limits. (I still have that rule.) If it's important, the person can leave a message, but family mealtime is important to me and is quality time. The same night that the "bitchin" word came out, Gabe and I had just walked in the door and were eating dinner when the phone rang. The caller did not leave a message, and the caller ID said "unavailable." The phone rang five more times in the next fifteen minutes. Eventually, Colby admitted it was him. This was repeat behavior for him. There were many times when I would come home and look at missed calls on my caller ID, and he would have called numerous times—not leaving messages for me to call back, just constantly calling. It is a control thing with him and something I eventually learned about his personality.

Late one Friday night, Colby called me every five minutes for forty-five minutes, all because he wanted to talk about a ladder I had. After a long week at work and finally getting Gabe into bed, I did not want to talk with Colby, and I knew it could wait. The next day he called me again about wanting to take "his" ladder.

One of the things Colby would do to get under my skin was make annoying comments when he would come to the house to pick up or drop off Gabriel. He would say things like, "Wasn't I supposed to have that painting?" or "Are you sure you don't want to split the china?" He even said once that he wanted to have my old computer when I was done with it. I told him Gabriel was using it for his educational computer games. While I got to keep the china in the divorce, Colby was supposed to get the formal dining room furniture, but he kept it at the house since he had nowhere to put it. At one point when he owed me around $700, I told him if he let me keep the dining room set, we could call it even. He jumped at the idea.

"And the ladder belongs to me," I said. "It's been used several times to fix things around the house."

His response to that, as it had been with so many other things, was to threaten me: "When we go to court, I'm going to deduct money from what I might owe you. And my attorney has found something that will change our arrangement about the mortgage and cause you to lose the house."

Threats. I knew he was blowing smoke. He had bounced more checks to me than had cleared, hence the reason we went to court so often. It was not always about visitation. Sometimes I took him to court over money he owed in child support, and it cost me more in legal fees than what he owed. But it was all about holding him accountable and sending the message that I would always do what I believed was right by Gabriel, no matter the cost.

How would you feel if your five-year-old told you his dad told him he could climb on the roof of the house and help him hang Christmas lights? Or that his dad said he could use the staple gun? What if your child told you he already had used the staple gun? Poor Gabriel was constantly getting mixed information from his parents on what was OK and what was not. Who was he to believe?

It was a constant challenge for me to let Gabriel know what things he should and should not do, all the while wanting to but not saying his dad was an idiot. That is a delicate line to walk. You have to guide and teach your children about right and wrong whether or not the other source of information is the other parent, a friend, teacher, or coach. As Dr. Phil always says (and I did not know this back then), "The most influential parent in a child's life is the same-sex parent." I am glad I did not know that then because it would have made me even more concerned and frightened for my son's emotional future than I already was.

How would you feel if your five-year-old child told you when he went to the movies with his dad, he was left alone in the theater, so Dad could go get treats? One of my biggest fears was that Gabriel would be abducted while in Colby's care due to his poor decisions when it came to Gabriel's safety. So, once again, I had to tell Gabriel that he was not to be left alone in a theater and that next time he should tell Daddy that he wanted to go with him. You have no idea how badly my inner voice wanted to preface that instruction with, "That idiot . . ."

When you can't seem to get through to the other parent, you may resort to constantly educating your children on right and wrong and try to give them tools for how to handle the situation if it happens again. It's sad when you can't rely on the other parent to do the right thing, and you are trying to teach your toddler to do so.

A few days later when I addressed it with Colby, he lied and said no one would be able to leave with Gabriel because he could see the theater door from the concession stand. Once again, I had to forge the common-sense idea that there are numerous ways to abduct a child from a movie theater besides the main entrance, not to mention the fact that all theaters have emergency exits.

At the time, Gabriel was in pre-kindergarten at Jude Academy. One day while screening my answering machine, the school finance office left a message saying Colby was delinquent in tuition payments for November and December and that they had notified him by mail and were doing so again since he made no effort to contact them.

They asked for my help in the matter, as if Colby would listen to me.

Chapter 12

ROUGH SEAS

༄

January–October 2001

ON JANUARY 16, 2001, Colby told me he was seriously considering leaving the law to return to the sea, just not via the US Armed Forces, as was his previous career. He said he did not want to return to the Navy but instead wanted to become a merchant mariner or work on a pilot boat. One of his former friends was a merchant mariner and made loads of money, but he also worked seriously hard. I did not see that type of hard physical labor in Colby's DNA. He explained that although he would be gone months at a time, he would also be on land for months at a time.

"That would not be good for your relationship with Gabriel," I said.

"He'll be fine, Regina. Kids adjust," he replied as he rolled his eyes. Colby was always dismissive of my concerns, invariably blowing them off.

When I met Colby, he was a lieutenant in the US Navy and had already put in to leave the Navy to pursue law school. One would think this a great career change if he no longer desired to serve in the military.

As our relationship progressed, and we got engaged, I ended up walking away from a successful performance career and dreams of Broadway to support him in law school. As the years went by, he had more job and career changes in two years than many people have in a lifetime. After being let go from several law firms, he decided to hang his own shingle, financed, of course, by wife number three. He practiced general law at first and then tried representing athletes, with no success. Ultimately, he was disbarred by the Supreme Appellate Court of New York. Court documents state that he "threatens the public interest." A legal article regarding the chain of events the courts set upon to subpoena him to appear says he took legal documents and retainer fees from clients and then fled town. Years later he lied in an interview for a court-ordered Parenting Capacity Evaluation[2] three times about having lost his license to practice law, and he lied two more times in a written questionnaire about it.

He seemed determined to become a merchant mariner.

"Colby," I explained, "the only reason I stayed in Delaware was to keep Gabriel close to you. Our own issues aside, it's important that Gabriel have a relationship with his father, and a long-distance relationship would be too difficult."

When we divorced, Colby was living and working in Delaware and then chose to move back to New York, so, technically, I could have and probably should have moved right then and there back home to Virginia with Gabriel, but I didn't.

---

[2] A Parenting Capacity Evaluation is a diagnostic instrument used by courts in both custody and child protective matters to assist the courts in making determinations of custody, visitation, or fitness to maintain a parenting role with a child. They include a thorough and specific evaluation into each parent, involving interviews of the parent and child, psychological testing, observation, etc.

I Loved You More

"Colby," I said, "if you do this, I can't guarantee I will stay in Delaware, especially with my family back in Virginia Beach." He went on to say that there could be an opportunity for him to work out of one of the Norfolk ports, which was one city over from Virginia Beach.

In February 2001, Colby told me he bought Gabriel a $300 surfboard and was going to teach him to surf. He regularly bounced child and spousal support checks to me, but suddenly he had $300 to buy a surfboard for a five-year-old who could barely swim. When I expressed my concerns about this, that Gabe was not a strong enough swimmer and was still uncomfortable going under water, Colby dismissed my concerns and promised that Gabriel would never be in water over his knees. I'm no surfer, but I grew up bodysurfing, and I know you can't surf in water shallower than your knees. For the eight years I had known Colby, he had never surfed, nor had he ever mentioned that he had in the past. He claimed he got his first surfboard at age twenty-two, but he had never mentioned that to me.

Because of my fear for Gabriel's safety, I signed him up for swimming lessons prior to his month of summer visitation with his dad. Even the Blue Cross swim instructors at the Boy's Club were shocked at the thought of a five-year-old surfing without more swimming instruction.

In April, because it was Colby's rotation year for having Gabriel on Easter, Colby told me he had out-of-town plans and was unable to take Gabriel for the holiday, so I took Gabriel to Virginia Beach and spent it with my family. It was nice to be there with family. It was on that visit that I decided Gabe needed to grow up with family. So, I began my plans to move back "home," especially since Colby was considering a career that he said might take him to the area.

At some point during Colby's short tenure practicing law at the New York law firm, they overpaid him by $2,500 on reimbursements and did not catch the error for months. When they did find it, Colby had already spent the money, so they garnished his check a little at a time. When I asked him why he kept the money and did not tell anyone, he blew it off.

"It was their mistake," he said, "not mine, so why not keep it?"

"How can you look yourself in the mirror," I asked, "knowing that, technically, you're stealing?"

It didn't faze him.

In late 2000 Colby lent me his work-issued laptop for a file transfer. Despite regular visits to pick up Gabriel, for months he never inquired about the laptop.

"Don't you need your laptop?" I asked finally.

"They gave me a new one," he said.

I believed at that point that he had been fired, but I never asked.

"Well, don't you need to return the old one?"

"They haven't asked for it yet," he said, "so I'm not saying anything."

In March 2001, Colby said he wanted it back. "I want to give it to my mother," he said, rather than return it to the firm.

In April he told me he had been let go from his job at the law firm. He had a history of being quick-tempered, an annoying know-it-all, narcissistic, and bullying. I didn't even ask why he was fired because I was so used to him lying.

"What are you going to do?" I asked.

He said he had just interviewed for a job working on a pilot boat. "Going back to the sea is not lucrative enough. I've decided to stick with the law, and I'm looking for a job in Virginia Beach."

He knew I was thinking about moving back to Virginia at that point.

Colby always lived beyond his means. According to Gabriel, he still does today. Paying his debts does not seem to matter much to him. In fact, repeatedly over the last two years, Colby has borrowed money from our son. Gabe tells me he does not expect to ever be repaid the last chunk of money he lent his dad.

Despite still being behind with child support, after finding a job in Norfolk as an attorney, Colby rented a beach house and kept two cars.

That year I couldn't wait to write my letter to my now five-year-old son.

May 9, 2001

My Darling Gabriel,

I am starting your birthday letter early so that I can recall a few things you have done & said lately that I just had to document! First, I need to say how proud I am of you! You are such a loving, affectionate, and happy boy! Your hugs & kisses and our cuddle times mean so much to me! I sometimes find myself suddenly stopping to "take it all in" because I know that you will someday be too old to do the special things you do that make me smile. Yesterday I was doing our secret coded wave as your bus drove away and watched you in the window waving really big to me. I suddenly realized that I needed to take in that moment for fear of it passing me by and not appreciating it enough until it happened no longer. You truly are in my heart, and it's times like that that I get emotional. I want you to be my little boy forever, but I also want you to grow up into the man I hope you to be.

You are now playing T-ball and doing great. You scored the first run and got the first out for your team at the first game of the season. Your team is called the Sea Dogs. While you are sitting on the bench during your team's at bat, you are quite the cheerleader! So cute!

You are almost finished your pre-K year at Jude Academy and then on to kindergarten this fall. Wow! Hopefully, this time next year we will sell our house, and you and Mommy will move to Virginia Beach. I have been thinking about that decision for over a year and finalized it when we visited my family at Easter. I hope you understand that I need to wait until next year so that financially I am in a position to buy us a house when we move. I have always felt and now have decided that you and I need to be near my family, and you need to be growing up w/your cousins.

OK, now for a couple of funnies that you have come up with lately.

Recently we were in K-mart, and I had to buy a personal feminine product. I was trying to make it fast, but as soon as we walked into the feminine product aisle, there was a box of tampons w/the back side showing at your eye level. You saw the picture of the tampon w/the string and all and said, "Mommy, is that a stick of dynamite?" I thought I was going to die! I wanted to say, "Yeah, sometimes it feels like one," but I could not even laugh because I did not want to make a big deal out of it for fear of embarrassment. How funny!

By the following month, my nerves were frayed yet again. Gabriel told me that he and Colby were making a new cage for his hermit crab, and Colby used a circular saw to cut the chicken wire. They were not wearing protective goggles, and Gabriel said he was hit in the face by flying sparks. Everyone knows to use wire cutters to cut chicken wire, not a circular saw—especially without protective eyewear!

A month later Colby asked me to meet him and Gabriel at the beach in Ocean City to watch Gabriel surf. We spoke on the phone three times that day. I was beyond worried. "The weather report says high surf advisory," I kept telling him.

"We'll be fine," he said with a cavalier attitude.

When I arrived at Ocean City, there were strong wind gusts. The surf was rough with whitecaps, and the red warning flags were out, flapping violently.

"Are you going out in the water first to make sure it's safe and that there's no undertow?" I asked. "I'm not comfortable with Gabriel going out in these conditions." My pulse began to quicken as it thundered in my ears.

Colby dismissed my concerns. "We'll check it out together when we get out there," he said.

Off they went, despite it being incredibly rough. My heart was in my stomach, I felt short of breath, and I began to sweat with anxiety. I was worried sick about my small child as he walked to the water carrying a surfboard twice his size. Colby had to help him. Even today I get emotional and upset with my younger self that I did not demand they *not* go out in the water. But it would have resulted in a fight with Colby in front of Gabriel, and in the end, Colby would do what he wanted anyway. In hindsight I realize there will always be times, although it should be rare, that an argument in front of a child may be necessary, especially if their safety is at risk. That was one of the times I should have put my foot down and demanded they not go in the water. It was by the grace of God that Gabriel did not drown that day. In just minutes they were back onshore.

"We can't do this today," Colby said breathlessly as they dragged the board back onto the beach. It was 5:00 p.m., and almost no one else was in the water. That's how rough it was out there that day.

That night I spoke with Colby on the phone. "I'm concerned that Gabriel was not wearing any type of life vest out there when you guys were trying to surf."

"There's no way I'm going to undermine Gabriel's confidence in the water by making him wear one," Colby protested.

"But it would reinforce the importance of safety with Gabriel while learning a new sport," I said.

"I *will not* make Gabriel wear one!" he barked.

I was frustrated and scared for my son's life. "I may have to do something about it then," I said.

Colby paused. "If you go out and buy one, I'll take a look at it and decide if he'll wear it, but I'm *not* promising anything."

While Colby was teaching Gabriel to surf, he kept telling me that Gabriel was never in water over his head. He had originally claimed Gabe was never in water above his knees.

The next day I was with Gabriel at the beach. "Yes, we go in water where I can't touch the bottom," Gabe said, "but Daddy is with me all the time."

I was careful how I responded to such things with Gabriel. I didn't want to cause him any conflict or make him feel like he was in the middle of my battles with his dad. No matter how many times I wanted to scream, "Your dad is a pathological liar!", I did not.

In August that year I was about to cook dinner on the grill. "Can I light it, Mommy?" Gabriel asked. He wanted to push the igniter button.

"No, honey," I said. "It's too dangerous, and children should not be near fire and gas."

"But I light the grill at Daddy's house. Daddy says it's OK."

I Loved You More

I wanted to scream! Instead, I reminded him that it was not safe for him to do so. I felt so bad that my child was continually getting mixed messages about right and wrong from his parents. At every turn I was trying to keep him safe while not throwing his dad under the bus.

One day that August Gabriel came home from his weekend with his dad and had a terrible cut on his elbow. "I got it skateboarding," he said.

It dawned on me. "Were you wearing your elbow pads, Gabe?"

"No, Mommy."

"Were you wearing your helmet?"

"No, Mommy. Daddy forgot to bring them to Mom-Mom's."

Oh for the love of God.

Meanwhile, when checking messages, I discovered that Jude Academy had called saying the August tuition for the new school year had not been paid. I had to call Colby and leave him messages to pay it.

As I wrote Gabriel's letter again that year, I made a decision.

. . .

> *You are growing up so fast and are so precious to me. This next year will be a big one for us both as we begin our journey to move to Va. Beach! It will be so nice to share you with family and to have family around all the time. No more long trips on all the holidays! May God bless you, cherish you, guide and watch over you, and protect you. I love you, Gabriel!*
>
> *Mommy*

Chapter 13

MONEY

November–December 2001

> *Regina-I have less than 200 dollars in my account right now. If I give that to you, I cannot pick up Gabriel on Friday (the roundtrip cost is over $100 with tolls and gas).*
>
> —Email from Colby, November 14, 2001

COLBY MOVED BACK TO VIRGINIA well before me and had been working for the past five months at one of the largest law firms in Norfolk, so I couldn't understand how he had no money for child support or to see his son that week. Only recently did I discover it was a matter of what he was spending his money on at the time. Colby knew I would not keep his son from him. He knew I always put Gabriel first.

That November Colby postdated the check for his half of the mortgage for mid-month. The bank withdrew the full amount from my balance well before Colby's check was any good. Once again he bounced so many checks to me that I again incurred $250 in fees from my bank. Meanwhile, he was asking to change his child-support payments again. He was already in arrears for over $10,000 in legal obligations to Gabriel for child support, medical expenses, and tuition, among other things. Colby was also on the title to our home in Delaware, which we were selling, so I could move back to Virginia Beach. Money issues were getting even more complicated with Colby.

He often resorted to stall tactics.

"I'll draft something we can agree to on December fifteenth," he told me. Later that day he emailed me a draft without any dollar amounts filled in.

"What are the blank spaces all about?" I asked.

"What do you want, Regina?" he asked.

"You emailed me an offer, remember?" I said.

On November 12th Colby emailed me.

> *Consider this—from December through June I will pay you $500 every two weeks. That creates a deficit of $5,400. At closing take $10,000 from the proceeds. And after June I'll resume paying you $900 a month for at least another year.*

When I reminded Colby of his offer in his email, he acted as if he had never named those dollar amounts. I forwarded him his own email as proof, but he rescinded his offer. I didn't know where all of Colby's money was going, but he was constantly driving me nuts!

A couple of weeks earlier, Colby had said he only had $200 in his bank account. On November 30 while telling me about a speeding ticket he had gotten, he let it slip that he was flying to

California for Christmas with his new girlfriend, that he had gotten a massage in the last week, and that he had flown with his new girlfriend to New York City recently for a weekend getaway. (This woman turned out to be wife number three. Ultimately, years later, after they divorced, she and I became friends.)

On my way back to Delaware with Gabriel one night, I had to stop by Colby's beach house to get some of Gabriel's things.

"Just walk in, Mommy. Daddy never locks his doors," Gabe said.

Later on in private, I confronted Colby about this. "It's just the way I do it," he said. "I don't lock my doors." Fear shot through me again. I worried about all the things that could happen to my son because of Colby's blasé attitude and carelessness.

December came and went with no child-support payment. When we spoke on December 4, he got very angry with me. "What was good enough last month is suddenly not good enough now? They won't advance me money at work, so I have nothing to pay you."

The next day Colby told me he had been fired after less than six months on the job in Norfolk. My attorney told me that an insider informed him Colby had gotten angry and stormed out of a meeting which initiated the termination. Knowing his violent tendencies and that he had attended anger-management classes twice in the past—once during our brief marriage counseling and once when he was in the Navy—I believed this could be true, but with Colby I never really knew.

Chapter 14

BREAKING HEART

January 2002

AFTER THE NEW YEAR HOLIDAY, Gabriel told me, "Mommy, I was with Daddy at his client's house." Colby was unemployed at the time—in fact, he was unemployed throughout that last December. "And we watched Rush Hour II and Pearl Harbor," Gabriel added in his cute, lisp.

"You should not have watched those movies," I calmly said.

"We only watched the opening scene in Pearl Harbor and all the fighting stuff," he said. I knew that *Pearl Harbor* doesn't have any fighting in its beautiful opening scene. Clearly, he saw far more than the opening. Now I feared my son was learning how to lie from his dad.

On January 4 I called Colby. "Did you mail the child support check you promised to mail three days ago?"

"I have not," he replied.

"What about the severance payment you told me about from when you were fired? Where did your settlement money go? And why did you take a trip to California if you have no money?"

"It's none of your business," he sneered, "but we should reconsider Gabriel's going to Jude Academy."

"Do *not* threaten our child's education just because you can't seem to manage your money or keep a job."

"Regina, you can file whatever you need to file to get support from me," he said. "I'll just claim a loss of income, and you'll end up paying me support."

It was very hard at times not to tell our son what his father was putting us through. He was always using intimidation and fear with me, giving me horrible anxiety in my belly, feeling it bubble to the surface again.

January 6, 2002

You fill my world, and everything I do is with you in mind. Merely typing these thoughts, I have a lump in my throat. Someday when you are older, you will understand what a "sensitive and emotional" person I am. It doesn't take much to make me cry, whether they are sad or happy tears. I think I am feeling especially sensitive today because when we were at mass this morning, something struck a nerve in me. As I turned around at the sign of peace, there was a family behind us (a mom, dad, and child). The child was obviously going through cancer of some sort because he/she (I wasn't sure as I did not want to stare) was losing most of their hair from treatment. When I turned back around I immediately prayed for that child and family, and then thanked God that my child was healthy and happy. I prayed that you always will be and asked God to protect you from all harm. I love you, my son, and am so proud of you every day.

January 7, 2002

I did not think I would be making an entry so soon after last night since I tend to go weeks or even months without journaling things in your letters. But today was a very, very sad day. Last night I was called by your teacher, Mrs. Lowrey, and she told me that a little boy, Brett Smith, was very sick w/a bacterial infection and to watch out for certain symptoms. Then as quick as this morning she called again while I was at work and told me that he had passed away. My heart aches for him and his parents. As a mother I could not imagine what they are going through, and it was their only child.

Selfishly I am thankful that you will be fine. I took you to the doctor's today, and you were treated for the carrying stage and the infection stage of what was diagnosed as meningococcus, a particular type of meningitis that attacks the blood as opposed to the brain. It was so hard to tell you about what happened to Brett. I was afraid I would cry in front of you, but somehow God helped me to be strong, so I could help you to understand a little. When I was done, we held hands and prayed together for Brett and his parents. I held you a little tighter (like I don't already) tonight and thanked God for your health. I always pray for that and for Him to keep you safe, but today those words took on another meaning. I love you, Gabriel, you are my whole life, and I would give it for you in a second.

Colby hadn't paid child support or his portion of the mortgage. Then he claimed he would pay child support on January 5. It arrived on January 7. On January 10 his check bounced, and I received no mortgage payment in January at all. Yet, just four days later Gabe told me, "Daddy and I are going to Hawaii over the summer."

I called Colby about this. "I'm worried you're filling Gabriel's head with dreams," I said.

"It's true," Colby said." "We're going to Hawaii." He would not say anything else about the matter. I waited almost a week before bringing it up again.

January 18, 2002

I found out today that your daddy is getting married again. Suddenly, my heart hurts, not for his new life change but for the fact that there will be another woman in your life, someone that your dad only met two months ago and you hardly know. It is not that I am insecure. I know deep in my heart that no one can take my place with you. I only hope that she is good to you and treats you nicely.

Many years later I noticed a pattern of Colby's using women to finance his lifestyle. When the money ran out, he tossed them aside, or they got smart and dumped him.

By the third week of January, I brought up the Hawaii trip with Colby. I was confused and cynical.

"How can you possibly pay for this trip?" I asked.

"Regina, I'm getting married." I felt a twinge in my stomach. The first thing I thought of was there was going to be another woman in my baby's life. It would be Colby's third marriage, all before the age of forty. "We almost drove to Mexico and eloped in December," he continued, "but I realized I want Gabriel to be there as my best man."

Gabriel was six years old.

January 20, 2002

You and I talked today about how things will be different in Va. Beach. I tried to make you understand that we would have a much smaller house and you would not have a separate toy room as you do here in DE. We talked about a pool and how it would be great, but I would not be able to afford it. In your sweet voice, you offered to give me all your money in your banks, so we could buy a pool anyway!

What scared me was Colby was constantly telling Gabe he was his best friend. Every phone call and drop-off ended with that being said as their goodbye. Sometimes Colby would ask it as a question to Gabe, "Best buds?", and wait for Gabe to confirm. I thought then, as I do now, that it was too much emotional responsibility for a child to carry. But Colby never could maintain friendships. He still can't. While it was highly inappropriate to treat Gabriel as a best friend, he probably was the only one Colby really had. Or maybe his son was the only "friend" Colby could totally control—for the moment.

Four days later I was informed of an issue at school. Apparently, Gabriel stole some beads and then lied about it twice. When I told Colby what happened, he said he would talk with Gabriel, and if he heard about other lies, he would not get Gabe the puppy he had promised him. Two days after that issue, Gabriel proudly announced that the dog would be there the following week. This despite the fact I had told Colby I would need to have Gabriel tested to make sure he was not allergic, as I had been growing up. It seemed they were moving ahead with the dog regardless, and the consequences for lying were out the window.

I happened to be visiting in Virginia Beach at the time. There was an open house at my elementary school alma mater, St. Francis's, which was where I wanted Gabriel to attend school once we moved back that summer. At the open house, Colby did not have the money to pay the application fee, something he was responsible for. He also told me he would pay child support "soon." It wasn't long after that while Gabe was still attending Jude Academy (his pre-K and kindergarten school in Delaware prior to the move to Virginia) that I received a letter saying if tuition was not brought current, Gabriel could very well be taken out of school.

This was a constant stressor for me. I was always having to chase Colby down, not only for child support but also for Gabriel's tuition. It never added up for me because if Colby really was an attorney making six figures between salaries and bonuses, how could he not meet his financial responsibilities to his son even as he declared how close the two of them were?

I began keeping meticulous records of these things because Colby was so regularly breaking promises, bouncing checks, and paying late, all while living a rather luxurious life otherwise. I decided to hold him accountable.

Meanwhile, my heart was breaking even more than it had before because I seemed to be losing my son.

January 26, 2002

I know you don't realize this now, but you often say, "I miss my daddy" after he has dropped you off at home. It just crushes me. I know you miss him, but what you don't understand is that he wants to just be your "buddy." He doesn't parent you in any way that I can see. This past week you lied to me twice, and one of the lies was in combination w/stealing some colored beads from the bead bin at school. I made you take them back and tell the teacher what you did. You told me you didn't know you weren't supposed to take them. But when you spoke to Mrs. Lowrey, she reminded you that she had indeed told you not to take them home, so you did know, and you took them anyway. I didn't tell your dad about the first lie (about some craft paint that you said came open by accident but you had taken it downstairs and pried it open yourself, making a mess). But after the second lie, I had to. I told him you were on restriction and that you would not be handing in your Goals to Last a Lifetime checklist at karate for a blue star this week.

Your dad turned around and announced that he was going to buy you a new dog, yet he told me it would not be for a "couple of months," and since he found out about the lies, he would make you wait. But that is not what he told you this weekend. You are now getting a dog in the next week. What you don't know now, but you will someday when you read this, is that your father is $2,000 in arrears of child support. Although he was let go from his job back in Dec., he was given a settlement (of $15,000) that would sustain him through mid-Feb., but as in the past, he spent it and hasn't paid your child support, yet he took a trip to CA for Christmas w/his girlfriend and now is buying you a dog. Of course, he's telling me the girlfriend is paying for the dog because he can't say anything different. He still has two cars and pays $1,650 in rent because he wanted to live at the beach. Well, so would I, but we have to *honor our responsibilities first, and that is you! I have given up so much of my singing and theater in order to keep you as my first priority. After work and karate 3x a week, there's really no time left for me to do anything but that is because you are my life, and I have only one shot to be your mom and to do right by you.*

I just feel as though I am the bad guy because I work so hard to teach you morals and discipline, and all your dad does is buy you whatever you want and "have fun" with you. I can only hope that one day you will see my actions as ones out of only love and devotion to you and your future. I can't and won't compete w/your dad for your love by materialistically spoiling you. You don't want for anything, and love and guidance are more important than "things." I love you, my son, even though at this moment my heart hurts because I have to constantly hear how you miss your dad, the dad who left Delaware two weeks after our divorce to move to New York City where he always dreamed of working. He had a great job here making great money, and he was close to you, but he was money hungry and took off once papers were filed w/the courts. Now he is your hero, and I can't compete w/the innocent thoughts of a young, impressionable boy who doesn't know the "whole" story.

I was always covering for Colby, and not just with Gabriel.

Chapter 15

SNAFU

February–March 2002

I HAD TO CALL GABRIEL'S SCHOOL and explain the circumstances of us missing tuition payments. They said it was possible that Gabriel could be pulled out of school if this went on indefinitely. They needed some sort of letter of explanation. I told Colby he needed to call the school and give an explanation regarding payment of tuition. He said he would call.

February 6, 2002

Last night was a "first-time" experience. We were joking around in the kitchen and putting frozen yogurt pops up each other's backs when you slipped and hit your toe on the trashcan. I immediately tried to grab you and to comfort you, and you ran away from me real angry as if I had intentionally hurt you.

You didn't want me to touch you. Well, although you've done this before, it (and always does) hurt my feelings. Add to that two previous nights of insomnia, and you get a real, real tired, sensitive mommy. I got upset and a little angry with you for treating me that way. I realized I was going to cry, so I went upstairs in my bathroom and closed the door to "get it out" without you seeing me. When I pulled myself together, I opened the door, and you were standing right there, ready to cry. My eyes were all puffy from lack of sleep and crying, and you looked so sad, saying you were sorry. I held you and explained why I was crying and that although it wasn't your fault, it did hurt my feelings how you reacted after getting your toe hurt. We hugged for longer than I can imagine and kissed each other, both promising not to do that again. I told you I was sorry for getting angry. As a mom, I felt awful that you heard me cry like that. It was bound to happen sooner or later, I guess!

As of March, still no child support or mortgage money from Colby. Yet, I found out that Colby had a new office close to the oceanfront, which is very expensive real estate. It had six rooms, a conference room, and new desks and computers. He had yet to tell me anything about any of this and was in shock when I called his new work number. He had been very secretive about the whole thing and told me always to call him on his cell phone. When I asked how he was paying for it all, he said it was none of my business.

I received a phone call from Jude Academy's finance office. Colby's partial tuition payment check for $500 bounced and was returned by the bank. It was now March. Colby promised again to send money, but first he wanted to pick Gabriel up early on Friday.

"Colby, Gabriel has karate class on Friday, but he will be ready at the house between six o'clock and six fifteen."

Agitated, Colby sneered. "This *karate thing* is becoming a problem. Maybe I'll ask Gabe what he prefers, to be with his dad or go to karate class."

"Colby, you are *never* to put Gabriel in the position to choose like that. It's wrong. And since Gabriel has to miss the Saturday karate classes, he cannot also miss the Friday class. I pay a tremendous amount of money for his karate, and he loves it. He will not pass his next testing if he does not go three times a week for the black-belt club that he asked to belong to."

A few days later, instead of the $500 Colby had promised, I was served court papers for a huge reduction in child support retroactive to June 2001. In the papers Colby lied about his reason for relocation to Virginia Beach, saying he moved because *I* wanted to move back. But he was the one who brought it up to me first, and I made no promises at that time, not to mention I was still living in Delaware.

I still didn't receive any money, but that Friday I had Gabriel ready for Colby at 6:15m as promised. When Colby picked Gabriel up, I gave him a full update *again* on the information from Gabriel's allergy doctor as well as the patient handout.

The previous March, in 2001, when I decided to move back to my hometown of Virginia Beach, I gave myself a year to get the house ready for sale and to prepare to move. I intentionally did not date anyone that year in Delaware because I didn't want anyone or anything to alter my plans to relocate. Near the end of 2001, as I got closer to getting the house ready to put on market in the spring, Colby suggested *I* sell the house.

"I'd rather see you get the commission than a real estate agent," he said.

Well, put your money where your mouth is, I thought. I didn't trust Colby to honor that, so I had my attorney draft a commission agreement stating that after the sale of the house, I would get a 6 percent commission, common for listing and selling a home in Delaware at the time. Because Colby owed me over $10,000 in child support, health insurance for Gabriel, and other incidentals, I had it included in the agreement that after the commission, the money owed would be paid, and only then would we split the remaining proceeds fifty-fifty. It was the only way Colby would get current on his debts to Gabriel.

In February 2002 I asked Colby if he could get the commission agreement notarized that coming weekend because I wanted to put the house on the market.

"Just go ahead and email it to me," he said.

"Colby, I don't have the final draft yet, and the dates need to match."

"OK. I'll just tell my paralegal not to date it."

I felt sick at the thought—a lawyer with such disregard for the law—again!

But none of that happened. You see, he only wanted me to sell the house, so we didn't have to pay an agent, and there would be more money to split. But I was not going to do all that work and not be compensated for it. So, once I was holding him accountable to sign the commission agreement, he kept finding excuses to put it off, probably thinking I would let it go. This went on for over a month!

About a week later he brought Gabriel home from his weekend and, in front of me, signed the final version of the commission agreement in duplicate. It still needed to be notarized, but I wanted a copy in my hands with his signature, notary or not. He claimed he would get it notarized and back to me before I flew out of town.

A week passed, and Colby had still not contacted Gabriel's school about tuition, he had not notarized the commission agreement, and he still had not paid his child support. I was about to fly out of state that Thursday (Valentine's Day) to perform with my dad and my brother with the Eastern Symphony Orchestra, and Gabe was going with me. True to form, Colby said he would wire the money on Friday, the day after I left town. The following Monday I called my bank—no wire transfer, no funds. Another lie.

The day after I called my bank, on February 16, while I was still in Illinois, Colby called my cell phone to talk to Gabriel. When we talked, I did not mention the money he owed me, but out of earshot of Gabriel I did ask him about the commission agreement because that was far more important to me, encompassing over $10,000 in money owed.

"I still don't have it notarized," he said, "and I see no reason for a notary since you have my signature on one copy."

"Colby, on the advice of my attorney, it must be notarized. Hey, I'll even pay the five-dollar notary fee and reimburse you for an overnight FedEx fee."

"OK, I'll need your credit card number then."

Does he think I'm an idiot? I refused, and my frustrations mounted.

Three weeks after first asking for the notarized document, Colby called again. "I have it notarized," he said. "I'll bring it to you at the end of the week when I pick up Gabe. I've also called Gabriel's school, and I'll send them a check. You should also know, I've found the money to buy Gabriel a purebred boxer puppy."

He omitted anything about his child support.

March was no different from February—no child support and no tuition, although he did write the school a check that bounced, as I was informed by the finance office at the school. Ugh!

"We need to talk about my visitation arrangement," Colby said in the midst of this, "and how Gabriel's karate classes are interfering with my pick-up time. I'll keep the dog out of his room. I won't let him sleep with the dog either, and we'll get an air filter," he claimed.

Later, I found out Gabe was sleeping with the dog all the time. I even gave Colby a handout from the allergy doctor to help him better understand Gabe's condition. Yet, when Gabriel came back from his next weekend with his dad, he was horribly congested.

"Gabe, did you get your allergy medicine?" I asked.

"I only got it twice all weekend."

He was supposed to get doses every four to six hours. I had even made it easy and cost-free for Colby by giving him his own bottle with the directions written in large letters on the label. Poor Gabriel was so miserable! Did I want to tell him that his dad was irresponsible and didn't care enough about his health and well-being? You bet I did! But I kept my mouth shut. I wanted to keep him from getting in the middle of our disagreements, as always.

Gabriel continuously told me of expensive things they did that Colby could not possibly afford like going to dinner at the Melting Pot, trips out of town, and so on. For a man who was months behind on his child support, how could he afford that? Later, I learned that Colby wasn't paying for those things; wife number three was footing the bill.

Gabriel wasn't just bringing home new ideas about materialism though. "Mom, we watched a movie last night that was about streetwalkers and how a bunch of women were being killed," he said upon coming home one weekend, "and there was this knife that when the street people touched it, they knew who was killed with it!"

I was horrified. That was what my six-year-old told me happened while on his most recent weekend with his dad. I also found out later, after wife number three divorced him, that they would all watch *Scrubs* together, a TV show that constantly talked about sex, strip clubs, and other topics not appropriate for a child. And when wife number three told Colby it made her feel uncomfortable watching a show like that with a child (she would often leave the room), he got pissed at her, claiming she didn't want to do family activities.

After they separated, she testified that Colby had pornographic screensavers on the computer that Gabriel used to do his homework and play games on. She went on to say that Colby had a huge stack of printouts of prostitutes' profiles with personal handwritten notes on many of them detailing things he noticed or liked about them. Finding these was the final straw for her, and she divorced him.

One day Gabriel and I were having a conversation about different types of jobs people have. "I want to have lots of money when I grow up, Mommy."

"Having lots of money is not what is most important," I said. "Loving what you do, working hard at it, and taking pride in it is important. And *family* is most important in life."

He looked at me. "Mommy, people who sell cars don't make a lot of money."

That floored me because he would have no knowledge of that on his own.

"Who told you that?"

"Daddy did, a long time ago when you were dating Adam."

Adam was a sales manager for an auto dealership. Aside from Gabriel having an unhealthy focus on money at age six, it certainly was not appropriate to say something negative like that about an acquaintance of mine to my son. But this was just the beginning of such comments from my ex. I found it ironic that Colby would talk to Gabriel about making lots of money when he was never able to hold onto his money or his jobs. He has always lived beyond his means and has the empty bank accounts and multiple job changes to prove it.

When Gabriel's second set of allergy tests rolled around, it was no shock that he was "a very allergic patient," as the nurse stated. The doctor had trouble measuring all the allergic bumps and redness because they blended into one another. Gabriel was miserable. Despite how bad his allergies were, the doctor and I talked about how upsetting it would be for Gabriel if we took the dog away. So, in lieu of that, Colby had to take extra precautions, like an air filter, keeping his room a sterile zone, using a humidifier in the winter, and definitely no sleeping with Georgie, the dog. The doctor went so far as to ask Colby to come in with Gabriel, so they could discuss what was in Gabriel's best interest going forward.

I spoke with Colby that afternoon and asked if he was willing to meet with the doctor, and he agreed. However, a week later when he came to get Gabriel for his weekend visit, I told Colby, in front of Gabriel, that Gabriel and I had talked about the necessary precautions to be taken to keep his allergies under control and the various things that needed to be observed. I also said that Gabriel understood and was OK with everything.

Colby went ballistic in front of Gabriel and began pointing his finger at me and yelling. "No one is going to tell me Gabriel cannot sleep with his dog! Gabriel is *not* allergic to Georgie, and I was *not* consulted about taking him off of Zyrtec for his allergy tests to be done. I will not listen to *some doctor* and be told what to do. I'll get my own doctor and have Gabriel retested."

I gently put my hands on Gabriel's shoulders, turned him around, and sent him upstairs to his room as Colby's behavior was getting out of control. I did not want Gabe to be a part of this. Colby continued yelling. "Do you want to know what a bastard I can be? I'm not going to sign these papers after all!"

There was language in the commission agreement he wanted removed relative to how I was paid the commission, so these were revision papers. I pleaded with him for ten minutes to sign the papers as he had repeatedly promised—even in writing via emails. He snatched the papers from me and was very threatening in his verbal communications with me. This was nothing new, but it was new to be happening in front of Gabriel, who was still within earshot.

When they were about to leave, I took Gabriel aside and gave him a big squeeze, what we called "our hugs." "Please don't let this upset you," I said. "I'm proud of you for understanding the importance of what the doctor said about your health being a priority and for being a big boy and accepting that you should not sleep with Georgie. Please, Gabe, don't worry about anything this weekend. We'll deal with all of this another time."

My first concern was for Gabe not to go through any distress due to Colby's behavior and his treatment of me in front of Gabriel. I always believed in consistency with my son, both in my discipline choices and how I communicated with him, not to let things said between his father and I upset him. While I realize that things like that will upset a child anyway, I felt he needed to hear that I was proud of him and that these things were not his fault.

Consistency in parenting, discipline, love, and teaching is paramount for children's upbringing because it allows them to predict how their parents will act. Consistency also allows children to be in control of their own behavior. Consistency means that as parents, we follow through on what we say we will do. While change is part of life, consistency, as much as possible, is necessary.

Then, a shocker! During this same pickup encounter, Colby informed me that he'd be mailing me a check for $2,000 on Monday. "We closed on a second mortgage on my fiancé's house. I would have brought you a check today, but I didn't know how much money we were getting."

What? Why is he getting any money from her second mortgage? They weren't even married yet!

What struck me was the dramatic switch in Colby's behavior during that incident. He went from normal to ballistic and then back to normal when telling me about the check.

After they left I got on the phone with my ex-mother-in-law because Colby and Gabe were on their way to her house in Baltimore and I told her what happened. "And would you please make sure Gabriel is OK?" I asked. "Will you speak with Colby about Gabriel's allergy issues, please?"

"I don't want to speak to Colby about it," she said, "because it will do no good."

"Well, please don't tell Colby about this call then because I'm afraid he will retaliate."

"OK dear," she said, "we'll keep this our secret."

Parenting is a constant journey of learning. One day while Gabriel was on the phone with his dad, I asked him to see if his dad still planned on taking him to the allergy doctor on Friday. After he asked, Gabriel quickly added that it was not his idea to ask, and he said that three times! I realized I should not have put him in that position; I should have done so myself.

"Why did you tell your dad that it wasn't your idea to ask?" I inquired after he got off the phone.

"I didn't want Daddy to get mad at me."

Poor guy! I felt terrible! "I'm so sorry, buddy. I should not have had you ask. That's Mommy's fault."

That was one of several times I acknowledged to my son that I had made a mistake and that I was sorry. It's important for children to realize that parents also make mistakes, that we are not perfect, and to let them know we will try not to do that again. This will help them do the same and to live by our example.

DURING ANOTHER WEEKEND visit to his paternal grandparents', Gabriel and I were talking on the phone, and he told me he was watching *Pearl Harbor* again. While I understood Colby's lack of judgment in letting a six-year-old watch a violent, R-rated movie, I did not understand why my in-laws allowed it, unless they, too, didn't want confrontations with Colby.

It was no surprise that when Gabriel returned from his weekend visit, he smelled like dog—again—and was very congested and had a runny nose. At dinner I asked him if he slept with Georgie.

"That was Daddy's plan, and I started out sleeping with her, but she was biting me too much on the first night. On the second night, I did not want to sleep with her because I was too tired and wanted to get some sleep."

I had Gabriel bathe to wash off all the dog dander and then put him to bed. I'd kept an air filter in his room since birth, and at the direction of the allergy doctor, I ran a humidifier when the heat was on. Since he was a baby, I would always read to him before bed, snuggling beside him and reading one of our favorite books that we have saved to this day, *Love You Forever* by Robert Munsch.

Cherish the moments.

REGINA ROSSI VALENTINE

PART 3

"The secret is not to give up hope. It's very hard not to because if you're really doing something worthwhile, I think you will be pushed to the brink of hopelessness before you come through the other side.

—George Lucas

Chapter 16

SIGNS OF WAR

April–July 2002

IN MY FRUSTRATION over the numerous delinquent and bounced child-support checks, which had been going on for several years by that point, I did a little Internet search on the law in Delaware. On April 11, 2002, I emailed Colby.

> *Are you aware that in the state of Delaware, your visitation rights can be suspended until you come current on your child support? You have made it painfully clear that you do indeed have money, but you are selective in how it is dispersed, which seems to be at your discretion and not what the courts have determined and ruled. What happened to the statement you made to me several months ago when you said, You are right, Regina. Gabriel's money should come first? Do I need to take this up with my attorney? I am more than prepared to do so.*

I Loved You More

Later, I found out from my attorney that this was incorrect, but Delaware did take delinquent child support very seriously. In most divorce cases where there is child support due, many times the parent who has to pay the support does not see it as money going to their child and the child's needs and expenses. Rather, they see it as money going to their ex, and that burns them up inside. I never used child-support money for anything other than Gabe. My conscience would not allow me to do anything else. I think even Colby would acknowledge that, then and now.

Colby responded to my email by saying he had filed an action against me.

Gabriel will be more than thrilled to hear of what Mommy is doing. He is a lot older now, Regina, and undoubtedly has a memory and an inquisitive way about him. I would encourage you to tread lightly. These things have a way of biting.

Livid, I burned off a reply.

I am sure you would inform Gabriel of the legal issues that go on between his parents as you use him as a tool to make yourself look better. So, heed your own advice as things biting you back will haunt you, not me. When he is an adult and can think for himself, he will come to his own conclusions based on what he has experienced and lived in each of his homes. I have never involved him or put him in the middle as you have. He is a child and, unfortunately, a victim of your selfishness, yet I have never communicated anything negative about you or your negligence to him. That would be wrong. Can you say the same?

Colby falsely claimed that he had never said anything negative about me or my parents to Gabriel, nor had he indicated anything to Gabe about our legal issues. Then there were the countless things that, down the road after their divorce, Rene, wife number three, revealed to me that Colby would say to Gabriel about me daily.

My email went on to itemize all the things he had not paid in regard to child support, school tuition, and so on. Since I was aware they were in Florida, because Colby made the mistake of calling me from their resort room phone, I pointed out that while his financial obligations to his son were not being met, he was nonetheless parading around on vacations. When Colby called me from the resort phone later that night once Gabriel was in bed, I called the number back and asked for their room number and when they would be checking out. I couldn't believe the clerk shared that information with me, but it allowed me to go online and have a good idea of what they paid for that short trip. It was around $1,100, and it was *not* an all-inclusive. That was just for a three-night stay, and remember, this was 2002. But there was no money for Gabriel's needs.

We don't all marry Prince Charming or Cinderella. How you choose to handle each and every situation with your ex is what matters. Choosing to handle things in ways that are best for your child means swallowing that humble pill at times. It may not matter all that much to them when they are young, but trust me, it will make all the difference in how they evolve into young adults and, eventually, adults. Everything we say and do shapes them, for better or worse. Children deserve better. Who cares if you don't get to vent your frustrations at your ex? In the long run, it's not about you; it's about your children. When you decided to become a parent, whether you realized it or not, part of that contract was that your children come first, always.

As I was planning our move back to my hometown of Virginia Beach once school was out, I was also setting up job interviews. In trying to keep Colby in the loop on various things, I always communicated with him as much as possible via email. It was my method of keeping records of things he would say to me. I found it very interesting that while he and Rene were away at the resort, he stayed up on all his emails with me, but then he went silent. Things were about to change, and since we would be living in the same town very soon, we needed to revisit visitation.

I had strongly encouraged Colby not to discuss anything with Gabriel until we hashed it all out in court because I did not want Gabriel to be disappointed. But, knowing Colby as I did, I knew he would continue to discuss summer plans with Gabriel to get his hopes up. The idea with Colby was that if the courts changed anything that affected his unrealistic plans, he would blame it on Mommy, so Gabriel would be upset with me, not him. It wasn't right on any level to set a child up for disappointment like that.

That night when Colby called, all I asked him before I handed the phone to Gabriel was if he had received my email.

"No," he said.

I knew it was a lie.

I WAS CONCERNED the next morning at breakfast when my innocent six-year-old told me, "Daddy says I can go to a massage therapist who works in his office building!" My concern deepened when Gabe added, "Daddy told me if I feel uncomfortable taking off all my clothes, I can leave my shorts on."

What? I thought I was going to throw up! I had serious concerns with anyone other than a doctor examining my child or touching his body in a way that he may confuse what is acceptable and what is not, especially when his dad was allowing a stranger to do so when Gabe had no medical need for a massage.

I was barely getting over the massage conversation when the next day Gabe asked me a question. "Mommy, why do women scream when they are about to be murdered?"

Oh my word!

"Gabriel, where did you hear such a thing?" I asked after I got over my initial shock.

"In a movie." Once again, Gabe was exposed to inappropriate movies at the tender and impressionable age of six.

That same day I had an appointment with the allergy doctor I had scheduled after the previous Friday's scene. I made sure not to speak in front of Gabriel and had him wait in another room. "You should know what happened last week," I told the doctor. "Colby reacted violently to all the medical issues concerning Gabriel's allergies. I want you to be aware of what to expect just in case Colby comes in for Gabe's appointment."

"Well," the doctor said, "again, make sure you are documenting *everything*."

"I am," I assured him.

"I have no worries about a potential meeting," he said. "I've been in practice over thirty years. I know how to handle the situation, so it's not upsetting to Gabriel. I'm giving you copies of Gabriel's medical records. I'll have my nurse give you two copies, so Colby can have one set."

That night I told Colby on the phone that I had copies of Gabriel's records to give to him. Around the same time, I opened the mail. There was a check from Colby for $2,007.50 with a breakdown of what it was for relative to back payments and other matters. He had paid me what he thought he should be paying for child support, not what the courts had mandated. There was still no money for Gabriel's medical insurance, prescription co-pays, or mortgage money, and Colby still owed more than $900 for Gabriel's tuition. It was April 2002.

The next day I discovered Colby was taking Gabriel for his summer buzzcut, even though he had never taken Gabe for a haircut previously, and that Colby and his fiancé had a large wedding planned. There would be wedding photos, tuxedos, a diamond wedding ring, brunch for all the wedding guests, and a photographer but no child support or tuition for his son.

As if all this wasn't enough, Gabriel called me the next day to tell me his dad had gotten him a parrot! I actually thought he was joking, but he wasn't. "Rene took me to the pet store and bought me a new bird with a new cage and everything! There was one that cost a hundred and ninety-two dollars, but they bought me one that was sixty dollars."

I felt sick but said nothing to Gabe about the fact that he was also allergic to bird feathers. I did not want to upset him.

"Mommy, I like living here," he said. My soul was crushed. But why wouldn't he say that when he was being spoiled all the time? To make things even worse, Gabriel said that while Rene was speaking with the saleslady, he was free to walk around the store looking at all the animals. He was six-and-a-half years old; he should not have been left unattended like that.

As if pouring salt in the wound, Gabriel told me the next day that he was "given a new diamond ring." In the background I heard Colby saying it was "for the wedding," but Gabriel couldn't contain himself. "It's real gold, Mommy, with a real diamond!" They were also on their way to get Gabe a tuxedo for the wedding.

I felt my stomach churn and my eyes fill with tears as fear overwhelmed me, thinking I might be losing my son to all this attention and material things.

Two days later Gabriel came home from his dad's very congested, constantly coughing and clearing his throat. "We forgot to give me my allergy medicine for a few days, Mommy," he told me at bedtime, "but I was OK."

"It's not your responsibility to take your medicine, Gabe, it's Daddy's." I did *not* say this in a derogatory way, although I really wanted to.

"Well," he said, "I mean *Daddy* forgot to give it to me."

"Did you have a humidifier or air filter in your room?" I asked.

"No."

"Gabe, do you still sleep with Georgie when you're at Daddy's?"

"No."

I was shocked. "Why? What happened?"

"I told Daddy I didn't want to sleep with Georgie anymore because she kept me awake at night. Mommy, that is part of the reason. The other part is that I don't want to make my allergies bad, but I didn't want to tell Daddy that because he would get mad at me."

"Gabriel, you're very smart to understand the importance of your allergies and your health. I'm proud of you for doing the right thing! Way to go, Gabriel!"

It reinforced for me that my way of trying to educate Gabriel on his health was getting through.

On our way to school the next day, Gabriel complained in the car about the dog hair on his windbreaker.

"I'll wash it tonight, Gabe," I said. "I'm sorry I haven't already done so, as in the past."

Since he got the dog, I had always washed his winter and flannel coats when he got home from his dad's because they always smelled strongly like the dog. Colby let the dog travel with them from Virginia Beach to Delaware. This was a new jacket, and since they arrived late on Sunday, I had forgotten to wash it.

The dog hair conversation prompted another comment from Gabe. "Mommy, I hate when I get cat hair up my nose. Sometimes I have to pick them out of my nose and then wash my hands because one time I was at the dinner table when it happened." Rene already had a cat before Colby met her.

Even more upsetting, Gabriel told me he had had a bad dream the night before. "I dreamed I stabbed my friend, Ryan, with a knife in his forehead, and his blood glowed."

I could only imagine what movie prompted that type of nightmare.

The next morning Gabriel woke up with a terrible bloody nose. Blood was all over his hands, his pajamas, and his pillow. This whole allergy thing was so frustrating, but Colby didn't seem to care. Colby seemed to care more about doing things his way instead of what was best for Gabriel.

That night at dinner, I had a conversation with Gabriel. "Gabe, you and Daddy will be going to see the allergy doctor together."

"I remember the doctor asking to see my dad," Gabe said, "and I'm fine with him going. But why is Daddy going with me instead of you, Mommy?"

"Well, the doctor wants to help Daddy better understand how important your health is and how serious your allergies are."

"Sometimes when we talk about the dog, Daddy says that Mommy thinks she's the boss of everybody."

I took a deep breath and patiently went through a fairly long explanation about what the dog, cat, and now the parrot had to do with his allergies and with the doctor testing him to see if they made him sick. "Dr. Seltzer has been taking care of people with allergies for a *long* time," I said. "He knows more than me and more than your dad about what's best for your health. The only thing the doctor cares about is that you stay healthy and happy. I am not trying to be a boss. I am trying to do what is in your best interest because *you* are the most important thing in my life. Gabe, what you just told me will be kept between the two of us. I would never tell your dad what you said."

"Don't tell a soul, Mommy, because I don't want Daddy to be mad at me."

My heart wanted to break in pieces for my little boy, who clearly was terrified of making his dad mad at him. "Gabriel, anything you tell me is private between the two of us," I assured him. If my sweet boy only knew all the things I was keeping from him about his dad in order to protect him.

I didn't pump Gabriel for information because I did not want him to feel as though he was in the middle of his parents. If he offered something up, it might have been good for me to know, but I was not going to drag it out of him, although I was discovering that was exactly what his dad did on a regular basis. Of course, I said nothing about this to Colby, despite the fact that I once again wondered who was paying for another trip. I didn't want him to know that I knew.

Knowledge is power, and over time, I learned to keep things under wraps until we were in front of a judge.

Chapter 17

RENE

August–October 2002

BOTH COLBY AND I were now living in Virginia. Because "co-parenting" was nonexistent, the courts insisted we go to co-parenting counseling with a therapist. When we started, Gabe was six and a half years old. Our therapist worked with us for two years. He's a forensic psychologist, and he eventually reached a point—because Colby often wouldn't show up, and when he did, he wouldn't listen, on top of all of his narcissistic behavior—that he actually "fired" Colby, making him the only patient that our therapist ever fired. "I will never be in a room with him alone again because of his violent outbursts," he said. "In my entire career, he is the worst sociopath and narcissist I have ever met."

Even with therapy, co-parenting didn't exist. It was always a battle, and for Colby it was always about winning. He never did anything, if you ask me, geared toward love for his child. It was always about winning and attacking me because that's what narcissists want. They want to control, and Gabriel was controllable by him. As I said, Colby called Gabe his best friend. I always cringe when I hear parents say to a child, "You're my best friend." *They're children*. You can't afford to be best friends. They need a parent, at least while they are young. I told Gabriel several times, "Look, I am not your friend. I am your parent and your mother. One day we'll be friends, just not now." It's too much emotional responsibility for a child when a parent tries to be their friend.

Colby was now with his third wife, Rene. I don't remember the date, but on one occasion when I dropped Gabriel off at his dad and Rene's, I noticed a large diamond ring on Rene's hand along with her wedding band. Meanwhile, Gabriel mentioned that Colby was still trying to get a job on a cargo ship, but he was also trying to be a "policeman in the sky." When I told him his dad didn't know how to fly a plane, he said he could learn. In speaking with my father, he figured it meant an air marshal. I wondered how many jobs Colby had actually had or would have. How many job changes was he willing to go through? And why? Offhand, I could name four jobs he'd had just that past year, two of which, both law firms, supposedly fired him. He was now looking for career number five. To think I gave up my career for him to get a law degree, and now he wasn't even using it (I learned why eventually). Additionally, Colby had lived in at least five different places in five years, which was neither good nor stable for Gabriel.

The practice of "forgetting" his checkbook, of "it's in the mail," never to be seen, and of short payments and of "hold this check for a few days" continued, all while living the good life with his new wife while Gabriel and I struggled.

On August 20 my father called me at work and asked if Gabriel had told me about the time the lifeguard had to come save him. What? I said no, but so as not to betray Gabriel's confidence and willingness to share things with my parents, I decided to wait a couple of days and get Gabriel to tell me about it himself.

I Loved You More

One night while Gabriel and I were eating dinner, I broached the subject. "Hey, buddy, I now go to a different street at the beach where it isn't as crowded, and people are allowed to surf," I said. "But I wouldn't want to take you there because there aren't any lifeguards, and I want to make sure we have one wherever we go as added safety. Have you ever talked to a lifeguard?"

"Yes, Mommy," he said exuberantly, "when we were at the beach one day, and I had a question."

"That's cool," I said. "Have you ever seen them save someone?"

"Yes, Mommy. One day not too long ago, I was in the water playing with this kid, and while we were talking, I missed a wave, but the other kid rode it in, but the wave pulled me even farther out. I couldn't get back in, and I was scared because it was over my head. The lifeguard and Daddy had to come out and get me."

My stomach did a flip. "Very cool." I said calmly as I speared a forkful of food. "How deep was the water you were in before the wave came?"

"Up to my neck."

Good lord.

Colby had repeatedly assured me Gabriel was never alone in the water when it was that deep, "never deeper than his knees," he said. Well, you can't surf in water that shallow. The fin alone would get stuck in the sand.

Five days later, Colby informed me that he and Rene were taking a trip to California. Five days after that, on August 30, Colby called from his cell phone and told me again he was indeed going to California.

"Colby, I know that; you've told me. Why are you telling me again? Wait, do you mean this might change my time with Gabriel on Sunday?"

"No, no," he said, "we'll be back by then."

"I don't understand."

"Well, Gabriel's going with us."

Really?

"I understood from our conversation last week that you and Rene were going alone on Sunday or Monday."

"Well, yeah, and taking Gabriel with us."

I was concerned. Gabriel hadn't been feeling well that week; in fact he had a fever. I questioned the intelligence behind taking a six-year-old across the country while sick. I sought the advice of my attorney as well as Gabriel's principal in regard to missing school. I called Colby to discuss it, leaving a message and asking him to call me back when we could talk in private, away from Gabriel's ears. He called me from his cell phone in his car, with Gabriel by his side, when he knew I was at work. I told him I'd call him back from a private office.

"OK, are we alone?" I asked. "Gabriel can't hear us, can he?"

"Regina, what's the problem?"

"Colby, please call me back when we can discuss this alone."

"If this is about California, we'll be together," he said. "He'll be by my side the whole time, right, sport?"

"Is Gabe right there with you?"

"Don't be such a pain in the ass, Regina!" He was shouting into the phone, driving, with my son probably in the front seat—again. "You're freaking out over nothing!"

"Colby, I just want to make sure you take Gabriel to the doctor first and make sure nothing is wrong before you guys make this trip."

"Not yet. Maybe after karate tonight."

"But that's too late, and Colby, Gabe's health is more important than karate. Please take him now in that case!"

"Do you plan on making the co-payment?" he asked.

"That's your responsibility," I replied.

"Great, then I won't take him. Right, sport? You don't want to go to the doctor, do you?"

"Fine," I said. "I have no problem paying, no problem putting my son and his health first. I've spoken with my attorney—"

"Dammit, Regina, you're being a pain in the ass! Go ahead, get a court order. We'll be on the plane by the time you do."

"Colby, if you don't stop yelling, I'll have to hang up on you," I warned.

Instead, he hung up on me.

I expected some form of retaliation, like more late returns of Gabe or not agreeing to visitation arrangements. It was not the first time Colby treated me badly in front of Gabriel.

But they did go, and at about 6:45 p.m. I got a call from Colby saying they went to the doctor, and he got a note stating Gabriel was able to travel. When I pushed to find out what was wrong with Gabriel, he said he simply had a "red throat" and was given a "mild" antibiotic. They gave him Zithromax, which is not mild; it's a strong five-day dose, which meant Gabriel had a bacterial infection, not just a red throat.

Colby picking fights and arguing in front of Gabe got progressively worse—and uglier. Something had to give. Colby was demeaning and angry, seemingly all the time now. A dozen times I had to say, "I will not have this conversation with you right now!", to no avail. He continued to badger and belittle me in front of Gabriel. On one occasion I told him we could not have a conversation like that in front of Gabriel again and to call me later.

"Fine!" he shouted loud enough for Gabe to hear. "I can't wait to hear why you won't let me have my son!"

Gabe was visibly upset, so I walked him into the house and had a talk with him, as I had done many times before. I explained that I was sorry he had to hear that and that his dad and I had been told that we should not discuss things in front of him.

"It's OK, Mommy," he said sadly. "I just wish you two would get along."

It was not OK.

Meanwhile, child support was nowhere to be found, and when it finally was, it was late, too little, or the check bounced. There were long stretches without even twenty dollars in good faith. Yet, Gabriel told me one morning on the way to school that his dad said he would buy him ninja swords for his Halloween costume. I had already told Gabe I would not buy them since he already had ninja nun chucks at home that matched his costume, and it was an unnecessary expense to buy a different prop.

Ugh.

October 2002

Well, I've been a bit remiss at journaling in this since I was so overwhelmed with the move, end of the year, looking for a job & a house in Va. Beach and making arrangements for your new school, St. Francis's. I am so excited that you are going to my alma mater and with your two cousins, too! You think it's pretty neat that Aunt Leslie works at the school, and you keep asking me to work there. But no matter how I try and explain it, you don't understand my need to work at a job that pays the bills. I keep telling you that someday I will be able to pick you up from school each day, maybe be a homeroom mom, and be able to do my voiceover work instead of working at a desk job. After all, dreams do come true!

Something else you've been saying for a long time now, more so since your dad remarried again, is that you keep wishing I would "find someone and get married and have a baby, so I can have a baby brother or sister." I never, ever wanted to just have one child. I had always dreamed of having 2-4 children especially since I am from a big family. But that's not how it worked out, and the older I get without being in a relationship, the less chance of my having another child. I'd love to give you a sibling, but sometimes we don't have control over those kinds of things. So, I will just have to shower you with all the love I have in my heart and hope it is enough.

...

Well, I am excited because I am going to buy you a new bike for your birthday! I picked it out yesterday and hope you like it! It's a 24" bike. You are so tall, and I can't see getting anything smaller since you are growing so fast! We are having a party with my whole family and 4 of your friends. Three are from school (Justin, who is the son of my best friend when I went to St. Francis's, Ian, & Kevin) and Alex, your new neighborhood bud. I will wait till after the party to write more about what happens.

...

The party went great! We played games, had a piñata, and bobbed for apples where each of the boys ditched their shirts like you to "dive in"! Since you were an experienced bobber, you won with the most apples!

It was the last time I hosted Gabe's birthday parties alone.

In October we had our first parent-teacher conference at St. Francis's. Afterwards, Colby called me on the cell phone to say that all the good things that had transpired with Gabriel, both academically and with his behavior and respect were "all you, and I wanted to say thanks." I was stunned he would compliment me, and I wondered what might come next.

I picked Gabriel up at Colby and Rene's house and had an interesting conversation at their front door with Rene while Gabe waited in my car.

"Regina, can we talk?" she asked, concern written all over her face.

"Sure, Renee, what's up?"

"I'm worried," she said. "I'm concerned with Colby's motivation to work and whether he *has any*," she said.

"Rene, I don't know what to say," I replied. "He has not been known for being very industrious."

"How much so?" she asked. I could see the distress on her face. Rene had straight dirty-blond hair, beautiful blue eyes, and a great smile with really white teeth. She had a friendly personality. I believed—and it was borne out in later years—she truly loved Gabriel and desperately wanted to be a family with him and Colby, almost at any cost. I wanted her to know what she had gotten into. Without elaborate description, venom or excuses, I simply looked at her and told her the simplest, truest thing I could think of.

"He owed us $9,800 in back child support and mortgage payments," I said. "That's as of the closing of the house this past May."

Rene took a step back and thought about it. Then she looked at me. "Where has all that money gone?"

"What money?" I asked.

Chapter 18

THROW ME A ROPE

November–December 2002

I SOLD OUR HOUSE in Delaware in less than two weeks in the late spring of 2002. When we moved to Virginia Beach on June 1, we lived with my aunt and uncle for several months while I secured a job and a new house for Gabe and me. Between the proceeds from the sale of the Delaware house and money I had put aside (a little here and there when I could), I had 22 percent to put down on our new home in Virginia Beach. I was thrilled to be able to get a mortgage without paying mortgage insurance!

In the divorce, we each took one some of the credit card debt based on our income. Colby took the MBNA credit card but never made so much as one minimum payment, ever. A couple of years before my move, I needed a new lawnmower and couldn't even get a Sears credit card to buy it due to his negligence. While I was aware of this issue when I applied for the mortgage, I thought that by putting 22 percent down, along with my great credit score, there would be no issue. Surprisingly, the bank would not approve me for my conventional mortgage due to that MBNA delinquency. My name was still attached to it. I ended up having to get an FHA loan with PMI (private mortgage insurance), paying $2,200 up front, then $60 more a month for 5 years—almost an additional $6,000, all because Colby didn't honor his financial and legal obligations.

While Colby was always financially irresponsible, he also continued to be reckless when it came to Gabe's safety. One afternoon I picked up Gabriel at Colby's office, excited to take him to see our new house.

"Mommy, when I was out on Daddy's boat," he told me on the car ride there, "it was so windy Daddy had to throw me a rope two times to pull me back in!" (Yeah, forgot to mention that Colby now had a boat too!)

What? I thought I was going to throw up as I tried to stay focused on my driving.

"Gabe, what do you mean? Were you on deck or were you guys trying to dock or something like that?"

"No, Mommy, it was while I was swimming in the bay."

"Was your dad in the water with you?"

"No. I was alone."

Panic bubbled up inside me, and my knuckles went white as I gripped the steering wheel even tighter.

"Was your stepmom, Rene, on the boat?"

"No. Just me and Daddy."

"Were you wearing your life vest?"

"No."

Oh, for the love of God! Stay calm. Stay calm.

"When we drop anchor, I'm allowed to take off my life vest," he said.

I Loved You More

I pulled the car over and, as calmly as I could, looked him in the eye and explained to him, "Gabriel, first, you are *never* to take off your life vest at any time on the boat, and second, never swim alone."

"But Mommy, Daddy has to stay on the boat, so if the anchor doesn't hold, the boat won't get away from us."

"Gabe, *you* are more important than the boat. What you are telling me is unacceptable and unsafe. Promise me you will *not* take your life vest off at any time while on the deck too, OK?" Once again I was having to teach my child about safety measures without throwing his dad under the bus for his stupidity.

"Gabe," I continued, "please understand that sometimes parents don't always make the best decisions, but your dad does love you, as I also love you."

It was ironic that Colby chose to move back to my hometown first, making it easier for me to move there and be with family while still being able to keep Gabe close to his dad. For me, though, it was a chance to reconnect with childhood friends and to reestablish those relationships

By November Colby's child-support payment was late. That put him $1,500 in arrears, again. I called him on November 2 to make sure the dinner reservations that he, Rene, and Gabriel had that night were not at the same restaurant that I was going to. I was going on a date with someone Gabriel had not met. Colby said their plans were locked in because they had invited fifteen people to go to the Japanese steak house for Gabriel's birthday.

"That's an expensive birthday party for someone not paying child support," I said.

"Yes, it is," he replied.

On November 3 I had to pick Gabriel up from Colby's house. Colby had been working on a tugboat since the previous night, so Gabriel spent the day with his stepmother, Rene, instead of me.

When I got there, once Gabe was secure in the car, Rene apologized.

"I'm so sorry, Regina," she said. "Please, let me know if Gabriel had a bad weekend."

"How come?" I asked.

"We had a bad weekend here. All our financial issues came to a head, and I wasn't very patient about it, not anymore." She reached out and held my arm and then spoke to me in a softer tone. "I used to have everything. Now, I have no more credit, no more savings, and I may have to take on a second job."

"Rene, I understand."

On the afternoon of November 13, Colby called me and announced he was at work on the tugboat and would not be back for two weeks. The following day was to be his Thursday night with Gabriel, as was the coming weekend. I had to plan and pay for sitters for Thursday's choir rehearsal and Saturday's auction at the school, for which I had purchased tickets. He said he would return on either November 25 or 27. He also said he had mailed me a check but did not disclose the amount.

On November 14 I received a check from Colby for $1,000 for other expenses for Gabe, which he owed. The check was written by Rene, from his business account. I called and left her a message thanking her for the payment. On November 25, Colby called me and asked when he could get Gabriel for Thanksgiving. We agreed on a time. Meanwhile, despite Rene's check, by November 30, there was still no child-support payment, putting Colby $2,000 in arrears.

November 2002

I am excited because this is the first time ever to have my family for Thanksgiving dinner in my home (our home!). Unfortunately, you are with your dad this year, and I am so sad that you will not be able to share it with us. Also, you will be with your dad for Christmas dinner, which also stinks, but it's the crazy schedule that we have—doesn't make sense!

Ugh. On December 3, Brother Dominic of St. Francis's School called and said Colby was over $450 in arrears with tuition. He also owed $100 for book fees, which was due by September, so he was two months behind in tuition payments. I was walking through life the best I could, but in private, I was pulling my hair out—when I wasn't crying in the shower.

On December 7 Gabriel told me his daddy had two boats, one they sailed and another that he was fixing up. Still no child support. By that December Colby was again $2,500 in arrears. On December 16 he called to tell me he was going out to sea for the next three weeks, and Gabriel would be with me for the entire Christmas holiday. Yay!

After Christmas Colby called from the docks and said his schedule had changed again, and he wanted Gabriel for the weekend since it was "his" weekend. I apprised him of our plans for the weekend since he was supposed to be gone three weeks and offered that he could pick Gabriel up that night at 6:00 p.m., have the following day with him, and I'd pick him up at 5:00 p.m. on Saturday, so we could go to my big family party at my uncle's.

"That's fine. I understand," he said. "But I want him on Monday!"

"Colby," I replied, "I already have plans for Monday."

"I don't care about your plans!" he screamed. "I want Gabriel *Monday*. And Regina, you'd better rethink your answer before I give a final one!"

I was at work, so I hung up. Then I sought advice from counsel.

December 2002

Our first Christmas in our new home, and you got to be with me on Christmas Eve! Wow! That was cool but a ton of work for me since I (Santa) bought you a new basketball hoop, which I had to carry downstairs and wrap myself, but, as always, I managed, for you! You were so excited, and I made you wait till the end to open it. We had a wonderful night together even though I was unable to speak. I lost my voice four days ago and did not get to sing my solo or anything at midnight mass! Thank goodness you can read as you were my phone caller to my boss and the family after I would write down the messages. Since I couldn't do it, you read me "The Night Before Christmas," and that was cool. We had a fire and hot chocolate and put out goodies for Santa!

This has been a busy but great year for us, and I am so happy to be back in Va. Beach with our family for you to grow up with them! I love you, my darling son. I am proud of you, and, as always, you are my life. All I do is for you and for your future. May God, in His infinite goodness, continue to bless us and watch over us as we continue our life journey together!

I'll love you forever,

Mommy

Chapter 19

FAMILY

2003

I WAS SINGLE FOR SEVEN YEARS from the time of the divorce in 1997 to remarrying my current husband, Rob. I had two or three long-term relationships in those seven years, but they weren't the right ones for many reasons. When I knew I was moving back to Virginia, I didn't want to date anybody for a year because I didn't want anything stopping me from my mission to move my son back to where my family was.

Somewhere along the way, I don't recall the moment, I got to this place. I looked in the mirror one day and I liked who I was. *God*, I thought, *I don't need to be with someone if it's unhealthy or it's not bringing me joy or they don't love my child the way he deserves.* That was literally what I said to Rob when I met him, "I don't need a man." It wasn't the whole "Oh, you complete me." It was "You've got to bring as much as I bring to the table."

I have always prayed my son will meet and marry someone who loves him as much as he loves her and who deserves him and likewise. It's an equal thing.

I had just gotten to the place where I knew I was worthy, that I was a good person, and that I didn't want anybody to try and change me. The behavior that Colby brought out in me when we were married consisted of responses to his triggers. From the age of nineteen to twenty-five, I worked on ships and at Opryland. I met Colby when I was twenty-five, got married at twenty-seven, and had Gabriel at twenty-nine. So, the only other time anybody ever pulled that response out of me where I would fight back, where I would yell and scream, was my mother while growing up. So, for all those years, from nineteen to twenty-five, that behavior was completely dormant in me. Then all of a sudden, when I married Colby, I was behaving like I did as a teenager and a young adult. *What is wrong with me?* I wondered. *This is not who I want to be.* That period in between had been some of the happiest times in my life. So, naturally, I thought, *I've got to get back to that place. I've got to get back to who I am because the yelling and the fighting is not who I am.*

It's natural to feel like you have to fight back when your child's in the mix. Children can't fight back, so you have to do it for them. But through it all, once Gabe was born, I never behaved or responded like that in front of him, ever. So, I did get to a place before I met Rob where I had this epiphany of, *I like who I am, and I am worthy*. It happened naturally, and I imagine my faith and my personal growth played a part.

When you decide to become a parent, it is an unwritten contract, and so much comes with it. A key part of that contract is that your child comes first. That's why I didn't go back to my performance career when my marriage ended because Gabriel needed me present. In the entertainment world, you don't know when your next job is or where it will take you geographically, and Gabriel needed stability. It didn't matter what I wanted or what I was afraid of. It mattered that I had to do what I had to do to protect my son because he wasn't able to do it for himself.

I Loved You More

I met my current husband, Rob, of seventeen years through the personals on Match.com. It's funny because when I met him, my dad said, "Please tell me you didn't meet him the same way you met Colby."

"Oh, no," I replied, because this time it was the Internet, not the newspaper personals, as it was with Colby "in the old days." I fudged that just a tad.

ON JANUARY 3, 2003, I got a call from CPA Group. "Hello," the caller said, "we are trying to update contact information for Colby Baxter and to locate the 1988 Bayliner twenty-five-foot Ciera boat. It was purchased on September 20, 1997, with a $3,000 down payment from a Citibank account." Then, not long after that, Key Bank called about the same thing. And then, on January 6, my parents had a message on their answering machine from PHEA (Pennsylvania Higher Education Agency) also looking for Colby regarding his law school loans, which he still hadn't paid back. I am also in possession of another 2008 document from a creditor for over $78,000 to American Education Services outlining the debt. Those creditor calls on Colby were a regular thing, and they still are today. When we were married, he actually suggested that we file for bankruptcy, not because we had financial issues but because he just didn't want to repay his student loans! This financial irresponsibility and total disregard for his obligations is common-place for narcissists because they believe the rules don't apply to them.

Two nights later while Gabriel was on the phone with his dad, Colby told him he wanted to speak with me. I told Gabriel to ask his dad if he could call me back later when Gabriel was in bed. I was making dinner and considering our legal battles and his history of picking fights with me in front of Gabriel, I did not want to risk that the conversation would be unpleasant, especially with Gabriel there. Colby never called me back.

Meanwhile, child-support arrears reached $3,500.

On January 16 while Gabriel was eating his breakfast, I opened the pantry door to look for something. I noticed a container of nuts, and it looked like one might be bad. I made a passing comment (which I'd done before) to Gabriel about it. "We definitely don't want Grandma to eat these!"

He agreed. "Mommy, we have macadamia nuts at my daddy's house, and one day he handed me one and said to take it home to Grandma."

I was mortified and upset. Seeing this, Gabe responded immediately. "Daddy was just kidding! He didn't mean it!" I had to explain how ugly and unkind that was and that I never wanted to hear him joke about anything at the expense of another person. Gabriel knew well what happened to my mom when she had the violent food poisoning attack that led to her heart attack. He understood that macadamia nuts caused it and that she needed to stay away from all nuts.

On January 24 I received a check in the amount of $1,100, leaving Colby still in arrears by $2,900. Through February, Colby delivered checks that finally cured the arrears three days before we were to go to court. Convenient. We met there more often moving forward.

On July 16 Colby and I were in court for his motion to reduce child support. Colby did not get the ruling he desired. As a result, his fuming temper, with which I was so familiar, reared its ugly head, this time toward my attorney. He was on our heels as we left the courtroom, slinging his briefcase back and forth. "I am *not* going to pay the school tuition!" he shouted. He was in a rage.

He physically blocked Saul, my attorney, from turning to leave the waiting room and faced off with him, towering over him like an irate giant. Three times he got in his face and with his cheeks ablaze and his chest puffed out, he threatened to hit my attorney just outside the courtroom.

I Loved You More

"I'm going to get a police officer," I said after the third threat. Thankfully, an officer just around the corner had heard everything and ordered Colby to leave the courthouse.

In August Colby began driving around in a brand-new red Audi Roadster convertible. He said it was Rene's. He still owned his boats, although his creditors seemed to have other plans, and he still was not paying tuition.

We were getting more familiar with the court. We had a court-ordered mediation in 2003 with a mediator, Karen. Initially, Colby charmed her to the point where she said, "He's just a dad who wants to spend more time with his son." I told her I had serious concerns, based on history, which were my basis for not wanting him to have additional visitation. However, an hour into the session, Colby lost his cool and blew up at me and the mediator, yelling and getting belligerent. It was so bad that another mediator came into our room to make sure everyone was all right. About twenty minutes later, Colby stormed out in a tirade.

I broke down and cried in Karen's arms.

ON OCTOBER 28 THINGS GOT even uglier. I had to call the school because the day before a note was sent home saying that the finance committee was sending out letters due to non-payment. I called Colby and told him the school would have to kick Gabriel out if he continued not paying and not calling them. I'd been after him for months to call them and to pay at least something in good faith to show an effort, but he refused. This same thing had happened repeatedly in Delaware with Gabriel's school there. Colby was livid. However, upon hearing Gabriel could be kicked out, he finally called the finance office.

"Well, you and your attorney said you were going to file a show cause against me but you haven't bothered to do so," as if to throw it in my face.

When Colby finally called the school, he said he could only come up with $200 and would do so along with a letter of explanation by Thursday, October 30. Then, he told *me* to come up with the $200, and he would then come up with $300. But things quickly changed, and Colby sent me an email stating he was going to pay nothing for Gabriel's tuition. Then things got much worse.

When I picked up Gabriel from school, the director told me Colby had come to visit with Gabriel. When Gabe got in the car, I asked about his day, but he didn't mention his father's visit at all.

"Hey, buddy," I said, trying to sound positive, "I heard your dad surprised you with a visit today! That must have been nice."

"Yes," he replied.

"What did you guys talk about?"

"Don't you already know, Mommy?"

"Well, why don't you tell me, and I'll tell you if I'm right."

"He just wanted to say hi and see how I was doing."

"Wow," I said, "that was cool!" I left it at that. But about thirty seconds later, Gabriel explained more.

"Well, Mommy, actually that isn't true. Daddy told me he quit his last job because it took him away from me and Rene too much. So, his money was low, and I might have to change schools for a year." I was furious that he would put poor Gabe in the middle of his financial burdens like that, trying to play on his sympathies, but I held my tongue.

Later, when Gabe was not around, I called Colby and said I would do or give up whatever was necessary to ensure Gabriel remained at St. Francis's.

Two days later I went into the finance office before picking Gabriel up early for his birthday. They said they had received nothing from Colby. I said I would get *something* to them by Monday, but I was not sure how much I could come up with. When I got home, miraculously, there was a letter from the Virginia Department of Taxation stating I was due a refund and would receive a check in fifteen days. When the check came, it was in the amount of $676. I wrote a check to the school for $500. The remainder went to my attorney.

On November 14 while in the car that evening with Gabriel, he told me his dad was no longer teaching "college" (another quick job change). I did not question him further.

Four days later while on the way to school in the morning, Gabriel and I were talking about Spirit Week when I was in high school and how I walked backwards on backwards day. I told him it was hard because the halls were so crowded.

"I've been to college, Mommy, and the halls are not crowded." (He was referencing his dad's brief teaching stint at the local trade school, which was not a college.) Renee told me later that while she could not prove it, she believed Colby had an affair with one of his students at that school.

"Oh, Mommy," Gabriel said, "I know where my dad is working now that he's not teaching. He's a lawyer in New York. That's good, right?"

"Yes, Gabe, it's good that your dad is working." That's what I said, but it was not what I was thinking.

The next night Gabe finished his call with his dad and could not wait to tell me what Colby had said to him. "Mommy, on Thursday my dad is going to court for a guy who wants more visitation time with his kids, and his wife beats him and the kids." Wow, nice. Just the thing to share with an eight-year-old.

Colby was late with child support in December. I had to ask several times, as usual. When he did drop it by, the check was signed by Rene, this time from her personal account.

December 2003

This has been a very big year for you, son! You are in your second half of the 1st grade!! You are growing up *so fast, and I love you to pieces!!! In February I met a wonderful man. His name is Rob Valentine—what a cool last name! He is a firefighter and also is in the US Air Force. I have not dated for almost a year and a half because I felt it important to focus on our move to Virginia Beach, and I did not want to have any attachments in Delaware. Rob is wonderful. He is so kind and caring and is honest. Integrity, you will come to learn, is so important to one's character and a quality you must strive to find in those you associate yourself with in life. Rob has two children—Megan is almost 13 and Justin is almost 18.*

We have done some things together, the five of us, and all you kids get along very well. I am so happy to have met Rob. His father was in the fire service for 41 years, and his brother is also a firefighter. How cool is that?

. . .

Well, a few months after meeting Rob, he proposed to me. You know, Gabriel, I have always said in my letters and to you as a young boy, that anyone I dated had to pass muster for you, meaning, was this person good enough for my son? It is not strictly a decision about me and what or who I want. It is mostly about you. It is important to me that anyone I am involved with is a good influence on you, loves and cares for you, and is worthy to be in your life and mine. Rob is that man.

We are planning on getting married in the summer in the Outer Banks, NC. We want you kids to be included in it, and for that reason, we will not take a honeymoon right away.

I Loved You More

. . .

    Our life is really coming together, buddy. We have a wonderful family with the Rossis, and now we have added the Valentines. They are a great family who love us, and we love them too. Everyone gets along so well and really enjoys our get-togethers. Grandpa & Grandma Valentine have included you as if you were one of their blood grandchildren. They treat you no different from the others. You, "we," are so lucky!

    I guess this will tie up your annual letter. I wonder what lies ahead for you and me and our family. Time will tell. I am so blessed God chose me to be your mother. I take that so seriously, and it is the most important responsibility I have ever had or will have in life. I love you, Gabriel. God bless you, son, in all you do. May He always protect you when I can't.

    All my love,

    Mommy

Chapter 20

GROOMING

January–October 2004

COLBY HAD BEEN GROOMING Gabriel not to say anything about what went on in their house while at the same time Gabriel was required to report to his dad everything that happened at our home. When Gabriel was in court-ordered therapy, his therapist told us it was evident that Gabriel was conditioned not to say anything to the therapist. He said occasionally Gabriel would get distracted with a toy or gadget in the therapist's office and start to speak about something and then immediately pull back and shut down. The therapist got to a point where he had to stop seeing Gabriel because he couldn't help him, since Gabriel wouldn't speak to him.

It was years later, when Gabriel was older, that he finally started to exercise his independence.

I Loved You More

Right from the beginning of 2004, child-support payments were, not surprisingly, late. In fact, Colby seemed to stop responding to my emails, probably because he learned I was documenting my communications with him. But payments were always late, I was still being asked to hold them "a couple days" even when I did get them, and despite the hardship of paying child support, I was still hearing of (and at times seeing) Colby living a comfortable lifestyle.

In early February I received a letter from St. Francis's school saying that if tuition was not paid and made current by February 15, Gabriel would no longer be enrolled at that school. I informed my attorney. I heard nothing from Colby on this subject.

On February 6 we were in court regarding Gabriel's tuition and unpaid child-support issues. Colby did not show up, choosing instead to be in New York City to represent a client in court there. As a result of his constant violations of both Delaware and Virginia courts' rulings on his child-support obligations and his contempt of court expressed by not showing up, the judge ordered a *capias*, a warrant for his arrest. Even though it was the judge who ordered the capias, Colby told everyone (Gabe, Rene, and Colby's parents) that *I* had him arrested.

At 7:00 p.m. on February 16, Colby brought Gabriel home from his weekend. He gave me the child-support check late. Gabriel and I talked that night about his weekend with his dad. I told him I had three things to ask him, and I wanted the truth. I found when I prefaced my questions this way, he would think about his answers first and be honest with me.

"This weekend, did you brush your teeth?"

"Yes, Mommy, but only one time," he said. This had been an ongoing oral hygiene problem while at his dad's place.

"Gabriel, did you shower at your dad's?"

"Twice," he said, which was acceptable.

"Did your father take you to church?"

"No."

Taking Gabe to church was something we had both agreed to do when we originally signed our parenting agreement. Colby never complied.

He also told me that his dad, again, did not give him allergy medicine all weekend. I left it at that and made no comments to him about his answers.

February 15 passed, but Colby made no contact with the school—no payment, nothing! So, I paid the school $500 and held my breath that this would hold Gabriel in there for a while. Then I spent $100 on school uniforms, but Gabriel still needed new pants because he had outgrown his existing ones.

Colby made no attempts to share the cost of Gabriel's braces with me either, for which I had already paid $2,715.

I got a hold of Colby on February 17 and asked him about the tuition for St. Francis's and whether he had received the letter I had gotten as well. First, he said, yes. Then when I asked what he planned on doing about it, he changed his story and said he did *not* get a letter from the school. I told him everything that was said in the letter and asked what he planned to do.

"I've told you many times before," he griped, "I'm not going to pay for tuition. There are plenty of other, public schools that won't threaten to kick him out, but this is the one *you* want him to go to."

A few nights later when we both attended Gabriel's karate ceremony, Colby made another grand gesture in front of Gabriel, saying he would pay half of Gabe's orthodontist expenses. This was the second time he had done so, but I doubted anything would come of this offer until we were in court.

The next day I called St. Francis's School and spoke to the finance office. They said Colby never called and had made no payments. The only monies received had been the $300 I sent in October and the $500 I sent two weeks ago.

As the year dragged on, Colby's child-support payments were still always late, short, or "in the mail," and I could not get help with tuition or the orthodontist from him. When he did deliver checks, they had to be held, or they bounced.

In April, Colby arrived with Gabriel. When Gabriel went inside the house, I asked Colby if he intended on paying his child support, which was in arrears.

He laughed sarcastically. "Yeah, eventually."

I became aware that Colby was spending more and more time in New York while Gabe spent more and more time with Rene instead of me, his mother. Time and again Rene was the one picking Gabriel up and dropping him off.

June 11, 2004

My Darling Gabriel,

Gosh, it's been another one of those "difficult" weeks for me. I have to keep telling myself that one day when you are a grown young man and can think for yourself, that you will see all that I did was because I love you more than anyone in this world!

As is the norm, your father has been making my life very upsetting lately. Although it's taken me a long time to get to this point, I have learned over the years not to let him know how he upsets me as he seems to gain satisfaction in this. However, putting on a strong and tough front isn't always easy, and inside I am still the same person who is sensitive and emotional and does not like conflict or confrontation.

We have been in court so many times, and even though I know that God has been on the side of fairness and what's best for you, it is still such a difficult journey. Prior to every court hearing, I have always prayed for our Lord to give the judge the wisdom of Solomon and to rule fairly, according to the knowledge God has of our true intentions and motivations. Only He knows what's in our hearts and souls. Every time I have left court, it has been a major victory for my attorney and me. I don't understand why your father does not understand that what we put into this world is what we get back. "What goes around comes around." I believe and live my life that if you put good out there, that is what comes back to you and vice versa.

Being a parent is a difficult but rewarding job. Being divorced makes being a good parent even harder. It is a constant challenge because each parent has different rules and beliefs as to what is important and not important in raising a child. I made the decision years ago that I would not compete for your affections with material things and lack of parental guidance so you would think of me as the "cool" parent. It would be an injustice to you and, in the end, would only hurt you. I want to do everything in my power to give you all that you need to become an honest, caring, strong but sensitive, young man, a man who knows how to love others and how to treat others.

. . .

I want you to know and understand that nothing in this world comes easily, and only with hard work, dedication and commitment can we reach our goals. I believe that children learn most of these things by their parents' example, not just be being told. I have tried and will continue to try and do my best by example and by explaining things that you don't understand.

I Loved You More

Years ago you would ask me if I liked your dad. Back then I didn't want to upset you, so I would tell you that we were friends but just didn't want to be married anymore. Now that you are older, you have, once again, begun to ask those questions. You are so incredibly bright and smart, and as you mature, I need to be honest with you. So, I've had to try and help you understand that the reasons I do not care for your father is because of how he treats me and the things he does to hurt both you and I. Right now you do not see how anything he does hurts you. You idolize him and think he can do no wrong. As a young boy, you probably should think that way. He is your dad, and you are very trusting and naïve right now.

Last month you kept expressing an interest in taking electric guitar lessons. I looked into them for you and found a teacher. I explained that we would initially rent a guitar, and if you really like it, stuck with it, and were committed, then I would buy you one. Before I had a chance to schedule your first lesson, your dad bought you a used, autographed guitar. Although it defeated what I was trying to teach you about "working for something" and not just being handed something because you asked for it, I still showed you my excitement at the "new" guitar. However, in an effort to be hurtful, last week your father told you and me that the guitar was to come back to his house and that you could not keep or use it at ours. So, I have had to go out and scramble to get you one. Thankfully, my friend, Keith, who owns a musical instrument store, offered me a guitar at cost.

I have to tell you, Gabriel, that every time your father has done something vindictive or hurtful, something wonderful seems to follow in its path to *smooth out his indiscretions. It is the most amazing thing; however, I know it is God at work, so I should not be so amazed. I am truly thankful! This doesn't mean, though, that your father's actions aren't hurtful; they very much are. Many times I have cried many tears in the shower. It is my "place away," so you do not know how I am hurting.*

You are the greatest joy of my life! Being your mother is the most wonderful gift from God! What a blessing to be honored with the chance to give birth to you and then to have the trust from Him to raise you to be the best person you can be. WOW! How awesome!

I feel it is important to note that I pursued an annulment with the Catholic church in an effort to follow church doctrine and guidelines. I hoped to remarry in the church one day. I began the process before I married Rob, and it took until June 2004 for the church tribunal to approve the annulment. While writing this book, and after the passing of my sister, I came across her witness testimony, dated September 2003, written on my behalf.

When Colby & Regina first returned from their honeymoon, they lived with my brother, Michael, and his wife, Kris for about a month and half. At the time Michael remarked to me how concerned he was about the way Colby bullied (verbally) Regina and nagged her incessantly, trying to start verbal fights. If memory serves, I believe he reduced her to tears on some occasions, but Michael can best address that himself. Once they moved to Delaware, and over the next few years, Regina would share very little in the beginning of the marriage but began sharing more at the end.

I Loved You More

Through that summer, Colby was regularly away, often in New York City, and on one occasion he took Gabriel with him to California when I was unaware they were going. Our calls became increasingly heated and abrasive, often with Gabriel witnessing Colby picking fights with me despite my perennial requests to speak out of Gabe's hearing or sight. On occasion it brought Gabriel to tears, as it did me. But I never let Colby see me cry. I would not give him that power. On July 22, 2004, I put Colby on notice that I wanted no more contact with him in person or by phone due to his hostile nature, especially in front of Gabriel.

On October 8, after Gabriel's football game, he was to come home with me for the weekend. His dad had him walk to his car with him, and I pulled my car around to pick him up. When I got out to help Gabriel with his things, Colby, right in front of Gabriel, served me with court papers. Colby's car door was open, and there was a teammate sitting in his passenger seat. I was not going to have Gabriel ask me questions about what he gave me, so I tossed them back in Colby's car, on the driver's seat.

A few weeks later when Colby brought Gabriel home from football practice, he caused a scene at the front door, badgering me about basketball information.

"Regina, who is the coach?"

"I'm not sure, Colby."

"Well, when are the practices?"

"I don't know yet. Gabriel just decided to play on Sunday night. I just sent in the money and registration yesterday."

"Oh, I'm *sure* Gabriel decided," he said. "Gabriel told me he wanted to play rec ball or nothing. I bet you don't know anything!"

"Please, don't do this," I pleaded.

Gabriel ran into the room. "My dad's not doing anything!" he shouted.

I closed the front door on Colby, and Gabriel ran to his room and began to cry. Within about a minute, Colby called from his cell. For the first time in seven years, I listened to his phone call with Gabriel. I did that a few more times until my attorney told me it was not allowed, so I stopped. They talked for thirty minutes, and Colby took every opportunity to badmouth me, saying things like the following:

"Your mother needs to realize I'm a parent too."

"I know she knows who your coach is and when practices are. Don't worry, I'll find out and be there for you."

"I wish you would play rec ball instead of playing for your school. You would learn so much more from the recreation league. It's OK, I know it was her doing and not yours."

"I'm sorry I got angry with you on the driveway when you told me about basketball. I didn't like that you pulled away from me, and I'm sorry I made you cry. I know it's not your fault, and this is your mom's doing."

"I have to deal with *Mommy Dearest* about which school socks to return, but she can't even return your cut-off T-shirt, which is your favorite. It's not at my house!"

"So, are you still only allowed your one hour of TV a night?"

"No matter what your mom says or does she can't tear us apart. I'll make sure of that."

Chapter 21

FOOTBALL

October–December 2004

IN OCTOBER, A WEEK before Gabriel's ninth birthday, I was attending one of his football games. For all the public scenes and shit we went through, this experience will always stand out in my mind. It was one of the worst for Gabriel, and I usually cannot relate it without crying.

Gabriel was the quarterback. He was also the team captain. So many people there watching. His dad was coaching. During the game a team member's father named Rick came over to me after Gabriel had thrown an interception.

"I can't believe he just screamed at your son for throwing the interception," he said.

"Hi, Rick. Sorry, who? Colby yelled at Gabriel?" I had gotten distracted in a conversation with another parent and missed it.

"Yes, Regina. He told him that if he was scared to throw the ball, he'd better tell him now, among other things."

I wasn't surprised, but I was upset. Then Gabriel made another error in the game, and Colby screamed at him from the sidelines: "Time out! Gabriel, get over here!" He was enraged, grabbing Gabe by the arm and in his face, obviously ticked off. Then he turned Gabriel around and gave him a hard shove back onto the field. Gabriel was so freaked out and scared to make a mistake that he threw another interception. Colby was livid, and that was the end of the game.

When the rest of the team came off the field and went to the sidelines, Gabriel just kept walking. He was by himself, and he kept walking as far as he could go. I give him credit for not making a scene by storming off, but once he cleared the crowd, he began to cry. I went after him. He noticed me following him.

"Go away!" he shouted.

"Gabriel . . ."

"Go away! Mom, just go away!"

He didn't want me to help. I didn't know what was happening. It wasn't until I hid behind the pole he was sitting under that he let me stay. "I won't let anyone see me," I said. "Gabriel, you were doing fine. You made a mistake, but you did not deserve to be yelled at like that."

Then another father came over. "Hey there," he said, "you did a great job!"

Gabriel was crying hard by then. "No I didn't! I did terrible! Everyone just leave me alone!"

Concerned, I told him I would leave for a few minutes but would be back to check on him. As I walked away, a few of his teammates came over to cheer him up. Then his father grabbed the bag of balls, in a rage. His lips were tight, and his face was puffed out and red. He went after Gabriel in a fury, but I was taking

I Loved You More

Gabe away by that point. Once we cleared the crowd I turned on Colby. "Stay away from him!"

"Mind your own business, and don't you ever walk my son off the field again!"

"I didn't!" I yelled. "Your son was humiliated. You embarrassed him in front of the team and the parents!"

Colby kept coming. He went up to Gabriel, who was with his other teammates by then, and jabbed his finger in Gabriel's face. "Don't you ever walk off the field like that again!"

"Leave him alone!" I yelled. Gabe's teammates looked scared.

Colby grabbed Gabriel's arm and dragged him farther down the field, hollering back at me, mocking what Gabe had said earlier. "Go away, *Mom*. We don't need you. Go home, *Mom*. Just go home!"

"I'm not going to leave you alone with Gabriel."

Then Gabriel turned around and, through his tears, told me to go away. I believe he thought my being there would make things worse for him. It was the most ungodly experience, and it was public. I couldn't get anyone to help until, finally, I went over to an assistant coach.

"Can you please go down there and make sure my kid's OK?" I asked. "If I come close to him, it makes it worse for him. My ex is so pissed right now that I just don't want to make it worse. Can you please go make sure Gabriel's OK?" He agreed and went over to Gabriel for me.

Once Gabriel calmed down, about twenty minutes later, I went over to say goodnight to him since it was Colby's weekend. I kissed him, told him I loved him, and then walked to my car.

Later, I reached out to that dad who was there when it came time to testify in court. He was a lawyer, but he didn't want to get involved, although he did remove his son from the team. It infuriates me because there were other people there too. I understand that people don't want to get involved; however, if any of them had done so along the way, decisions could have been made sooner for Gabriel's best interests. I believe Colby's enraged behavior made them afraid to get involved, but I'll never know. After all, if people behave that way in public, how bad is it behind closed doors?

ONE WEEK LATER, on October 25, with a court date the next day, I was at a point where I refused to be in the same room with Colby in an effort to avoid things turning ugly. He brought Gabriel home that night and hung around the front door for a long goodbye. I stayed at the top of the stairs. Gabriel had begun to come inside when his dad called him back to the door. I repeatedly told Gabriel to come inside, but his dad physically held onto him. Colby's feet were outside the storm door, but his entire body was inside. I heard him tell Gabriel that he had something to give me. Gabriel was trying to get me to come to the door.

"Gabriel, say goodbye to your dad, and come inside," I said. "If your father has something for me, he can mail it or give it to me another time."

Colby refused to leave. He continued to hug Gabriel, so he could keep him at the front door to lure me there. Finally, he threw a check onto the stairs. Still at the top of the stairs, I calmly said I did not want it. He was argumentative and yelled back, "Good! I hope you throw it out!"

Gabriel wanted to know what it was and what I was going to do with it. After I shut the front door, I told him it was nothing for him to worry about.

A few days later, Gabriel spent some time at his cousins' house. When I came to pick him up, my sister-in-law, Leslie, opened the door. Gabriel was sitting on the floor in hysterics. Leslie said he and Danson had been playing a little rough, and they both were corrected, but she found it odd that Gabriel reacted the way he did, crying uncontrollably like he was.

I Loved You More

I took him out on the porch, but I could not get him to calm down. I had him get in the car to go home, but he still would not stop crying hysterically. Finally, I had to pull over in a store parking lot, get in the back seat with him, lock the doors, and hold him in my arms while he cried it out. It was thirty minutes before he calmed down.

"I was afraid Aunt Leslie would hit me," he said. There was no reason for this; Leslie would never do that. "I never want to go back to *that house* again," he added. Then he claimed that my brother had thrown him to the ground the previous year at Danson's birthday party. However, my entire family was there, and that is not what happened. They said Danny merely raised his voice at the boys for playing too rough. Gabriel continued to make false accusations against my brother and his wife and saying he was never going back to their house.

We talked about how we felt when someone yelled at us.

"Only my mom and dad are allowed to yell at me," he said.

"Gabriel, I know no one likes to be corrected or yelled at. When we had that problem on the football field with your dad, you must have been very upset that he yelled at you in front of so many people."

"That was not my dad; that was my coach!"

"Well, regardless," I said, "it was not OK for him to treat you that way."

He began to cry again. "I don't want to talk about that anymore!"

"OK, but can I ask you why not?"

"Because I'm afraid you'll tell someone."

"Gabriel, who would I tell?"

"A judge."

I was stunned.

"What would make you say that?" I asked.

"I don't want you to tell the judge because I'm afraid you'll take my daddy away!"

October 30, 2004

It is now the fall, and this has not been a good year for you at all! I won't waste space in this letter and give you all the ugly details, but it has been one event after another where your dad picks arguments with me and causes scenes in front of you no matter how many times I've asked him to keep you out of it. No matter what happens, you are loyal to him to the death. Once when I asked him to please stop doing this, you ran down the hall and said, "My daddy isn't doing anything wrong." He had started berating me in front of you at the front door, and I kept asking him to leave, but he wouldn't.

My files show everything that happened and all that you suffered because of it. I ended up putting you in therapy because I didn't know what else to do. No matter what I said or did, I was the "bad guy." I didn't want you growing up thinking that your father's behavior and treatment of me in front of you was an acceptable way to treat others. You are seeing a therapist, and I pray to God this helps you. You have been reticent to really open up to him, and he feels it's because you are afraid to say anything about your dad for fear of getting into some kind of trouble. I need to give this a lot of time for you to work through it all.

. . .

I love you with my whole heart and soul. I know that I have no intentions of sharing these letters with

I Loved You More

you until you are an adult. I want to apologize now that this letter is less than positive. This year has been a living hell for me because I have had to see your tears and your little heart hurt over and over again. I will try to be better about sharing all the joys with you instead of all the hurts. You are the joy of my world, and I love you to the moon and back and then some!

All my love now and always,

Mommy

On Halloween night, Colby called to talk to Gabriel and again. I listened as I still did not know it was not allowed.

"Did you tell your mom I gave you a BB gun for your birthday?"

"No, Dad."

"Good boy, Gabe!"

Gabriel asked if he could get goggles in case the BBs ricocheted off something, but foolishly his dad said he didn't think he needed them.

The next morning I asked Gabe, again, what his dad gave him for his birthday because all he had said so far were clothes, and I knew Colby would not just give that to him. Plus, I had listened in on the call the night before.

"Dad also gave me a PS2 game called Sly 2," he said.

"Cool!" I replied. I did not reveal that I knew differently.

Later that night Colby called Gabe from his New York office, and yes, I listened in again.

"What are you doing?" Colby asked.

"I'm going around collecting the house trash."

"Gosh, I'm sorry you have to do that, buddy."

"Dad, my mom asked what else I got for my birthday, so I told her you gave me a Sly 2 game. And I almost blew it at Toys R Us tonight when I saw it and said I wanted that game. My mom said, 'I thought your dad gave you that,' and I had to say he did." (Both of them laughed mockingly.)

"Dad," Gabe whispered nervously, "I'm worried Mom will find out about the BB gun. She's sticking her nose in our business."

"If she does just tell her I gave you permission to lie to her."

Gabe changed course. "Dad," he said with enthusiasm, "they start digging our pool tomorrow! I'm so excited because I've never had one!"

"Oh, the pool I'm paying for? Well, I'm glad *my* money is going to good use," he said sarcastically. Clearly, he had been discussing money issues with Gabe. By that point I was a very successful real estate agent for the biggest condominium builder in the area, and Rob was a captain with the Virginia Beach Fire Department. We were doing well financially.

Later in the call Colby said, "Thanks for looking out for me, buddy."

"What did I do, Dad?"

"You take care of me by standing up for yourself and indicating that you want to come and live with us. I'm proud of you for that."

Colby was not only teaching Gabe to lie, he was praising him for it, and I was about to find out how easily Gabe let a lie roll right off his tongue. Throughout the entire conversation Colby used profanity like "shit" and "crap" as if he was talking to a friend instead of his son, trying to be cool and act like equals.

A little over a week later, Gabe was writing a letter to Santa and asked for the PS2 game, Sly 2. Imagine my surprise.

"Wait," I said, "I thought your dad gave that to you for your birthday."

I Loved You More

A lie just flew out of his mouth in response. "Oh, I want another one, so I can have one at each house."

"Gabe, you have never had two copies of any game because you bring them back and forth with you in your collection case. Are you sure you got it for your birthday?" He offered another lie as if it were his normal dialogue.

This had gone on long enough. I went to the kitchen to gather my thoughts. Then I called him in. "Gabe, something is going on, and I think you are being less than honest with me. I want you to go to your room and think long and hard. After dinner we are going to have a serious talk, and I want the truth."

After dinner we did talk, and he ended up telling me the entire truth, without difficulty.

"Gabe, why did you lie to me?"

"I was afraid I would get in trouble, Mom."

"Did your dad tell you to keep this secret from me?"

"Yes, he did. Are you mad about me having a BB gun? Are you going to take it away?"

"Gabe, I have no control over what goes on at your dad's house, but, yes, I'm not happy about the gun, and I'll tell you why." I went on to give him specific examples of times in his life when his dad did not make good choices when it came to Gabriel's safety and explained that if I felt he made better choices, then I would not be so concerned. I gave him specific instances when his father made poor decisions, and Gabriel could have been in serious trouble.

1. The time Colby left him alone in his apartment in New York City to go to the drugstore and get medicine.
2. At three years old, Gabe was left alone and locked in his dad's NYC office to take a conference call on another floor for well over thirty minutes.

3. At seven years old, Gabriel was allowed to swim in the bay off his dad's sailboat without a life vest, and he could not swim back to the boat due to the strong current,
4. His dad left him alone at four years old in a movie theater, so his dad could go and get treats,
5. There was also the infamous breakfast with Pooh at age three.

Using these examples helped me explain my concerns to him. I also told him that his dad loved him very much and that these decisions were not intended to hurt Gabriel but were just poor choices his dad made without thinking things through.

Later that night when his dad called, Gabe told him everything we had discussed. I happened to be putting linens in the closet, which was directly next to his room, when I overheard Gabe mimicking me, saying, "My mom said she doesn't trust you."

I went straight to his room and told him that was not what I said, and he had better be truthful in relaying our discussion to his dad. He got extremely upset and asked why I was listening to his private conversation. He began to cry hysterically. I told him he had to get off the phone until he calmed down and to tell his dad he would call him back later. Gabe was out of control emotionally. We talked until he settled down, and then he called his father back. He seemed fine when he went to bed.

A few nights later at another one of Gabriel's football games, one of the parents, Lori, and I were talking. She told me she planned on reporting Colby to the chairman for his excessive profanity on the field. She and her husband went to every game and practice, and she couldn't believe how much Colby cursed in front of the children. I reminded her what Colby had said to the team and parents after one of the recent practices. He told them something that happened to him when he played quarterback in college. I was appalled.

I Loved You More

After that practice I confronted Colby. "Colby, you never even played football in college, let alone played quarterback. You just lied to all of them."

The sides of his mouth curled up in a sneer and with a single cocked eyebrow he chuckled and said, "Regina, it's all in how you spin the story."

REGINA ROSSI VALENTINE

PART 4

"If you have never been hated by your child,
you have never been a parent."

—Bette Davis

Chapter 22

REVELATIONS

2005

IN 2005 IT BECAME CLEAR that Colby was not fully exercising all his visitation with Gabriel. Gabe's additional day of Monday on his weekends was, more often than not, spent with Rene while Colby remained in New York City. Gabriel had told me several times that his dad was in New York, so Rene picked him up after school and brought him home to me. Yet, when I was off from work on Mondays, he could have been spending that time with me.

In December I wrote Gabriel a new letter, sealed it, and hid it with the others to give to him one day. Writing those letters got me through the next couple of years.

I Loved You More

My Darling Gabriel,

This year has brought about many changes for you. The therapy you have been in with David has really done wonders. It has taken you a great deal of time to feel comfortable with him, but it has definitely made a change for the positive in your behavior.

You're doing very well in school, as usual, and we've discussed having you tested for the Phoenix Gifted School in your mid-5th grade to enter in 6th. I could not be prouder of you! You did such a great job in football this year despite the challenges w/your dad's behavior again. It is hard for me to see and hear things from other parents and not be able to discuss them with you because no matter what, you defend your dad or deny there are any issues with him. Even Brian, Grif's dad, told me one night that your dad must have had a really bad day because he seemed to take it out on you at practice. I can only say that I pray for you all the time that you will be stronger because of all of this and that you will soon be your own person.

When it's just you and me at home or even when it's the four of us, you are so cuddly with me and sweet and loving. But when your dad's around or you are on the phone w/me while at his house, you are different to me, and it hurts. But I keep telling myself that the Gabriel I know is the one you are when you are here.

This fall you finished football and began basketball—finally! Last year your father interfered with your playing and discouraged you from it. Later on when we were in co-parenting counseling, he admitted he hated the sport. It's a shame he deprived you of the experience because of his disdain for me. At the end of the season last year, Coach Matt knew of the situation w/you trying out, then quitting, then asking to play, then quitting, all while you were trying to please your dad. So, in an effort to give you a chance to experience the game, he invited you to play w/his varsity boys and girls in an exhibition game right after the Harlem Globetrotters game. You were the only younger boy, and you had a blast! Our deal was if you accepted his offer, then you had to play for St. Francis this fall, and you are. You are such an awesome athlete, and you do exceptionally well at all three sports (football, basketball, and baseball). I can't wait to see what you end up pursuing as a potential career, just so long as it's YOUR decision and not from pressure from your dad. It's funny, when we were married, he had no interest in football or sports, for that matter. While we would visit your Mom-Mom and Pop-Pop, I was always the one watching the pro football games w/them, not your dad. You and I even watched the Superbowl together the past few years, but your dad never has had an interest. Now he is trying to coach you and also get a high school coaching job, yet he has no experience. Your first year of flag football, he didn't even let you boys have water breaks. I had to fight w/you to bring a bottle of water or Gatorade to practice and games. It was absurd.

. . .

You also found out about Santa recently. You had been asking questions for a long time, and you are so smart that I began to think you already knew but were checking to see what I would tell you. I know kids at school were talking about it too. So, one night we talked about it, and I told you. You were initially upset with me for telling you, but as luck would have it, if I hadn't, you would have found out from Danson, your cousin. I know if you had found out from him you would really have been upset that he was told before you, and he is younger. He was openly talking about it in the pool on the last day of school. I think if you had found out that way, I would have been upset that it hadn't come from me. I assured you it would not change anything for you at Christmas, except that you would "know."

This summer the four of us went to Knot Campin' Cabin in the Blue Ridge Mountains right on the Shenandoah River. It was amazing! We went for four days and did all kinds of fun things, plus it was great family time. We did a float trip down the river, we went horseback riding, and we went hiking in the mountains. We watched movies and popped popcorn. We canoed and tried to fish from the canoe behind the cabin. The weather was spectacular, and we all loved it. I am so glad that you and Megan get along so well and that you are both good kids. We are a very blessed family.

WOW! October has been an unbelievable month! I was promoted to site manager of a brand-new condo site, and we began pre-sales this month. AND Megan—who three years ago was not happy about Rob being a Christian and the fact that we "prayed" as a family at meals and went to church—well, she announced to us that she wants to be a Christian and to move in with us! The sad side of it that I have not shared with you is that when her mom found out, she literally kicked Megan out of the house that same night. It was very ugly and hurtful for Megan and sad for all of us. It has been a bit of an adjustment as it came about 6–8 mos. sooner than we expected, but

Megan is so much happier with us. She said there is too much yelling at her mom's house. You were thrilled that she was living with us. My only concern is that when you get older, you will want to live w/your father, not because you are unhappy with us but because there are no real rules or boundaries at your dad's, and you are treated like an adult there. Megan came to live with us because she was very unhappy at her mom's, and her mom didn't support her activities and sports or youth at church.

This year has been my very first opportunity to be your room mom at school, and you were very excited about it, at least that's what you said ☺*. Anyway, we had a great Christmas party for you kids with crafts, games, food, and a movie. Our class was the envy of the others, who we heard only did pizza and a movie.*

For your birthday this year we had your party at Motor World where they do go-kart racing. It was a lot of fun for you and your friends.

Christmas was really nice in that I had you both Christmas Eve & Day, but the trade-off stank as your dad then got you for a whole week to go to CA. I really missed you and didn't have you or Rob at the big family Christmas party.

Well, I am going to close out this letter with a big fat X (kiss). I love you, son, and you are turning out to be a wonderful young man. May God shower His blessings on you always, and may all that you do in life be with His guiding hand and protection.

All my love always and forever,

Mom

Chapter 23

THE CHOICE

∽♡∽

2006

February 26, 2006

Hi, Sweetheart,

 Tonight was a bit rough. We were on the phone (you were at your dad's), and I wanted you to bring your baseball glove to school tomorrow, so you could have it here for us to practice for drafts on Saturday. On Friday you didn't even want to bring it to your dad's, but I talked you into it, yet tonight on the phone you denied having said that because your dad was right there. Anyway, for some reason the reminder to bring it home caused an argument w/you and I, and your dad feeding you thoughts of "me putting you in the middle" when I don't do that. This was not between your dad & I but between you and me and simply to bring your *glove home. Then your dad got on the phone w/me and pursued an argument in front of you, letting you hear everything he said to me and saying some things I said out of context, so it sounded ugly. I hung up the phone and was so upset that I broke down and cried in the driveway (I was just getting home from your Uncle Danny's house). I am so very tired of your father trying to manipulate you and situations so that they become confrontational.*

. . .

Your dad and I had another co-parenting counseling session, and in the first 10 minutes he threatened to leave. Although he stayed, he yelled at me three different times. The therapist had to tell him to lower his voice and made your dad see that he was yelling at me, but he wasn't upset "with" me; he was upset with your attorney, the GAL (guardian ad litem). Nevertheless, he took it out on me, as always. Your attorney wrote a letter to Judge Wallace and said that, based on his extensive investigation of your situation, he did not feel that additional visitation with your dad was in your best interest. He said that he felt as though you were being coached in what to say to him, to me, and to your therapist. He said you behaved the same way with him when he came to our home to meet you and just simply chat. This infuriated your dad, yet, it's something I have felt was true but could not prove w/out involving you, which I would not do. Your therapist, David, also has these same concerns.

I just wish this would all go away. I worry constantly about you and your heart and your emotional well-being. I fear that your father, although he loves you in his own way, is hurting you emotionally, the way he did with me. When I came in the house, I called my friend, Maureen, and asked her to pray with me because this was so difficult for me, and it never seems to end. I told her that my biggest concerns and fears were for you and that, at the age of ten, I didn't know how "real" I could get with you in our conversations to help you see the truth. You so easily lied to me on the phone about never saying you didn't want to bring your glove to your dad's because he was sitting right there. I feel you are afraid to say or do anything that may upset him—I just can't prove it. And I won't push things with you because this is not your fault, and you should not be in the middle of anything.

I hope our Lord will give both of us strength to get through this. If it were not for my faith, I would truly not make it through everything that happens with your father. I pray that you will not be scarred emotionally but will grow up to be a strong, sensitive, loving, and honest man. I love you so much it hurts my heart just thinking about all you've had to go through these past few years. Your father also said in our sessions that he was not in favor of your going to therapy and felt you still did not need it. Pity he is so blind to the fact that it is one of the best things I've done for you. Everyone who knows you has seen a change for the best since you've been seeing David! You and I both cry much less than we did this time last year, and THAT is so good!

. . .

I have to tell you what happened last week on Valentine's Day. That morning I had gifts and a card for you and Megan when you ate breakfast. You had come home from your dad's the night before, and although it wasn't the worst time, you were not in your best mood or behavior that night. After you opened your gifts, you said, "Thank you so much, Mom, and I wasn't very nice to you last night!" Then you came over and gave me a big Gabriel hug and kiss. Your admitting that to me so quickly told me that you are very much aware of what is going on and how you are acting w/me at times. The fact that you were so thankful and acknowledged your misbehavior meant more to me than you know! I know in my heart that you will be a wonderful young man one day.

In May 2006 Colby intentionally falsified Gabe's date of birth for the Florida Gators Elite Quarterback Football Camp, so he could attend the camp. It was for sixth to twelfth graders, but Gabriel was only in grade four. I don't recall how I found out, but, knowing me, I likely did an Internet search about the camp. I emailed the camp and asked how someone Gabe's age was allowed to attend. They gave me the age requirements that were on their website, but I explained he was not old enough. They pulled the application and faxed it to me. Clear as day, Colby put a different year for Gabe's date of birth on the form. (We used this in one of our court hearings.) Unfortunately, all this happened after the camp's completion. To make matters worse, Gabriel's roommate at the camp was in eighth grade. I was so angry about how inappropriate it was for Gabriel to room with someone that much older than him.

I put this letter aside for quite some time as I could not bring myself to write. My heart was/is breaking inside. Despite the deep concerns from your therapist and your attorney, your father went another route and pushed for you to meet with Judge Wallace, so you could tell her what you wanted, or rather what most of us believe he coached you to say. At age 10, no child wants to hurt either parent, especially you, my son. I was so unbelievably upset that your father put you in this position because I did not want you to feel any pull of loyalty to either of us or to be manipulated in any way. But, despite all that he has done to us in the past, the judge allowed for your meeting. To my disadvantage, it was on a Monday, I believe, right after your weekend with your dad, so there was much room for influence on his part.

Much to everyone's surprise, it was made clear that if we did not come to an agreement on visitation, the judge was probably going to rule for a 50/50 split on visitation. I remember that I was leaning against the wall outside the chambers and just slid down the wall, crying and crying and crying. We went back & forth between my attorney and your father to "negotiate" a schedule. When we were inside with the judge, it was the first time in 9 yrs. of being in courts with your dad that I could not maintain my composure, that I just sat there and continued to cry. The only saving moment for me was when she told us that in all her years on the bench, never had she met a more respectful, polite, well-spoken, and nice young child as you. WOW! Then she turned to me and said, "Mrs. Valentine, in light of the ugliness of this case over the years, I attribute most of that credit to you because your son has been with you most of the time. You should be congratulated."

As part of the visitation agreement I asked her to make it mandatory for your father to continue to attend co-parenting counseling with Dr. Alexander and me. He was not in favor of this, but the court mandated it, thank God! The sessions have been very ugly at times and put me into serious anxiety and issues with my breathing and stress. But I know in my heart it will be for your benefit. If we can find a way to co-exist peacefully, it only helps you.

I was having a hard time putting past problems with your dad aside in dealing with things at hand. Dr. Alexander helped me see that, although I will not forget those things, we need to try and move forward. The treatment of you by your father with all the confrontations in your presence, the berating of you on the football field in front of everyone, etc. and how much he has hurt you were and still are very hard for me to forget and let go of. I was the victim of his anger and rage when we were married, and I was NOT going to let my child be the same.

In one of our sessions, your father admitted that he had been on and taken himself off of antidepressants. He said that even Rene and their friends had said he was acting very differently for a while and that he was very short tempered. I have known this in your father for many years as it is also a trait from his side of the family. But it was definitely heightened in the past few years. He said he went to his doctor to get a prescription to go back on them, so hopefully this will help.

What I love about Dr. Alexander is he is a straight shooter. He calls a spade a spade. He gave both of us things to work on in an effort to help us better communicate and get along. There were several times your father either did not show up for an appointment or cancelled at the last minute, so I would take the appointment as a one-on-one with Dr. Alexander, which, although it was helpful to me, it also angered me that your dad did not always take its importance seriously and make time for them.

I Loved You More

  This fall we agreed that your dad could coach you in football again; however, if there was any treatment of you as in the past, I would pull you from the team. This was agreed in a session with Dr. Alexander. Also, he was to do it on a team that was closer to our home, which was Courthouse Estates Recreation League. The Great Neck Recreation League also got several complaints about his treatment of the kids, so he could not coach there again, anyway. This season went much better than last year, although several parents were not happy with how your dad would go to the opposite side of the field with the kids, and parents could not hear all that was going on at practices. They also commented that he yelled at the kids too much. My concerns were more that he did not single you out again and embarrass you, as in the past. At the end of the season, the league fired him because he refused to step aside for a game and acknowledge that he made an error on the roster with one of the players. The league's choice was that he step aside so the child could play, but he refused. So, they fired him on the spot at the game because the kids are more important. I also believe, after hearing numerous complaints from parents, that this was the league's way of getting him out on a "technicality." I was stunned that he would not be the bigger person so this child could play in the game, but in the end, it only embarrassed and hurt your dad.

  Also, this fall I decided, along with you, to apply to the prestigious Phoenix Gifted School, where your cousin, Nicki, has been attending. I have been working on the application and the requirements with letters of recommendations from teachers, etc., so I am excited to see how it goes. On a much-needed positive note in this letter, you have been amazing with your grades in *school. You are so blessed by God with your knowledge, your sports abilities, and your guitar playing. You will have so many choices available to you in your future. You just need to see what is the most important and loved thing to do. Above all, the choices need to be yours and not what you think one of us wants you to do with your life. My parents were so great by giving us both a love of music and sports. They exposed us to so many things, and then the final choices were ours to make.*

Gabriel, I love you more than you can imagine. There are so many times in life that I question "why" with what has happened in both our lives. I wanted to have 2–4 children and never wanted just one because, coming from a big family, I know how great it is to have siblings. I never wanted to "leave you alone" when I am gone one day. But that is not the deck of cards I/we were dealt. We have to go forward, make the best of what we have, and always, always guide our decisions with love and faith.

. . .

Gabriel, one day when you have your own children, you will see how important it is to be a parent first. Later on in your child's life, you can be your child's "friend." But when children are growing up and learning about the world, parents are their teachers, guide, and the ones to set boundaries and good examples. You can't be a friend to your children when they are still children; it doesn't work that way. What I mean by that is, you should have friends who are your own age and parents to be your parents.

Well, enough for now. Life is not easy, and more often than not, it is not fair. I continue to pray that I am doing my best for your sake. My parents were very

I Loved You More

good examples for me, and I see that my four siblings and I all turned out successful and very good people with many, many friends who love and respect us. We are blessed, even though at times we wonder why we have the very hard times that we do.

All my love—to the moon and back and then some!

Mom

Chapter 24

DREAMS & JOBS

2007

I FEEL MOST ALIVE when I'm on stage. Performing is thrilling. And so much of what I do with my singing is to serve others. When I sing in church, it fulfills me to know it is bringing some sense of healing to someone somewhere. Music is healing. When I was singing at one hundred funerals a year, it was a healing ministry. I did have to back away from it because it was draining me emotionally because I was so emotionally invested. But it wasn't just a job and a paycheck. It was personal. When I feel like I have the ability to touch someone else's life, that brings me joy. It's so gratifying.

I came to the arts through genetics. As mentioned, my father was a full-scholarship opera student at Juilliard in the 1950s. Between his third and fourth year at school, he was told, "Why don't you go audition for Broadway, and see how the other side lives?" So, he auditioned for *the* Rogers and Hammerstein and was immediately added to the original Broadway touring cast of *South Pacific*. He met my mother there, who was also a singer, and cast in *South Pacific*. Then they did *Kismet* together. They got married when *Kismet* was on the road in Cincinnati because it was the most central for my dad, being from Canada, and my mom, in Norfolk, Virginia. Like every good Catholic girl, she immediately got pregnant and left Broadway. Meanwhile, my dad went on to do more shows. I still have the playbills, with Dad, Sammy Davis Jr., Carol Burnett, Tony Randall, and Robert Weede.

I almost wasn't even born because my mom told my dad when they met that she wanted ten children because she was the third-oldest of nine. He still married her. After three kids he felt like, *Isn't this enough?* Then my brother and I, the two musicians in the family, were born. So, of the five siblings, my brother, Richard, and I, the two youngest, carried on the music tradition. Richard is stronger in conducting, composing, piano, and organ. For me it is singing. Growing up, we thought we were the Carpenters, and we would do all their music together. It's something that brings a high. When you're on stage and performing for other people, it's like an escape into another world. And I *love* musical theater. Richard loves classical music more.

During the holidays, wow! There was always a lot of singing when we got together. I have forty first cousins just on my mother's side, so we had big family parties once or twice a year. It was tons of singing and tons of showcasing. "You do a solo! You do a solo!" It was incredible, lots of fun, and it gave us an opportunity to really hone our skills because in a family with that many artists, always singing, everyone's always critiquing too. Everyone has to be *on*. In addition to singing professionally, I've also sung in church choirs all my life.

During my brief college stint at UNC Chapel Hill (1984), I received the largest music scholarship in the history of the university and was the only undergraduate to sing with the university chamber choir. But I was unhappy and just wanted to perform, so I left to pursue a career on stage.

In 1986, when I was nineteen, I moved out of my parents' home and into an apartment in Virginia Beach for about a year. During that time I worked in the corporate world while auditioning for things. Then I moved away from my hometown and started working and performing at Opryland USA in Nashville. I was a singer and dancer on the General Jackson Showboat, a paddlewheel riverboat—more specifically, a showboat—on the Cumberland River in Nashville. Then I spent five years performing on cruise ships with Holland America, Royal Viking, and Royal Caribbean cruise lines, with dreams of Broadway, like my parents.

It was when I met Colby in 1991 that I decided to leave my blossoming career in entertainment to support my new fiancé and see him through law school from 1993 to 1996. During that time I took a job as a sales manager at First Valley Bank, overseeing all loan officers in five counties in Eastern Pennsylvania. I gave up my performance career and my dreams of Broadway to put Colby through law school because that was something my mother had groomed me for, to believe that was what I wanted.

With my mother, it was a constant mantra. Whether I was calling home from an overseas port while working on cruise ships (having the time of my life!) or on a visit home in between contracts, she constantly said to me, "You don't want to do this forever, do you? Don't you want to get married and have a family?" Over and over and over again. After a while I started to believe what was being fed to me.

I always wanted a family. I just didn't realize that my mother was grooming me in this way, to *her* expectations. As a result I was sizing up every guy in my life as husband and father material instead of enjoying where my life was at the time. She groomed me to her expectations, and Colby groomed Gabe to his.

Looking back I think I gave up my career too soon. I still had a lot more performing to do.

After all Gabriel and I had been through leading up to 2007, Colby kept being verbally abusive, and he kept getting fired from jobs. The domino effect of that spilled over to all the ongoing financial issues with child support. Through court papers and everything, I had a laundry list of his job history. Colby took half of June and all of July 2001 off from *any* work just for the heck of it, all while still behind in child support and tuition. What I wouldn't give to take the summer off and play! Then, after moving to Virginia in August 2001, Colby had a string of jobs.

- From August 2001 to December 2001 (just four months), he worked at a law firm in Norfolk, VA.
- In January 2002 he started his own law practice, Baxter & Associates.
- By March 2002 he was working at Big Boats Resources (his "newest" business).
- By May through July 2002 he had gotten bored and started job hunting again.
- In September 2002 he was an executive VP at Professional Efficiency Systems, but he quit after just two months.
- On October 20, 2002, he started with a local towing company, working on a tugboat as a deck mate.
- In the fall of 2002, Colby went to school for a captain's license.
- By the winter of 2002, he was hired at a different towing company as a deck mate.
- In the middle of 2003, he worked for only a few months on a ferry boat as a relief captain.
- In the fall of 2003, he was hired at a local trade school as a law teacher for budding paralegals.
- In the winter of 2003 into 2004, he resurrected Baxter & Associates, commuting to New York City after Judge Wallace scolded him for under-employing himself.
- In 2005 he launched another company, managing professional athletes.
- From January through March of 2006, Colby attended a local college's accelerated program, seeking a teaching certificate, financed by wife number three.

- In the fall of 2006 Colby worked at a local high school in Norfolk as a math teacher.
- Also in the fall of 2006 he was one of many assistant football coaches at a Virginia Beach High School.
- In the fall of 2007 he quit the Norfolk school and was a math teacher at that same Virginia Beach High School where he was also an assistant football coach.
- He was soon fired as an assistant football coach at that Virginia Beach High School before the end of the season.
- Beginning in the fall of 2008, Colby was a math teacher at a high school across the water in Newport News.
- At the Newport News school, he was also an assistant football coach. Colby confided in me that he would not be at that school the following year.

Colby tended to leave a trail of broken jobs and debt in his wake. When things eventually didn't work out, whether it be a job or something else, it was always everyone else's fault. This pattern is a typical trait of a narcissist.

In 2007 the Supreme Appellate Court of New York suspended him pending an investigation, potentially ending his career as an attorney, for abandonment, neglect, and failure to return documents and fees to clients, then skipping town. Any frustration I felt with how unethical and simply stupid that seemed was eclipsed by my own sense of what I had given up for him in terms of sacrificing my ability to pursue a Broadway career. It was one more thing that broke my heart.

On January 23, 2008, an official determination was made. It detailed that Colby had become delinquent in his registration with the Office of Court Administration. The rest of the bullet points seemed such silly, pathetic reasons to foul a career in law, but these measures were taken to protect the public.

- In 2006 there was a complaint that Colby took a $1,200 retainer and then stopped returning telephone calls and messages. That client tried to track Colby down, only to discover he had moved, and his website had been deactivated.

- Again in 2006, another client filed a complaint against Colby, stating he had neglected her divorce matter after she retained him with $760 to represent her in an uncontested divorce. When this woman did get a hold of Colby, he told her that her divorce had been "lost" and told her to try him again in a month. When she tried to find Colby after that, she discovered his telephone and fax numbers had been disconnected. He never completed her divorce or refunded her money.
- The disciplinary committee tried to reach Colby repeatedly, leaving multiple phone messages and sending multiple notices on approximately fifteen separate occasions. The letters were never returned, and those sent certified were returned as "unclaimed."
- Then he failed to appear for his deposition.
- An investigator with the Virginia State Bar was sent on behalf of the committee in New York to find Colby and give notice to him at his home address. When Colby answered the door, he refused to accept the documents once he learned they came from the committee.

Ultimately, the determination was because of "his lack of cooperation with the Committee's investigation of professional misconduct which threatens the public interest."

He was officially disbarred.

Chapter 25

CYCLES

2008

IN EARLY 2008, GABRIEL was twelve years old. The light in his eyes seemed lost, and he was stressed out a lot. He told me a few years ago that back then school was his escape and the only thing he could control, as his dad was controlling his sports and other things, on top of the fighting between his parents. His hair went through stages of buzz cuts for sports to a thick, curly mop. His voice got deeper in high school (naturally), and he had beautiful teeth (thank you, braces!). Despite his often-sullen appearance, he was becoming a "chick magnet" and popular in school. By his senior year in high school, he was captain of the football team. They went undefeated for the first time ever and won the state championship.

I continued to hold on. Today I have nerves of steel, having survived the pressure of all that I am writing about, but back then, especially in 2008 and the following few years, I cried *a lot*. I know I've mentioned that before, but it's true.

The constant late and missing payments continued into 2008. Colby would "miraculously" get caught up just prior to court dates. It always pissed me off. I was so frustrated with Colby's irresponsibility and apparent ineptness. It took years before I fully understood that Colby, in addition to using everyone else to financially support him, was spending a *lot* of money on prostitutes and escorts. However, he also saw money as a form of control. He wanted to anger me. It was a constant baiting. I believe narcissistic people like Colby thrive on confrontation and conflict. They like to rile others up.

I will never forget the day I found my power in 2008. Colby was dropping Gabriel off one day, and as he was leaving, he said something to me. For the life of me I can't remember what it was because it's how I handled it that stands out in my memory. It was something intended to get under my skin, trigger me, and make me mad. For whatever reason—maybe I was tired, maybe I just wanted him to be gone—I simply shrugged and said, "Whatever." It pissed him off, and I could see it in his face. His eyes had fire in them. Inside, I wanted to laugh, but it was that moment when I realized I should never again engage in such interactions with him, so that I could be in control. It was a huge moment. Personally, I hate confrontation, so this was one of the most powerful things I learned. It took me many years, until my son was almost a teenager, to see it. A light bulb went on.

I was now in a position of power. I wouldn't let him affect me anymore and get a reaction. That was a big deal.

Words have power, but sometimes silence has even more power.

Once Rene and I became friends, after their divorce, she told me that, during their marriage, Colby verbally abused Gabe all the time. He would tell Gabe he was stupid and lazy and that he would never amount anything. (Sound familiar? My mother said the same thing to my brother, Michael.)

In a recent conversation with Gabe while writing this book, I talked to him about being called stupid by his dad.

"You know about that, right?" I said. "Your Pop-Pop (his dad's father) used to say that to your Mom-Mom (Gabriel's grandmother). Pop-Pop would say, 'You're so stupid, Beth,' all the time. I was there, Gabriel, I witnessed it, and it upset me deeply"

Because I never had a good relationship with my own mother, I was very close to Beth, and the loss of that relationship hurt me more than the loss of my marriage. I was very protective of Beth. Gabriel feels like his Mom-Mom stood her ground and held her own because she could be just as bitchy in return.

When he was a young teen, Gabriel started calling our dogs "stupid." I told him to stop and explained it was a pattern of learned behavior in his dad's family. "We don't allow you to call others stupid," I said. "It's an ugly word and hurtful, and you need to stop, but you are copying what you learned. Your dad was copying what he learned, but that creates a legacy of verbal abuse."

And we needed to break the cycle.

As I was writing this book, I struggled with whether or not to mention my own childhood abuse for fear of what other family members would think, specifically my mother's siblings. "Don't worry about what Mom or anyone else thinks about it," my brothers advised me. "You have to say what's your truth and what's right."

"Had I not made the conscious decision in my early twenties not to repeat the history of abuse," I replied, "I believe that Gabe would have been raised by two damaged parents, and the outcome would have been vastly different. Just this year while writing the book, I've made the connection that Mom is also a narcissist, just like Colby. Why did it take me this long to make that connection?"

They say women typically grow up to marry a man like their father, but I married one like my mother instead. As a result, the manipulations and abuse of my childhood repeated in my marriage. Why didn't I look for a man like my dad? The truth was, the "package" Colby presented to me was very much like my dad. That's what a narcissist does. He kept who he really was hidden, for the most part, during our courtship.

My therapist has worked with me this past year in navigating all of my childhood abuse. He has helped me see many parallels between my relationship with my mother and Gabe's relationship with his dad. Hopefully, that will help me to better understand and help Gabe work through any conflicts he has down the road with his father.

However, it has also made me wonder, did my grandparents inflict physical or verbal abuse on my mother and her siblings? If so, was it to the degree that my mother inflicted such things on us? Did any of them break the cycle? If they were not abused growing up, how will they feel about what I am publicly sharing now about their sister, my mother?

My maternal grandfather died in his fifties after surviving multiple heart attacks and strokes. I was very close to my maternal grandmother. Of the forty first cousins on that side of my family, I was one of the closest to her. I actually paid a nurse to bring her to my wedding to Colby. I'd go see her several times a week on my lunch breaks. I'd feed her lunch and spend time with her. I really loved her. When we were kids, my brother, Richard, and I used to spend the night with her in her trailer and go with her in the morning because she taught swimming lessons. I don't know if my mom was physically or psychologically abused, like I was by her. I do know that my grandmother told me, and several of my mom's siblings have validated it, that of the nine children, my mother was the worst with back talking, breaking the rules, and getting into trouble.

What's odd is that until the conversations with my siblings over the past few years, we never really identified what our mother did as *abuse* because, growing up, we didn't know anything different. We would have a few choice words for her, but the honest conversations about it actually being abuse didn't start until 2016, a year before my sister passed away. If abuse is all someone knows, they don't know what to call it. What I know for sure is that her behavior prevented me from feeling love for her. I didn't want to be around her and could not wait to move out when I was nineteen. It also made me keenly aware that I never wanted to treat my children the way I was treated. I never wanted to make another human being feel the way she made me feel or hurt them like she hurt me. Hence, the conscious decision not to be like her.

I broke the cycle of that abuse.

People would tell me, "Well, her memory is bad because she's up in age." But she was like that my whole life and still is. She would leave me guilt-laden, condescending voicemails: "Regina, why haven't you called me? I've left you three messages. I need you to call me right away." Her voice was bitchy and nasty in a negative, nagging tone, and most of the time it was *not* urgent at all. During her time in hospice she would add, "I don't know if I'll still be around by the time you call back." *Geez, really?* More emotional blackmail.

"Mom, don't leave me messages like that," I'd tell her. "It doesn't make me want to call you back."

"You know, I'm so different with Gabriel," I told her on another occasion. "In a world where we text each other all the time, I will text him, 'Hey, thinking about you, love you,' with absolutely zero expectation for a response. I know he's busy, and he can't always stop to answer me, so I don't ask him to because I don't want to guilt him into anything."

"Well, you're just a better parent than me," Mom replied.

"No," I countered, "I've chosen to be a different parent."

None of us know how my dad stayed with her considering her constant controlling and abusive behavior. She was always the kind of person who believed everyone should live how she mandated. She believed she was the authority on everything from the Catholic Church's teachings to medicine. As a matter of fact, she made no bones about telling the priests how they could be more holy, and she pointed out if they did something she disagreed with. The same went for her physicians, as if she was their superior. They diagnosed a condition and prescribed a medication, but she always decided they were wrong, and she let them know it. As a result, I coined the name for her, Sr. Barbara, MD.

My sister would say Dad loved her. I remember a time when Mom and Dad were having marital problems, and Mom came to see me down on one of my ships. She was sharing things with me that I did *not* need to know about their marriage. My sister said Mom was trying to rally people to her side, but Dad stayed with her. He did a lot of things to keep the peace.

When I was a junior in high school, I was dating the senior valedictorian, Brian. That summer, I was also babysitting forty hours a week for a two-month-old and a two-year-old. On the weekends I was the church organist at the Naval Air Station. I was working a lot, and I had my boyfriend.

"Mom, can I go play putt-putt with Brian?" I asked one day.

"No," she said, "you've already seen him once this week." So, I went to my dad.

"Dad, I want to go see Brian."

"What did your mother say?"

I had had enough. "You never stick up for us," I said. "You always let her make all the decisions!"

That didn't go over well, but it was the truth. I've talked to my therapist about how my dad did a lot of things to keep the peace, always acquiescing to my mother.

Years later my dad and I were driving to one of our weekly appointments at Virginia Oncology. "You know," he said, "your mother's never going to change at this point in her life. And I know I'm to blame for a lot of why she is the way she is."

He was an enabler. He kind of created a monster because he let her do what she did. I don't mean the physical abuse because, as I've said, that always seemed to happen when he was not home.

I'm talking about her controlling, dictatorial behavior, wanting everything her way. He had the best intentions—to keep the peace and keep the family together—but we kids, and dad for that matter, paid the price.

In my recent conversation with Gabe about the Baxter family history of using the word "stupid," he told me that while his dad and Rene were married, Rene used to say mean things about him to his dad, usually when she had been drinking, and always within earshot of Gabe. But he realized she had no right to say those things. Gabe told me that Rob, my husband and Gabe's stepfather (of seventeen years now), "has more of a right to say something about me than she does."

After they divorced, Rene admitted to me that she drank while married to Colby.

"Well," I said, "as far as your drinking, I'd be an alcoholic too if I were married to Colby, you know, to numb the pain of everything."

"No, I was a drinker," she said.

When people are drunk, meanness can come out of them, and they don't really think about or care about who's around or who hears them.

Gabriel told me other things Rene would say to Colby about him like, "He's so lazy."

"So," I said to him, "what you're telling me is Rene would say to your dad the things that your dad would say to you, but it wasn't OK because she was your stepmom?"

"Exactly."

I know the pain of my own biological mother's abusive words toward me. It was like Gabriel was dealing with that from his own dad. It was not OK that Colby was saying those things about Gabe, and it was definitely not OK that his stepmom was saying those same things about my son. It's no wonder Gabriel has dated the wrong girls at times. He doesn't think he's worthy of better. I think he's finally starting to figure that out now though. We talked about it last year.

"I don't think you realize what a catch you are," I said. "You're so intelligent, you're beyond your maturity, you're good looking, and you're kind."

He tends to break up with girls and then take them back repeatedly. That's exactly what I did with his dad.

Rene was my son's stepmother for seven years. Sadly, once the marriage was over, I believe Colby turned Gabriel against her as well. Since she is not blood, Gabriel has never come around with his feelings toward her, which saddens me. She paid for almost everything over the years, including many child-support payments, all Gabriel's camps, and probably his tuition at high school as well. Colby used her, and she gave up her career with US Airways for him and the family that Colby made her believe they could have together. (Sound familiar?) Rene has told me on several occasions that she really did love Gabriel and desperately wanted that family that was promised to her.

In the recent past, Gabe shared more of his negative feelings toward Rene. He told us that she was a "big drinker," so much so that she would get drunk and pass out from time to time and that he even used to open her bottles for her. Rob and I both felt like he was exaggerating, that these things were probably planted in his head by his dad, so we didn't really give it much credit because we know Rene, and I have since become friends with her. I sang at her wedding three years ago when she remarried after Colby. I've gone out socially with her, and I've spent time with her in our home. I've never seen her overdrinking. But I'm sure she did while married to Colby. Can you blame her?

Her dad was a plastic surgeon. While she admits it's her own fault that she allowed it to happen by believing Colby's lies and desperately wanting the family he promised her, she burned through her entire inheritance, most likely on my ex and my son.

With all the financial troubles Colby left in his wake, Rene almost lost her home as well.

There would be other victims to come.

Chapter 26

FOOD & COURT

March–July 2008

OVER THE COURSE OF A FEW YEARS when Gabriel was playing football as a preteen and a teen, Colby wanted him to "play down" a division, so he could "shine." So, he made him diet and report everything he ate on a daily basis! Gabe was already tall and thin, so he didn't have any body fat to lose. Doctors got involved eventually. Then Colby abruptly changed course a year or two later and wanted Gabe to "play up." He forced Gabriel to bulk up, even giving him supplements like creatine at a time when his body was still developing. Our family doctor warned that it was going to give Gabriel a warped idea of proper nutrition because the message kept changing, including that he could manipulate the system.

On March 4 while taking Gabriel to his guitar lesson, Colby called to ask what Gabriel had eaten for lunch, annoyed that he ate a slice of pepperoni pizza. So, Gabriel claimed he only had two bites, along with a salad and fat-free dressing. Just as it was going somewhat well in the call, Gabriel got in trouble for eating peaches in syrup instead of fruit juice.

Gabriel refused to eat all his dinner that night, even though we stopped by Tropical Smoothie, which was our regular treat on those nights before he went to catechism class. He ate only half and claimed he was full, which had never happened before. Later I found an email from Gabriel to his dad apologizing for having eaten those peaches. My heart was breaking for him, and I struggled with how to handle the situation, which I felt was out of my control because Colby was controlling Gabe's every move.

That month Gabriel was required to call or email his father to report everything he ate every day, and he would stress about it if he had not done it by day's end, asking to get on the computer. I was concerned, so that same day I emailed Gabriel's teacher for—in addition to other things, including his stress over a math assignment—advice in the matter. Here is the email I sent.

> From: Regina Rossi Valentine
> Sent: Thu 3/04/2008 7:46 a.m.
> To: Ms. Smith
> Subject: Math Homework
>
> Dear Ms. Smith,
>
> . . .
>
> I have never had him forgetful like this and it worries me.
>
> On another note, I feel this is somewhat impacted by undo stress from his father relative to an additional 11 lb. weight loss his dad wants him to achieve to stay down a division in football (he has already lost 3 lbs.). This weight loss is over the next 5 mos. while his body is supposed to be doing normal growth and additional weight gain during a very developmental period in his life. I have had our Dr. tell my son this is not a healthy decision, nor does he endorse it, but Gabriel has an allegiance to his dad and will do

I Loved You More

"whatever" he wants him to do. Having said that, he has to report each and everything he eats to his father daily and I have noticed him not maintaining his normal eating habits and wasting food. Additionally, he gets very stressed when his father questions him as to things he has eaten and tries to justify this to him.

I truly believe that this stress is impacting him emotionally/psychologically and I know how important his academic performance is to him. If you notice anything unusual in his behavior, etc. please, please let me know. On my end I am trying to send his lunches to school (hoping he eats them) and make him breakfast, but he is even protesting some of what I want to make for him in order to opt for things his dad suggests.

. . .

Regards,
Regina Rossi Valentine

This was one of many emails about Colby's expectations for Gabriel's workouts each day. At one point Colby even had the following spreadsheet set up.

Regina Rossi Valentine

	A	B	C	D	E	F	G	H	I
5	Friday, January 26			(with Coach)					
6									
7	Exercise		Set 1	Set 2	Set 3	Set 4	RTBS		Max Lift
8	Bench Press		6 x 40	6 x 40	6 x 50	6 x 50	90 seconds		90 total
9	Incline Dumb		8 x 10	8 x 10	8 x 15		90 seconds		
10	Close Grip Bench		6 x 40	6 x 40	6 x 50		90 seconds		90 total
11	Military Press		6 x 30	6 x 30	6 x 40		90 seconds		30 total
12	Preacher Curls		8 x 20	8 x 20	8 x 20		90 seconds		20 @
13	Standing Calf Raises		30 x 40	30 x 40	30 x 40		90 seconds		100 total
14	Tricep Pushes		8 x 20	8 x 20	8 x 20		90 seconds		40 total

16 RTBS means REST TIME BETWEEN SETS

18 **Conditioning Workout #4**

20 Tuesday, January 23
21 Thursday, January 25   Friday, January 26
22 Saturday and Sunday, January 27 & 28

24 Warm-up/Flexibility   10 00 minutes

26 **Tuesday, January 23 --**
27 1 x 1/4 mile GOAL IS 1 minute and 45 seconds
28 REST 1 minute 10 seconds
29 2 x 1/8 mile (rest 1 minute 10 seconds between each) GOAL IS 45 seconds
30 **** Quick Feet Drill # 1 (see other attached sheet)

32 **************** all of the below will be done with Coach ************************
33 **Thursday, January 25 --   AND Sunday, January 28**
34 Quick Feet Drills with Coach
35 4 40 yard sprints for time with Coach   (Movement Drill #1 Sunday ONLY)

38 **Friday, January 26 --**
39 lift as above
40 Goal Line Tag with Coach
41 Balance Drill #1 with Coach
42 Quick Feet Drill #1 with Coach

45 **Saturday, January 27**
46 1 x 1/4 mile GOAL IS 1 minute and 45 seconds
47 REST 1 minute 10 seconds
48 2 x 1/8 mile (rest 1 minute 10 seconds between each) GOAL IS 45 seconds
49 **** Quick Feet Drill # 1 (see other attached sheet)

I Loved You More

Here is a workout routine from May 2007:

Upper Body lift

Bench Press 10 x50   10x60   15x60   10x70
Close Grips   10x30   10x40   10x50
Curl   20x30   20x30   15x40
Tricep Push   15x20   15x20   15x20
Military Press 10x30   10x40   10x40

3 sets of 25 GOOD Pushups

Neck Isos -- each direction for 30 seconds

BIG BIG Bond

Dad

When we talked about the weight loss, here is a screenshot of just *one* of Colby's many emails (March 2008) requiring Gabriel to report everything he ate:

Breakfast – what did you eat? How much

Lunch – what did you eat? How much

Dinner – what did you eat? How much

What was drunk during the day – watch high sugar drinks – soda, tea, juice, etc.

Workouts—what did you do and for how long????

On March 18 I told Gabriel I was taking him to see Dr. Anson regarding his diet for football. This was the first time Gabriel accused me of "not supporting him." I would later find out from Renee that, on a regular basis, Colby would tell Gabe that I did not support him or his football. On the rare occasion that I would miss a game due to work, she said he would literally ask Gabe in the car on the drive home if I had called him yet to ask how the game went. That would be followed by more of the same script about me not understanding or supporting him. I hadn't even had a chance to do so but it didn't stop Colby from feeding negativity about me into our son instead of a healthy diet.

Later that evening I was blindsided by his dad harassing me on the phone about going to the doctor. "What do you hope to accomplish by doing this?" he asked. "What makes him more of an authority than me on nutrition?"

Colby's grooming was working. Gabriel was not eating, in fear of his father's opinion of him, and starting to say he wanted to live with his father more and more. In late March while Colby was on a trip to Hawaii, Colby claimed Gabriel told him clearly and for the first definitive time that he wanted to live with his dad. (That summer, Gabriel confirmed that he said this.)

In April I started getting more reports from Gabriel's teachers that he was exhibiting erratic behavior. I was also told he threw up on a recent field trip. At the same time, I was reaching out to his teachers and coaches and starting to get signs of support from them.

On April 8 I emailed Gabriel's school for help.

> From: Regina Rossi Valentine
> Sent: Tuesday, April 08, 2008 12:07 PM
> To: Ms. Newell (etc.)
> Subject: Gabriel

I Loved You More

Importance: High
Sensitivity: Confidential

Dear Educators,

I have some serious concerns with my son, Gabriel's, behavior, and well-being. Please keep me informed of anything unusual you notice with Gabriel as I am trying to stay on top of this for his sake. Thank you all for all you do for our children. God bless!

Peace,

Regina Rossi Valentine

I received the following response less than an hour later.

To: "Regina Rossi Valentine"
Sent: Tuesday, April 08, 2008 1:05 PM
Subject: RE: Gabriel

Ms. Valentine,

In light of your email, I wanted you to be aware of Gabriel's illness on our recent school field trip to Charlottesville. Gabriel became sick on the bus ride from the university to Monticello. He was pale for most of the morning and kept squatting down in the grass and holding his head in his hands as if he felt really sick. Shortly thereafter on the bus ride, he vomited. He said he felt much better afterward and seemed to perk up a little. I reported this to his dad when he came to pick up Gabriel from school, but I wanted to be sure to share this information with you as well.

Sincerely,

Ms. Newell

Ms. Smith also wrote me back very quickly, adding,

> . . . The idea of Gabe's food being restricted is very worrisome. We do not eat lunch with the students, so I cannot give you any insight into what he is eating at lunch. However, I have noticed what I would describe as a bit of an "edge" in Gabe recently. In fact, other team teachers agreed on this recently. Just yesterday, Gabe simply had a "look" about him that was unsettling, he looked very troubled. When I asked him what was wrong, he said nothing. He is generally the up-beat boy that we are used to and really enjoy. I hope that there can be some resolution to the situation that does not have a negative impact on his emotional health. You are right, he is a GREAT kid!

Things were happening fast, and I was sick with worry. I asked Loretta for help and for her prayers, and she came through, of course. Colby and I now had a court date, on top of it all, where Colby was *again* trying to gain full custody of Gabriel and take him away from me full time. Through his grooming, Colby had Gabriel say he wanted to live with his dad. Loretta had other points for me to consider, and she was a great help to me through all of this. She even related it back to our experiences growing up. In an email on Friday, May 2, 2008, from Loretta, with the subject line, "Prayers," she wrote the following.

> *Of course I will pray for you and Gabriel. Give this a thought though. Have you ever noticed that we always seem to try to please the one who is the hardest one to please? For instance, we still want Mom's approval on a certain level even if we deny we do. The way it manifests itself is when we give her something or tell her something we think she will like or want her approval on. Meanwhile she was the hardest one to please our whole lives. It doesn't mean that we would*

want to live with her over Dad (theoretically of course). I think it's possible that Gabriel is just trying to prove to his dad that although he doesn't live with him all the time, he still cares about him and wants his approval. But in reality it's Colby who is hardest to please. He demands things of Gabriel that dig into his core. You may think you are the one that would be hard to please because you have to discipline him. But Colby looks for things from Gabriel that could mean changing the person that he (Gabriel) is. I don't know if I am being very clear. But this type of pressure is much more difficult, and this is why it manifested in Gabriel's attitude and stress level.

With you, Gabriel doesn't have any stress. He knows the rules and lives by them. If he messes up, he knows the consequences but how do you live up to a father's expectations of being the BEST at everything such as sports. Imagine the stress of relaying everything you ate for the day and having to hear that you may not be good enough if you don't do as Colby says. You don't put that pressure on him. You allow him to be himself. Gabriel may be writing things about being Colby's best friend but that is because that is what COLBY wants. He probably indoctrinated him with that thought process. Gabriel won't want to live under that pressure full time. He knows he is safe with you and the simplicity of what is expected. Just to be a good person.

Even if he ever voiced the thought of wanting to live with Colby, it just may be about manipulation or threatening you because he knows how much it will hurt you. If he says it to you again, I would not be emotional about it. I would point out the differences in how it would be for him. And then I would tell him if necessary that this is not his decision to make (no anger or tears). The decision was already made years ago. Don't let your child control you. I know he isn't doing it now, but he may in the future try. I am sure you, me and all of us at times in our lives have said things that hurt Mom and Dad to the core.

However, because they remained strong on their convictions (right or wrong), we had to abide by their dictates. We survived and so did they.

Gabriel is going to test you, maybe even in subtle ways. You are smarter than him so don't let him get the best of you. The only way he would be given to Colby is if you are unfit and that would never happen. It is Colby who has the unstable home, job, life, etc. Colby can afford to look good to Gabe because his time with him is limited to a certain point, so he can pull off looking like he would be great to be with full time. But if Gabriel got a regular dose of Colby's temper, I'm sure he would not think things would be so ducky.

He will hurt you . . . many times in your life. That is a given. Don't you think that you and I have hurt Mom and Dad more than once and in ways I hope we never get hurt? It doesn't matter if we thought we were right, the point is we hurt them. This too will happen to you but you have the control and the fortitude and you have to recognize that it is a part of life. Just plug on and remember he will not always feel this way. When he is old enough or mature enough as a man, he will know it was you who was the true parent. So tough it out and take the blows that parents have to take but stay strong in your convictions and beliefs and never give up. You will have to be hard on him *someday and he will resent it but he will be better for it.*

Gabriel is so blessed to have such a wonderful, caring, strong, intelligent, and loving mother. You are an inspiration. Do not ever doubt it although you may have days where you will. Go on with the knowledge that no one can take away from you the truly good mother that you are. Remember this because it always comes true: "What goes around, comes around"! That goes for good and bad.

Love ya, Loretta

In June Colby brought Gabriel to see Dr. Anson for asthma issues. The doctor emailed me after, reporting no success with the weight issue we'd discussed. I hoped our getaway to Florida the next week would help alleviate some of our issues, but instead my family directly observed Gabriel's defiant behavior and disrespect—not just with me but his aunts and uncles too.

Heavenly Father, please protect my son from the evils of the world, especially his dad. I beg of you to open his eyes to the truth about his dad and about me, to help him accept that truth and to live that truth so that my relationship with him will one day be close and loving, the way it should be between a mother and son.

That became my constant prayer for Gabriel, beginning in 2008 and throughout his teen years when our relationship was so bad. It had far more to do with his dad than Gabriel being a teen. The years 2008 through 2010 were by far the worst years of my life. My son hated me and my family. When I looked into his eyes, I didn't even recognize him.

At the start of July, I emailed Colby to request counseling with Dr. Alexander (he hadn't fired Colby yet). His response, when he came to pick up our twelve-year-old son to go to a workout, was, "Got your email. We're heading for court." Of course, he said it while within earshot of Gabriel.

But we made the appointment for counseling. Dr. Alexander was average height and weight (not slim but not overweight) with short, curly, salt-and-pepper hair, a traditional beard and mustache, glasses, and a fairly soft-spoken, calming voice. As a result of our July 9 session, we were informed that for a pre-teen, 10 percent weight loss bordered on an eating disorder, and Gabriel could have long-term issues with food as a result. Dr. Alexander repeatedly asked Colby why he had not sought medical advice on this decision, pointing out that it could lead to long-term psychological and health issues for Gabriel.

Colby admitted to me in the parking lot afterwards that he got angry with Gabriel for coming back from Florida "already one hundred pounds." Gabe couldn't win when it came to pleasing his dad. Colby also said he was angry with Gabriel for forgetting his Florida Gators duffle bag, which he needed for camp.

A week later I called Colby to see if we might work a few important things out and avoid a court battle. It went nowhere, so I told him I was filing. Later that night Gabriel told me on the phone that his dad now "forbade him to diet."

"What does that mean, Mom?"

"Gabriel, I love you, but I am not discussing that any further," I replied.

On July 16 I filed papers with the courts seeking an emergency hearing.

Chapter 27

PRE-TRIAL

July–September 2008

AT 7:00 A.M. I PICKED GABRIEL UP from his dad's work. When we drove away, he got serious.

"What's going on?" he asked.

"Gabriel, I love you, but there is nothing to discuss."

"Well, you're starting the whole court thing, even though I don't like confrontations."

"There's nothing for me to tell you, Gabe. It's obvious your father already has."

"But I want to hear it from you, Mom."

"Again, I will not discuss the legal matters with you."

"I don't know if I will ever forgive you for this, Mom."

That night after speaking with his dad on the phone, Gabriel asked to talk to me. It was about living with his dad.

MY ATTORNEY—AND NOW MY FRIEND, Saul Marshall, is medium height and bald with hazel eyes, and he always wears his glasses on a leash. He's a thinker. In an email from my sister that I forwarded to him when she found Colby's disbarment statement (highlights shared earlier), he stated, "Colby may be a schmuck, but this, in essence, says he's a thief too."

Meanwhile, my other problems had not gone away. In fact, they were getting worse. I reached out again to Gabriel's teacher, Ms. Newell, in an email. I started including Saul in the emails.

> To: "Ms. Newell"
> Cc: "Saul Marshall"
> Sent: Tuesday, July 22, 2008 7:46 AM
> Subject: Re: Gabriel-Time Sensitive!
>
> Dear Ms. Newell,
>
> Things have gotten very bad for Gabriel in the past couple of months. He has already dropped over 10 lbs. in weight, despite my having a meeting with his coach and dad, taking him to the doctor (who warned this would be a dangerous mismatch to his height and advised against the weight loss), and getting his father into a co-parenting counseling session with a psychologist who we have worked with for several years. Nothing has worked and Gabriel's horrible behavior towards me and others has escalated, not to mention his health and well-being.
>
> I am left with no other choice but to file an emergency hearing request with the court due to the health concerns. I am asking you, as his mother, and will be doing so with Ms. Smith, to please, please consider the possibility of appearing in court,

only to testify to what you know and have shared with me relative to his health and/or behavior changes in the spring when all this started.

My attorney is Saul Marshall, whom I have copied on this e-mail, as well as Mrs. Marin (guidance counselor), who was made aware of all this during the school year. Would you kindly provide me with either your home/cell # and/or address? If you are more comfortable, please call him directly. This is extremely time sensitive as we do not know how much lead time we will have on a court date.

I am praying you will be able to bring yourself to help Gabriel on this and thank you in advance for your kind consideration.

Regards,

Regina Valentine

In our dealings with the court, Gabriel was assigned a guardian ad litem to represent his interests. Colby requested this, thinking that, as an attorney himself, he would have some influence or control over one. Our guardian ad litem (GAL) was a man named William Garrison. He was always impeccably dressed in a suit, had green eyes, and was bald, which he wore very well. I rarely saw him smile because he was all business. He made it clear and actually told me that he did not care about me or Colby. Gabriel was his top priority, and he lived up to that.

With all my concerns, I emailed Saul to see if he had heard from Mr. Garrison.

From: Regina Rossi Valentine
To: Saul Marshall
Sent: Mon, 28 Jul 2008 3:08 pm
Subject: Garrison

Any word from him? If not, is it inappropriate for me to contact him with mention of my deep concerns and wanting him for Gabriel's sake as his advocate "of reason"?

Saul wrote me back with good news, which I desperately needed at that point.

> From: Saul Marshall
> To: Regina Rossi Valentine
> Sent: Monday, July 28, 2008 4:22 PM
> Subject: Re: Garrison
>
> I just so happened to have just finished a phone conference with him about 5 minutes ago. He said that the weight loss thing was ridiculous (from Colby's standpoint). He wants copies of the emails and text messages. I told him I thought a parent has a right to see those and he seemed to agree. He said he would try to meet with Gabriel prior to our hearing date on August 21.
>
> When is the weigh in? The 20th?

The text messages referenced above came to my attention when I took Gabe's phone one day and began to read them. Colby was texting things to Gabe like, "Good morning, team, need memory help today. What did I tell Gabe yesterday to NOT tell his mom so I would get the shocked and embarrassed look on her face in court?" or "You are only as good as you dare to be bad."

Dealing with the courts was an incredibly stressful thing. With major life issues on the line, I never knew how things would shake out or even if I would receive able and interested advocacy, but sometimes the courts were my last resort and my only recourse. That did not make things any less stressful. My progress through court cases was at first measured in battles, in wins and losses, and for me that period was filled with prayer.

I Loved You More

We were assigned Judge Wallace. She was very tall (or maybe her long black robe made me think she was) and average weight with short, straight, medium-blond hair. She was intimidating! She always had "cheaters" on the end of her nose as she looked over them at us from her high perch. She had a reputation for favoring the dads since she had a good relationship with her ex-husband. She expected everyone else to as well.

On September 23, I emailed Saul regarding what I hoped was a breakthrough in terms of Gabriel and what was going on.

>Saul,
>
>Dr. Alexander said to me in my last session (just before court and his letter) that Colby had alienated Gabriel against me. I had no clue this had an actual name! In the media recently has been a lot of talk about PAS (Parent Alienation Syndrome) and PAAO (Parent Alienation Awareness Organization). Of course, my sister is up all hours of the night researching things for me, God bless her.
>
>Below are two links. The first is a short article with a judge's ruling for a case in Canada—so like mine to a degree.
>
>The second has two video clips on the first page . . . make sure you click the one on the right. It is a mother, who as a child was the victim of PAS via her father, and her story. Oh my God, **it is exactly the development of how Gabriel has changed and treated me.**
>
>*I would strongly ask you forward these to William Garrison and Dr. Alexander* since you have their email addresses. I wanted to copy Garrison but wasn't sure if it was appropriate.
>
>Thanks,
>
>Regina

Desperate, scrambling, and dizzy, my life was on the line—my son was on the line. I was in over my head, and I knew it. I just couldn't let anyone else know it.

Chapter 28

OCTOBER

October 2008

October 6, 2008

My Dearest Son,

It is with an extremely heavy heart that I am writing this letter to you. I have really struggled with writing to you this year. I have had to keep putting it off because my emotions were too raw. I have been so deeply hurt, you can't even imagine. You and your actions to me this year have been so hurtful in addition to the things I always deal with relative to your dad. Even though I know deep in my heart that your father has put you up to most of it and encouraged it, the pain is still the same. One day when you have children of your own, you will understand that when your child hurts you, there is nothing worse for your heart.

I can't even tell you how much I have agonized over this past year in particular. I have cried many, many times and prayed with such intensity to our Lord to help you through all of this and to give me the strength I need to accept whatever His plan is for us both. I ask the Virgin Mary to wrap her mantle around you and protect you from any evils of the world. My constant prayer for you is that your eyes will be open to the truth and that you will accept the truth and live the truth. I know when this happens that our relationship will heal, and you and I will once again become close.

It all began this past spring when I found out you were dieting, reporting everything you put in your mouth to your father, and trying to lose more than 10 lbs. to play down a division in football. He put you on a diet and then, when I did not support the diet for health reasons, I believe in my heart he tried to turn you against me. The very day in March when I told you we were going to see Dr. Anson to see if this was a healthy choice was the first time you played the card to go live with your dad. You accused me of not supporting you but that your dad did. That is what you kept saying to me. How in the world have I not supported you, son? I have been your biggest supporter in all your sports, music, school, etc. I have also been your biggest financial supporter in all these things over the years. You just don't realize or know it because I do not discuss these things with you.

I have given you every opportunity to try anything your heart desires. I started you in soccer, then there was karate. When you wanted to quit karate early, we talked about commitment and finishing something you started, setting a goal and following it through. As

I Loved You More

a result, you finished karate and achieved your black belt. As a single parent, karate was an extremely expensive sport, and your dad did not contribute one bit. In fact, he fought me on putting you into karate in the beginning and then argued that your lessons on Fridays cut into his time with you. During karate I also got you started playing T-ball and baseball because you said you were interested. Then there was basketball. Do I have to remind you of all the hassles we had with your start in that and how your dad tried to change your mind about playing for St. Francis's at the 11th hour?

Thank God for Matt who blessed you with playing in that exhibition game with his varsity players right after the Globetrotters game! You were hooked and went on to play for St. Francis for two years, achieving MVP both years! I also started you in guitar lessons, and I had you signed up for football your first year at Courthouse Rec League, only to find out from you that your dad had signed you up for the Great Neck Rec League without my knowledge. You probably don't even remember that I had done this for you too because I tried not to make a big deal about my issues w/your dad. Now for your birthday I have gotten you a harmonica because you would like to try that too. So, I ask you, how is it that you can accuse me of not supporting you? I am also the one who spent a tremendous amount of time on your application for the Gifted School because you wanted to go there.

It was the dieting that I did not support, not your playing football. Cooking, baking, and providing these things for my family and loved ones has always been something that is near and dear to my heart. And you have always been a good eater, never an overeater!

Once you started claiming that you weren't hungry or you were full or not allowing yourself to eat things you always had, food became a serious issue with us. I watched my child reduced to skin and bones by the end of summer, and I was totally helpless to do anything for you. You and your father were on a mission, and I was disregarded in the actions you both took on your health. You are far too young to be making such a decision, especially when the medical doctors and therapists said this was not healthy or wise for you to be doing when your body was going through adolescence/puberty/growth.

Nothing I said or did this year mattered except to make you and your dad angrier with me.

Our relationship this past year has deteriorated, and it is breaking my heart. I know you. I have raised you. You are a loving, caring, and compassionate young man, but the person who has been living with us this past year is unrecognizable to me most days. You have been so hurtful, disrespectful, and at times, hateful to me. You are cold, distant, and void of any type of affection toward me. No, this is not due to your "getting older" or approaching your teens. It was directly related to the diet issues.

I would look in your eyes and not even recognize my own son. You stopped interacting and playing with the boys in the neighborhood over the summer. On July 23rd when I "made" you go and play with Peter and his brother, you got angry with me and stormed out. Then you ended up playing with them for 5 hrs. They stayed at our house for dinner, and you had a great time! After we walked them home, I looked at you and said, "You don't have to say anything. I just want you to know how happy I am that you had such a good time with your friends." Then right in front of me, it was like you transformed into that hateful boy I don't recognize and said to me, "I just don't like being made to play with my friends!" I was so shocked. We got the Gabriel we know and love back for five hours, and then you reverted back into the mean kid you had been to me for months. When you are at your dad's house, you seem to have nothing to say to me on the phone but one-word answers. But I know you, and the Gabriel I know leaks out every once in a while, as if to let me know he is still there inside—but hidden far, far away.

This past summer all the Rossi's went to Orlando, again. It was one of the worst weeks of my life. I have no idea how your memory will be of this week. I think you will pinpoint it as the time you "got in trouble for not eating a ham sandwich" because your dad kept joking that point with you over and over. The reality is that your disrespectful behavior and treatment of me climaxed while we were in Florida. On this one day we had all come back from somewhere, and you went outside to talk on the phone w/your dad. While you did, I made you a nice lunch of a ham, turkey, and cheese sandwich. I only gave you a small handful of chips because, due to the diet, you were typically not eating much, let alone chips.

You came in and said you wanted to make your own sandwich, but I already had it all waiting for you. What followed was total defiance by you. You had eaten this type of sandwich before and loved it. But for some reason you had it in your head that you could not eat the ham even though the chips had more calories than the ham. You were adamant that you would not eat it and began to argue at length with me. That, after 7 mos. of this behavior and defiance of eating, was the last straw for me, and I blew up at you, using profanity that I NEVER say. But I was at my wit's end. When I left the condo to cool off, I came back to find that you had eaten the sandwich but taken the ham off it to make a point. Gabriel, this whole scenario was not about the ham but the principal of your respecting not only my authority but also the fact that someone had gone to the trouble to make you a lunch you enjoy, yet you were defiant in eating it because of your dad's control over your weight loss. As a punishment for the continued behavior (you had also hurt your cousin, Danson, in the pool and mouthed off to Uncle Richard), I took away your cellphone.

I feel as if I am in the fight of my life right now for your sake. You say you want to live with your dad; however, with everything he has done to you and to me, I can't wrap my brain around it. I feel as though the physical manipulation he put on your body with this diet and the emotional manipulation to pit you against me is really the root of the problem.

I don't know if you realize right now how very hard it is for me to bite my tongue about your dad. I have done so for years, but recently it has been exceptionally trying. Everyone says that I need to start sharing things with you that have happened or that he has done because everyone knows he is poisoning you against me. They say that you are older now and should know. But I keep telling everyone that one day when you are a man, I know you will look back on how your father and I conducted ourselves during the course of your life. I want you to respect me and learn

I Loved You More

from my example on how we should and should not treat other people. I want you to see that my love for you was, is, and always will be stronger than my disdain for your father.

Speaking badly of him to you now will only hurt you, not him. That is why I constantly tell you that we both love you, and you need to feel free to love us both too. We may disagree on many levels, but that should not play a role in your relationship with either of us. You should be protected and shielded from all the ugliness and legal matters.

. . .

In two weeks we go to court over custody and who you will live with. Your father wants full physical custody with you seeing me "when you want." In 3½ weeks you turn 13. I wish this was not happening at the same time as your birthday. We have also been in the middle of a court-ordered parenting capacity evaluation.

October 11, 2008

I was so hurt today at your football game. It is a long-standing tradition that a mother wears her child's jersey to a game if there is one from a previous year. Today, several of the mothers were wearing their sons' jerseys from last year. Rene showed up at your game wearing your jersey—a jersey I should have been wearing. She even walked directly in front of me just before your game started and stood there for a few *minutes, I assume to make sure I saw it. Two of the other moms came up to me because they thought what she did was hurtful (it was!) and poor judgment on her part. I was so upset I had to leave the field and go to my car, call Rob, and try to pull myself together. The two moms both commented that she didn't bother to do it last week when she knew I would not be there, yet she did it today. I am your mom. I am proud of you. I should have been the one to wear your jersey, not her. She has been so hostile toward me the past month since this whole parenting capacity evaluation began. It seems at every turn my heart aches.*

WE WERE IN COURT again. And wow, what a day it turned out to be. So emotional. So difficult. Constantly praying for wisdom for me, my attorney, the judge, and Mr. Garrison. For years I specifically prayed for Judge Wallace to have the wisdom of Solomon, to rule on what only God knew were the true intentions of our hearts when it came to what was right and best for Gabriel. I resolved to trust God and His time, not mine.

But that was so darn hard!

End of October 2008

Well, after all these months, we finally went to court on October 22, 2008. I was not happy with court being so close to your birthday and the importance of turning 13! Not knowing how things would turn out, I did not want it to be a negative memory for you surrounding your birthday.

Going into court we knew that your attorney was going to recommend that you go ahead and live with your dad if that's what you wanted. Even though he told us that it was not the better place for you, he felt you were smart enough to try it out and then figure it out on your own. I prayed so very hard, as I always do before court and other difficult times, that the truth would come out, that lies would be exposed, and that all those in a position to make decisions about your wellbeing would be filled with the wisdom of Solomon (truth and wisdom)! Our prayers were answered! We were actually in court from 2 p.m. until midnight—no kidding! Judge Wallace was determined to hear all the testimony and evidence in your case, and by gosh she did!

I know this next part will be somewhat hard to hear. Your father made several attempts in court to discredit me and my integrity by misrepresenting documents and claiming I "lied" on them. One in particular was from my annulment. He showed one page that had seven additional pages with it, yet he tried to say I lied under canon law about knowing he was married before. I never lied about this, never! He, however, did lie to me about being married before when I first met him and asked him that question. He did not tell me until our third date because he said that, after speaking with me at length on the phone prior to our meeting, he knew from what I said that my faith was important to me, and he didn't want his prior marriage to negatively influence me.

Regardless of all that he attempted to do in court, none of it panned out because it was all lies. He even had your previous football team mom, Kelly, testify against me. She claimed that I was confrontational with her about being removed from the email distribution list for track. She, too, lied. Thankfully,

Judge Wallace saw right through her and in her closing statement said that two of your dad's witnesses, the team mom and Rene, hurt his case.

Rene—I truly feel as though I have (had) been her biggest advocate when it came to you. Well, after all that she did to me and to you this year, I am no longer on her cheering squad. In court when she took the stand to testify, if what she said hadn't been so over-the-top ridiculous, it would have devastated me. She actually said that you and she were so close that you did cooking together, homework together, reading together, crafts together—the list went on. She said you always greeted her at the door to help her carry her things upstairs, that you told her every day that you loved her, and she said she loved you too. She said you "followed her around like a puppy dog." At that remark, Judge Wallace said, "The fact that you would even say that a 12-year old boy follows you around like a puppy dog is disturbing to me." And the rest of us agreed. She went on to say that your dad always gave you my messages, but you just did not want to call me back or talk with me on the phone. Gabriel, even though I know it was exaggerated, it still hurt me to hear the person who I supported, say that about me and you.

When Rene was finished testifying, Judge Wallace looked straight at me and said, "I can't imagine how hurt Mrs. Valentine must feel after hearing all of that." I was stunned to see that, a judge who had been very hard on both of us for over six years, finally "saw the light" of what I had gone through. It was so liberating and validating.

I Loved You More

Once all the testimony was heard in court, it was time for closing arguments. It was 11:45 PM. Your attorney, Mr. Garrison shocked us! He got up and delivered a brilliant closing argument, with absolutely no notes, but he spoke intelligently and from the heart. He said he was struggling with what he was about to do and that in all his years in court, he had never changed his position as he was about to do with us. At that point I breathed a sigh of relief! He said he felt as though he was betraying you because he told you more than once that unless something significant came out at the hearing, he would recommend that you go live with your dad. He said that very significant information came out and that, in good conscience, he could no longer suggest that. He said that he was very disturbed at what he heard and that he had never been so conflicted about a case as he was about yours. He said that no attorney wants to worry about disbarment, but your father repeatedly ignored contacts from the courts, even though he had an obligation to see what charges were filed against him. He was also disturbed that your father denied more than once even knowing he was being disbarred—until he finally admitted it when Mr. Garrison quoted a legal article about it that clearly stated your dad knew what was going on.

Then Judge Wallace gave a compelling closing statement and agreed with Mr. Garrison completely. She said she wasn't even sure she was at peace with her final decision/ruling. She said she was very conflicted and disturbed at the testimony she had heard. She said she felt it would be wrong to reward you with living w/your father, considering your behavior toward me. She told your dad and Rene that they had a moral *responsibility to have corrected your behavior toward me and not encourage it. She also said that she felt sorry for me and wished me luck as I had a lot of work to do to repair my relationship with you given all that happened this past year.*

It was truly an amazing end to a long and difficult journey.

When I got home from court that night (Aunt Loretta stayed with you at home and took you to football practice for me), I laid in bed thinking about everything and preparing myself for more of the same bad behavior from you since you did not get what you said you wanted—to live w/your dad. I thanked God and His mother for answering my prayers, prayers for truth and wisdom! The next morning I got up extra early to talk to you about court. Much to my surprise you were already up at 5 a.m. doing homework (because your dad had taken you out of school against your attorney's advice, and your bookbag w/homework was in his car during the hearing). So, you had been doing homework.

I noticed a phone was close to you on the couch and asked if you had talked with your father. You told me you had, but you wanted to hear from me what happened. Because I wanted to protect you from information about your dad that you do not need to know at this point in your life, I simply told you that Judge Wallace heard a lot of information, and her decision was very difficult for her to make. I told you that although she understood that you wanted more time with your dad, she did not feel it was necessary that you live there full time; however, she gave you an extra day with him. I kept it simple with you and did not go into more detail. Much to my surprise, you finished getting ready for school, and when I kissed you goodbye, you kissed me back and went off on a very good note—not what I expected at all!

When you came home from school, the same thing—you were "normal," the Gabriel we all know and love. Rob best describes the change in you. He said it was as if a shade was lifted from your eyes and your personality that day. Grandpa told me that he believes you were relieved it was all over. I believe that too. You did everything you were told and/or expected to do, and yet, the decision was taken from you by Judge Wallace, but you did not get your way.

It was over, for now, at least.

Gabriel, son, I need to share this next part with you too. In court your father tried to make Rob look like a bad parent. He put him on the stand to testify. Rob was not supposed to testify and was only there to sit in court w/me as moral support. But your father expressed wanting to put him on the stand, so Rob had to wait in the waiting room for 10 hours. He brought nothing to read or do, and it was a long, long day and night for him as witnesses are not allowed to leave. Your father began to question him about Megan and how she drove to Virginia Tech once without our knowledge (she was 18 too!). He tried to make Rob look as though he did not even know what his own daughter was up to and that, quite possibly, that would not be good for you. Thankfully, the judge wanted to hear nothing of all that and put an end to it. So, Rob was not allowed to be there to support me and then went through a fiasco of questions that were totally irrelevant to the case in the end.

. . .

I did not make big plans for your birthday other than the whole family coming over for dinner and cake/ice cream. We actually had a great time, and we gave you a harmonica with a head/neck holder and several other things. We had pancit, lumpia, pepperoni bread, and chicken on a stick from the Filipino restaurant owned by my work partner's mom. The food was great! And for dessert you asked me to make Megan's cinnamon coffee cake!

Gabriel, all I can say is on October 23, 2008, you changed. The day after court, I got my son back, honestly. We were back to the previous days of snuggling on the couch to watch Ghost Whisperer *or rent a movie. When Rob is at the firehouse, you still enjoy coming into my room to read our books together. All I can tell you is God is in control!*

With every decision I make relative to you, I try to look at the big picture of your life, how this will affect you long term, not just in the here and now. It has been extremely difficult for me to "let go and let God," to give this cross up to him when it comes to the troubles with your dad. But I know that when I do, I am at peace. There is an inner peace I have that I can't explain except to say that I believe in the deepest part of my soul that you will survive all of this and be better and stronger for it. I pray all the time that our mother, Mary, will wrap her mantle around you and protect you from the evils that surround you. I know she does.

Well, this is by far the longest annual letter I have written to you, certainly not the happiest one; however, sometimes the truth never is. I anticipate

I Loved You More

that this may come up again down the road (your saying you want to live with your dad). I am not going to worry about that for now. Right now I am so thankful the darkness is behind us and I got my boy back. Your happiness means everything to me. I wish I could protect you from everything and all pain, but I can't. I just do my best with God's help.

I love you, son, to the moon and back and then some!

Xoxoxo Mom

As part of this 2008 court hearing, we were provided a thirty-eight-page comprehensive report from the parenting capacity evaluation, which consisted of diagnostic interviews with each parent and Gabriel, psychological testing of each parent and Gabriel, observations of each parent and Gabriel together, which included home visits, and a collateral contacts and records review in order to define Gabriel's best interests. The examiner, who holds a PhD and is a professor of psychiatry and behavioral sciences, also testified to his findings.

In addition to lying three times about ever losing a professional license and claiming there were no professional, ethical, or disciplinary complaints or hearings filed against him, the report went on to say that Colby's ". . . failure to report his disbarment in New York to the examiner, the history of court actions necessary to ensure his payment of child support, and his misrepresentation of himself as 'Dr.' . . . are all evidence of significant lapses in judgment . . . and the primary physical custody should be retained with Mrs. Valentine, and Mr. Baxter be granted reasonable and customary visitation."

I was also subjected to being cross-examined by Colby because he had fired his first two attorneys over the years, only to represent himself. His cocky attitude, as if he were in control of the courtroom, was palpable. Having him stare me down as he towered over my seat while questioning me was beyond unnerving, but I held my own and simply told the truth. After all . . .

"He who represents himself has a fool for a client."
—Abraham Lincoln

PART 5

"Healing takes courage, and we all have courage,
even if we have to dig a little to find it."

—Tori Amos

Chapter 29

DEBACLES

January–August 2009

Dear, dear, Gabriel,

    Gosh, I just have to begin this letter with how joyful I am since Oct. 23, 2008! Ever since the day after court, you have been the son we know and love! As of that day, I got my son back. We have been just great, and you and Rob have been growing closer with your interests in Flight Simulator and simply by our time together as a family. I thank God all the time, yet, I still pray for you daily for so many things and reasons.

    . . .

    Ya know, as I have written these letters to you over the years, I realize they get more and more disclosing *to you about what is going on, what I am going through. I know they do not paint a nice picture of your father. I realize he is your father, and right now while we are in this mess, I will not tell you these things. You have a right to be protected from the ugliness of his actions and cultivate your own relationship with him. I believe you know what is right and wrong. I also know that when you are an adult, you will thank me for protecting you now and not putting you in the middle or turning you against your dad or expecting you to "choose me over him," as he does to you. You will have to make your own decisions when you are older, and I do not want to be responsible for influencing those decisions by telling you now what goes on. By the time you read these letters, you will have come to your own conclusions about your parents. I am trying to "take the high road," and it is not always easy. I am also not perfect and realize I slip sometimes. I am human, after all, and when someone uses my child to hurt me, it is unconscionable, unforgivable, and hurts deeper than you can imagine until you have children of your own. You must love your child more than you dislike your ex. I try to remind myself of that every day. And I do love you more. I always have, and I always will.*

THE FIRST QUARTER of 2009 was magical. I had my son back! Then in April I was surprised when Colby came to my workplace, the sales office at a new construction site, unannounced, with Gabriel to tell me that he and Rene were divorcing. He called me just minutes before to say he was there and wanted to come to talk with me. I felt blindsided. It turns out Gabriel had known for a month but had said nothing to me.

It seemed the more time Gabriel spent with his dad, the more he grew to resent me again. Despite his dad's negative influences, at least he ended the academic year on a positive note.

> *At the end of the school year I was contacted by Mr. Boone, your English teacher. He told me you were getting the highest award given out at the ceremony. It is called the* **Phoenix of the Year**. *I was so very, very proud!!! Both Rob & I and Grandpa Rossi came to see you accept your award. Wow, what an amazing honor! Great job! Well done, son! I have been told by several of your teachers that you are such a polite, respectful, and wonderful student to have in their classes. Ms. Rachman (your science teacher) told me she wished she had a whole class of "you"! I told her to send that kid home because I had no idea who she was talking about! Ha-ha!*

Initially, by summer, we had minimal issues. Our summer plan was to go on our family vacation to Georgia, to the home of my brother, Michael, and his wife, Kris. We were all there on a lake in Monticello for a family reunion. The lake is gorgeous, and they had a pontoon boat and WaveRunners to ride. Thirteen of us were there, and we started out having an absolute blast swimming, riding the WaveRunners, eating great meals together, and just relaxing and chilling out. That week we also had multiple birthdays to celebrate—my mother and father's as well as Michelle's and Christian's, two of Michael's children.

Sadly, on my mother's birthday, June 29, we found out that Uncle Dave, my father's brother in Canada, went in to be tested to donate a kidney to his son, my cousin, Joe. When he was there, they told him he could not donate a kidney because he had AML (adult acute myeloid leukemia, a cancer of the blood and bone marrow), the worst type of leukemia there is. All of us were devastated.

The next day was not much better than the day before. Well, up until almost 5:00 p.m. it was. Even though we were having a fun time, Gabe's behavior was still slowly morphing into the son I didn't recognize, the son who hated me because of my ex. Most everyone except my parents had been riding the WaveRunners all day, and Rob said to me, "Come on!"

"No, I can't," I said, "it will hurt my neck. I can't." I have lost two inches of height from stenosis and arthritis in my neck, so I am super careful not to exacerbate the pain.

At the end of the day, Rob tried again. "Come on, Regina, I won't drive hard," he said.

I'm very adventurous, so I love that stuff, but I wasn't managing my neck pain like I am now. I hadn't paid much attention throughout the day as to how the kids were getting on and off the WaveRunners. My brother, Michael's pontoon boat was tied up at the end of the dock. It had a little door on each side, and we could go off the rear as well. The boat was docked all day because we hadn't used it, but that's how we were getting in and out of the lake. We'd walk across the dock onto the boat and then off the other side. I wasn't paying attention, but when they used the WaveRunners, the kids were going off on the boat's stern. So, when Rob called for me to join him, he was floating over by the side where I thought I was to get into the water and on the WaveRunner.

It was the end of the day, around five o'clock, and everybody was up at the house except my brother, Michael, Rob, Gabriel, and me. Rob and Gabriel had just been riding the WaveRunners, so Gabriel was getting off where I thought I was going to get on the WaveRunner. He handed me his life vest on the deck of the pontoon boat, I put it on, and as I went to get in the water at the side of the boat, Michael and Rob said, "No, go to the other way!" meaning the stern of the boat. So, I reached back to grab something to stop myself, but I went right into the water. I didn't know what happened next; I just knew it was bad.

I used my left arm to pull myself up the floating ladder thinking, *Oh my God! I lost my finger.* It had gotten caught in the hinge of that little side door and ripped off.

Suddenly in flight mode, I ran up the hill to the house. Meanwhile, my finger was sitting on the deck of the boat. It was oddly funny because at first Rob thought I had lost a fingernail. "I haven't had fake nails for, like, eight months," I told him later at the hospital. My poor brother picked my finger off the deck and ran up to the house behind me.

"Put it on ice! Put it on ice!" Rob yelled, running behind him. But it was *ripped;* it wasn't just a clean cut.

At the time Rob was a captain with the fire department. We had driven to Georgia, so he had his truck. He got his medic bag, and as he started wrapping me up, all I could think was, *Don't let the little ones see this! Don't let the little ones see this! Don't let the little ones see this!* I didn't want them to be traumatized.

It was 2009 and Gabriel was still thirteen. It's funny because in my mind he was so much younger. While we sat on the bottom of the deck steps to the house, and Rob was wrapping my hand, my kid who hated me, who didn't want to be around me, was sitting next to me with his arm around me. "It's OK, Mom," he said. "Just listen to my voice and stay calm. It's OK, Mom. You'll be OK."

It was instinctual. And you know how it is when you're a kid, if your parent gets hurt, you think they're going to die because your parents are indestructible, and such things just don't happen. It was a shift for him. It was also traumatic for him because the ambulance brought me to a field where they airlifted me to Atlanta to the hospital. It was funny because while in the air they asked me my pain level, but I didn't know what that was. I'd never had to give a "pain level" before. They blew out one of my veins in the ambulance trying to put in an IV line. I still didn't have morphine, just pure adrenaline. So, I was in the helicopter, thinking, *Man, I may never get to do this again!* I looked out the window at the incredible view, and they finally gave me morphine.

When I got to the hospital, they showed me the pain chart with all the smiley faces ranging from one to ten. In the helicopter I said I was a level four or five, but I was still in shock. Now that I saw the actual range, I told them I had been an eight!

I found out two years later (a colleague of my sister's was doing some research) those pontoon boats had a class-action lawsuit against them because other people had also lost appendages because of the boat design. My brother's boat actually had the fix—a ball on the top to prevent what happened to me—but I happened to go just the right (or wrong!) way into the water, and it ripped my finger off. Unfortunately, they could not reattach it and had to cut it down a little more to sew me up properly.

It's just a little pinkie finger missing now, but I do get phantom pain from time to time. Out of nowhere I'll feel like somebody is sticking a pin in it. It doesn't happen as frequently as it did in the beginning, but it still happens from time to time.

When I came back to Virginia Beach and had to have the stitches removed, I was sitting in the doctor's office having found out the day before that my dad had been diagnosed with the same cancer, AML, as his brother.

"Why is missing a finger upsetting me so much?" I asked the doctor. "It's a freaking pinkie. My dad has cancer." I was trying to process it all.

"First of all," the doctor explained as he was taking my stitches out, "you can't compare your crisis to someone else's because it's *yours*, and it's big to you. Second, it's a part of you, and that's a big deal."

I don't really miss my finger today, to tell you the truth, except for playing the piano, which is a real challenge. But it could have been worse; it could have been my whole hand.

That traumatic experience kind of started Gabriel's awakening to his mom. In time I believed that it was a "God thing" to help my son. When I look at that missing finger now, I am always reminded that the loss of it had a higher purpose. It was for Gabriel's sake.

BACK HOME, GABRIEL TOLD ME his dad asked if I had passed out when my finger was torn off. I had not! By mid-July Colby told me he was letting Gabriel take his cell phone to my house (against my wishes) because he was texting Holly, a girl from school, a lot, so I agreed to a trial run. Not surprisingly, we started having major issues again with disrespect. Even Megan commented on how Gabriel was treating me.

Once Gabriel went back to his dad's that first week after my accident, things started to change. I don't know if Colby was threatened by our recent closeness or what it was. Due to the new disrespect, after a couple of weeks, I banned Gabriel from having his cell phone in our home. I took it away for one week initially, and when I checked for all those supposed text messages from Holly, there was only one. He had been speaking with his dad all that time, and his behavior during the time he was using the phone was so much like the previous year's, full of disrespect and being argumentative, not typical teenage behavior either. Eventually, inappropriate texting between Gabriel and his dad escalated to an alarming level.

Gabriel went with his dad to Waters Edge High School's football team conditioning at the end of the summer. For several years Gabe had expressed a serious interest to us and his teachers at the Gifted School, in going to a different high school, one that had a math and science academy, but Colby had other plans and pressured Gabe to go to Waters Edge because he wanted him to be the quarterback for the football team. However, he made sure to have Gabriel tell (convince) the guardian ad litem that he was really interested in other cultures, which was that high school's academy program (global studies and foreign languages). That was a stretch of any potential truth because all of it was football driven, Colby's agenda, never mind what Gabe wanted.

Twice I had to pick Gabriel up from those practices. Both times concerned me. Gabriel had such a cocky attitude and demeanor, bragging about how well he threw the ball during practice and how he was better than their JV quarterback. He said they gave him his own locker, and the coaches really liked him. All that is fine, but it was the way he said those things that was worrisome. I didn't want him to turn out in such a way that others didn't like him because of bragging and thinking he was better than other kids. I had to explain that there was a huge difference in being confident and being cocky. Strangely enough, he would act that way while in the car with me, and then it would not come up again. As a matter of fact, Gabriel rarely talked about football in our home and would almost never work out or condition there unless his dad called and told him on the phone to go run around the block or work with his jump rope.

In a series of four games, Gabriel ran only three plays, all in the first game. He was on the sidelines for the other three games. I cried at that last game. My heart hurt for him. I knew how hard his dad had worked him all summer and again in the fall and how Colby had filled his head with things about himself. So, to watch Gabriel on the sidelines after working that hard for so long just killed me. Over the years of playing football, Colby continued to send Gabe workout schedules and drills that he had to complete on a daily basis.

My dad went with Rob and me to Gabriel's first game. I did not find out until the following week that doing this exhausted Dad. With his leukemia, by the time he walked all the way to the stands and then back to his car afterwards, he was wiped out. He never told me because my dad never complained about anything like that. I found out by accident from my mom the following week. We really wanted him to do things outdoors since he couldn't go to public places indoors due to his compromised immune system, but by the end of the day he was usually so tired.

In his later years, my dad had salt-and-pepper hair, which eventually went all gray. His whole life, he had a gentle kindness about him; however, when I was little, anytime he raised his voice, it would frighten me, even if he wasn't yelling. Boy, could he project! Most likely this was due to my super-sensitive hearing, which I believe I have because my vision is the pits.

It makes me smile now. That was enough to make me behave! He also put on weight as he got older, which was probably from sneaking ice cream out of the freezer late at night when we were all in bed.

It was just a few months after my dad retired at age seventy-nine that he was diagnosed with Stage IV AML.

"This is not how I envisioned our retirement," my mother commented to me. "I thought we would be traveling."

Are you kidding me? I thought. *Did you really just say that? You're blaming him for getting sick?*

I told my sister, Loretta, what Mom said, and she told me that Mom had said something similar to her.

A few weeks later my dad and I were on our way to his regular oncology appointment. "You know, I feel really bad for your mother," he said. "I know she would rather be traveling right now instead of taking care of me."

Oh my God! Such a selfish remark she'd made to my sister and me, and we found out she had said that to my dad too. How could she be so cruel? It wasn't his fault he got cancer! He had never really been sick his whole life.

Loretta got really upset when my mom made that comment too. "I don't get it," she said. "Mom had the career she wanted. She was on Broadway. She met the man of her dreams. She had the family she wanted. She traveled with him through his work years."

Loretta was right. They went to Hawaii and Tahoe and enjoyed a cruise-ship vacation, among other adventures. My dad won those trips for selling insurance as well as being a stockbroker. Then my dad's choir went on an amazing trip to Italy, singing for High Mass at the Vatican, and had a private audience with Pope John Paul II. My parents had a picture of each of them shaking hands with the Pontiff. The following year the choir toured France. Wow! She had so much, but she was never satisfied. It was never enough. And she always—oddly—had very expensive tastes. She bought designer brands and other expensive things. It was all about impressing people and what people thought, just like Colby. (I am the polar opposite.)

You might think her infatuation with the finer things in life came from her upbringing, but it didn't. She grew up the third oldest of nine siblings, and they were dirt poor.

Chapter 30

PRECARIOUS

August–October 2009

AT 5:00 P.M. ON AUGUST 7, I picked up Gabriel from his dad's. They had spent a week together, and I knew I was in for the usual "detox" we went through after exposure to his dad. The next day they talked on the phone for over thirty minutes. Shortly thereafter we had repeated problems with Gabriel's attitude, particularly his disrespect for me, so I gave him a warning that he had used up all his "free passes." He got nasty with me, and in the middle of his back-mouthing I slapped him with my right hand, the one with the amputated finger, which was still bandaged and swollen. It probably hurt me more than it did him! The "barely a slap" left no mark and was really more of an attention-getter for him to stop his behavior. It was a reaction to the constant, in my face, disrespect. It was wrong, but I had been pushed to the point where it happened before I realized what I'd done. I had never done that to him before, and I never did it again.

I Loved You More

I took his cell phone away for the remainder of the day and told him he was not allowed to use it until he had eaten his lunch and finished his chores, which included putting away clean clothes, purging old ones for Goodwill, checking on his school supplies, and practicing guitar. He claimed that "even prisoners get one phone call." Smart mouth!

While he was eating, we had a discussion.

"Gabriel," I said, "you are almost fourteen, and there are no more excuses for doing these things, for doing things that are wrong, like reporting things to your father that go on in our home and then exaggerating them to make me look bad. You are not the seven- or ten-year-old who doesn't know what you're doing anymore. Please think about your actions over these past few days. I'm a good mother! I don't deserve to be treated this way."

He made a fairly threatening facial expression. "You don't think you should worry about what you just did?" he asked snidely.

"When I did what, exactly?"

"When you slapped me, just now."

I made him sit on the couch and listen to me. "Gabriel, I will *not* discuss any specifics about testimonies or other matters from court with you, not yet. But I want you to know that no matter what was said about me in the past to your dad or what I was questioned about, the judge recognized that I had not done anything wrong. She said I had grown in the past six years, and the more I gave to and cooperated with your dad, the more he took. Despite your wanting to go live with your dad, Judge Wallace and Mr. Garrison feel that it is in your best interest for me to have primary physical custody and not make any changes. Mr. Garrison said in court—and he told me he would discuss this with you too—that he felt like he had betrayed you, that he *was* going to recommend you live with your dad, but after hearing all the testimony, he felt that it was in your best interest to keep custody the way it was. Both of us, your dad and I, love you, but we are very different people, different parents. That doesn't make either of us better than the other, just different. Judge Wallace gave your dad one extra day with you each week because she wanted to give him something and not totally disappoint him."

In response, Gabriel confidently folded his arms across his chest and leaned back into the couch. "That's all I need is one day at a time," he said sarcastically.

"What does that mean? That you'll keep getting one more day to eventually be at your dad's all the time?"

"Yes!"

"Because it's so miserable here?"

He did not acknowledge that.

"Is it that great at your dad's?" I asked.

"Yes."

"Gabe, I realize you're treated like an equal and an adult there, and I understand that is very attractive to a kid. However, you are not my equal, and even when you are forty, you will still be my son and should still respect me. My job is to be your mother, to teach you respect, to teach you to treat others with respect, and to prepare you for the world and society, to be kind and forgiving. Throughout your life you will be faced with decisions and crossroads to which there will be a right and a wrong choice to make. You need to learn to choose wisely and to listen to your inner voice because deep down you know what the right thing is. Those decisions will either come back to bless you or haunt you, and you must own them all. Now, if you continue to do things to intentionally hurt me—like reporting to your dad information for him to use against me in court—you will have to live with that for the rest of your life. Nothing you ever say or do will change my love for you, but think before you act. And choose wisely."

Amazingly, the rest of the afternoon and evening went very well. We went to mass, had dinner, watched TV, and he acted as if everything was fine. He had not talked with his dad, so that was reflected in his behavior.

However, Colby called at 5:45 p.m. while we were at church and again at 8:15 p.m., three calls in one day. For whatever reason though, Gabe did not call him back.

MY DAD HAD TO BEGIN chemo shots the next day. AML kills good white blood cells and produces bad ones rapidly. If not diagnosed and treated early, it is fatal within weeks or months. We were thankful that it was found early, as early as stage IV can be, because he had no symptoms. He merely demanded to be tested because his brother was diagnosed with it. We had to wait for four rounds of chemo shots to see if there was any positive change in his blood counts, but that wouldn't be until sometime in early December. We all prayed for his recovery.

Megan was home all summer from college and working at a vet clinic down the street. She came home for a weekend in September to go to a concert. On one of those nights, she and Gabriel went to Taco Bell together. Gabriel told me the following week that she no longer annoyed him, and it was pretty cool having her around. They got along great that summer. Both were maturing in their own ways, which was nice.

On September 29, Rob was driving Gabriel to catechism class after football. "How am I supposed to tell Mom that I want to live with my dad?" Gabriel asked.

It hadn't been a year since the judge ruled that Colby and I continue to share legal custody, with me having primary physical custody.

Later that night, Gabriel asked me to tuck him in, something he had not asked me to do in months. I knew he was doing that to get me alone to talk about it, and he did try. But it was 10:00 p.m. on a school night, not the time to have a serious conversation. We ended up talking about it the next day after dinner.

I did not freak out when we talked. I was calm and told him I valued and would consider his feelings. I also told him I would think about it and talk to those people who were influential in court last year when it was decided that it was not in his best interest to live with his dad.

Inside, I was crushed, of course. I found little solace crying that night in the shower, out of view.

I told a dear friend of mine about this, and she wrote me back. I was so touched by what she said; it was so beautiful:

> From: Jeanee
> To: Regina Rossi Valentine
> Sent: Saturday, October 03, 2009 9:49 PM
> Subject: Re: here we go again!
>
> Dang, I can't believe Colby puts you through so much pain. What kind of a person is this guy? Your son is so blessed to have you as his mother. He will be just fine, and believe me, when he is older and understands what his father has done all of these years, his love and respect for you will only grow.
>
> I look at challenges in my life as if there is a purpose for them. Your ex is like the sand in your oyster shell, all of the friction, the tension, the frustration, the anger, and the sadness he has put you through, you are taking it all and making a beautiful pearl. You are living your life with grace, faith, and love and a living testament to the power of God. The ironic thing is, if he is trying to break you, he is doing the opposite and making you stronger in every way.
>
> Love you always,
>
> Bean

~

Gabriel, I find that I do not call you every day at your dad's. I feel as though it puts a strain on both of us. I don't even know how to talk to you on the phone because your dad is always "right there," and you have nothing to say to me but one-word answers. We don't have this problem when you are home with me. It's as if you are afraid for him to know that you love me or want to talk to me. It's so very sad. I wait for the day when you are older and figure all this out for yourself.

I just didn't know if he ever would come to the truth about his dad.

Chapter 31

NEVER QUIT

October–December 2009

October 2009

Disappointed, what a way to start a letter. After your dad worked you so hard all summer to get ready for football and continuing to work hard this season, your dad is not only allowing you but giving you his blessing to quit football. You only have one game left and then a championship game. Unbelievable. It worries me that this will send a message to you that, when things don't go your way, you can just quit instead of sucking it up and working through something. Your dad has quit and been fired from more jobs and asst. coaching positions than I can actually count without having to go through my records of them. No doubt this has been a difficult year for you as last year with the Mustangs, you were the star. This year in middle school ball you have been sidelined for all 5 games, with the exception of running 3 plays in the first game and then 2 plays in the 5th. That 5th game was so upsetting that I was walking off the field crying on the phone with Rob that you had been so horribly embarrassed. With 1:47 left in the game, the coach put you and the 2nd string in. You had 2 bad snaps and he pulled you all off the field, put in the first string that ran one play and then took a knee. You all won, again, with a score of 20-6. It was horrible seeing you all taken off the field that way.

I left to go to choir and during choir got a text from your dad that you were going to quit, and he agreed. Gabriel, quitting is rarely the answer in life. Your father sent a very long, pontificating email to the school principal, who wanted to see you, personally. I took you in that afternoon, and he, the coach, and the activities coordinator met with us. They really wanted you to stay on the team, but you still wanted to quit.

I found out, but could not tell you, that the principal banned your father from attending any other practices unless he stayed in his car, and if he ever approached the sidelines during or after a game again, he would be banned from the stadiums altogether. Apparently, he did this after game 5 and went up to your coach and had a very argumentative/aggressive conversation with him. We, the parents, were all told at the first meeting that parents were never to approach a coach after a game. Your father was at that parent meeting, but he thinks rules don't apply to him. It was the way your father spoke to and treated the coach that led him to ask you to turn in your equipment, thus dropping you from *the team. You were going to quit anyway; however, the coach and the principal said that both your father and the coach were wrong in what they did.*

Your father met with the principal the following Monday and as a result, the principal wanted to meet with you personally. Your dad was not available that afternoon to bring you, so I offered. I also wanted to be there for and with you. The principal, the football coach and the student activities coordinator were all there, plus you and I. It was a very good meeting, and the principal told you that your dad and the coach were wrong. The coach felt very bad about what happened. They all practically begged you to stay on the team for your own self and for the learning experience that things don't always go our way, and quitting is not the answer.

. . . but you stuck to the script you and your dad had, and you chose to quit anyway. I am worried how this will affect things for you in the future. I asked you to leave the principal's office, so the adults could speak. I asked them if there was anything that you had personally done that was either disrespectful or unacceptable behavior to warrant what had happened. The coach said that, initially, he was looking at you as the starting QB, but this other player just stepped up his game and he also had the benefit of going to school with the kids (you attended the Gifted School) and being a role model for them to look up to.

He went on to say that your dad paced the sidelines all the time, and when he was there your playing was affected. You seemed to be intimidated and did not perform as well when your dad was around. He said you had a lot of skills and talent, but your dad's presence was not good for you. He also said that parents had complained that your dad was on the sidelines badmouthing the coaches to other parents (which he had also done with me, but I walked away from him). This does nothing but cause problems for everyone, including the players. It undermines and is disrespectful.

So, you quit. I was very disappointed yet torn as a mother, knowing that your allegiance to your father was stronger than anything anyone could say to you. I pray that someday your eyes are open to the truth about your dad. I am not saying that I want you hurt by this, but the truth will truly set you free to be your own person, to think for yourself, hopefully not to carry the bad influences of your father into your own life as an adult man.

November 2009

I recently typed in your name on Facebook and, to my surprise, there you were! So, I sent you a friend request, and you added me (you had better!) Sadly, I was very hurt that in the field where you put your parents, you only list your dad, not me. Just another slap in the face of something you have done to make him happy, at my expense. I know deep down that these are all things that you feel you need to do in order to stay in his favor.

A truly good father would not be doing to you what he has done, turning you against me, controlling you in ways that you don't see due to your immaturity and ignorance. In some ways I can't fault you. It is innate for us to trust our parents. Parents are supposed to protect their children. So, when they don't, sometimes children do not recognize this as bad. You are no different than an abused spouse or child. Abuse is not just physical, although I have my doubts as to whether or not your dad uses physical discipline on you. You say nothing to me, and Rene never saw this, so I don't know.

But things like that can be hidden. Abuse is also emotional and psychological, and sometimes these can be worse than the other. I know you are a victim of this, and it breaks my heart. The 8 months we had from the last court date of 10/22/08 until this past summer were wonderful in our home. You were "you." Your dad was so reprimanded by the judge last time about how he did and did not handle things with you that he laid low for a while, and you returned to normal. Then just after my accident last summer, I feel he noticed how close we had gotten. Plus, he and Rene split, and all his time was yours now. That is when your behavior changed again. He began pressuring you and telling you how to act, what to say and do, just like in early 2008.

The nightmare has resurrected. I can't remember how much I said of this at the end of your 2009 letter, but it has progressively gotten worse since mid-July, after my accident. You have become that dark and somewhat hateful son that we experienced during the first 10 mos. of 2008, prior to the court ruling in October. You argue with me at every turn, you shut me out from everything that is going on with you, you back talk and are a smartass a lot. It is getting unbearable, and I know this is all because of your father. And it breaks my heart to see how tormented

I Loved You More

you are inside. You seem lost to me. I just hope it is not too late to get you the help you really need.

Colby had given Gabe another cell phone privately, so they had a secret line of communication. I found the phone and read all the horrible things in their conversations, designed to groom Gabriel and vilify me as well as rampant profanity and an overall disregard for any real parenting, in Colby's interest of turning my son against me. Colby's plan ultimately backfired on him.

After Christmas that year, my mother called telling me that my father had to be taken to the hospital immediately. He was running a fever and had just been through a powerful chemo drug, hopefully to put him in remission. I had Gabriel go with me. (I did not want to leave him home alone because he had let Colby into the house previously.) Once we got to the hospital, I found that due to all the flu viruses, no one under the age of eighteen was allowed in, so I drove Gabriel all the way back home. When we got there, I sat him down on the couch and laid into him about what he had done—sneaking the phone into our home and the content of his text messages with his father. I had not been that enraged since the days when I was married to Colby.

Here's a sampling of what I mean in a thread of texts between Gabriel and Colby. At the time, Gabriel was fifteen (spelling and grammar unchanged):

Dec 13 2009, 3:54 p.m.

COLBY: R we going soon or should I take a shit?

Dec 15 2009, 7:11 a.m.

COLBY: And u know ur mom is gonna come get u at some point…so get ur txtg done this morning

Dec 15 2009, 9:11 a.m.

COLBY: When does ur mother go to work? Delete this msg.

Dec 24 2009, 8:12 a.m.

GABRIEL (to friend, Gracie): Ummm….im not sure …im leaving ma moms house in a few (sneaking ma fone) and im gonna go lift……

Dec 24 2009, 6:01 p.m.

GABRIEL (to friend, Gracie): Its not that she doesn't like u…she just…she just likes to be in control of everything I do…u have to kno her to understand

Dec 25 2009, 11:18 p.m.

GABRIEL (to Colby): Hey man…sorry it took so long…. can't really talk mom still awake…mele kaikawaka

Dec 27 2009, 10:54 p.m.

COLBY: Called six times…ring me if you can but don't get in trouble…don't use cell.

Dec 27 2009, 10:55 p.m.

COLBY: Ok…love u and know I was rough …but it is time…pls acknowledge if still there..

Dec 27 2009, 10:56 p.m.

I Loved You More

GABRIEL (to Colby): Still here…nother fite wit mom…bitch

Dec 27 2009, 11:02 p.m.

COLBY: What do you mean, why?

Dec 27 2009, 11:07 p.m.

COLBY: Lol…what fight? How big…whats up???

Dec 27 2009, 11:08 p.m.

GABRIEL: I don't think anything to worry about …just regina being a cunt…

Dec 27 2009, 11:09 p.m.

COLBY: Got it…ok…we relax on weds when I pick u up

Dec 27 2009, 11:26 p.m.

GABRIEL: Thanks dad…I gotta stop talking …I think I ate something bad and if I puke I don't wanna get caught wit ma fone

In the 2008 court hearing, when I had taken pictures of text messages on Gabe's cell phone, I was told there was no way to discern if they actually came from Gabe's phone. What? So, this time around, after confiscating the phone entirely, I provided the court with full transcripts of the text messaging that was going on between Gabe and his dad as well as the cell phone. It is important to note that in the courtroom Colby never denied the content of the transcripts and, surprisingly, acknowledged them as accurate.

Now Gabriel was pushing me to my limits. Nothing hurt me worse than the things he had said about me. Nothing. Rob kept trying to calm me down, telling me it is not Gabriel; it is his father. It did not take away the pain and hurt I felt. I was watching my son deteriorating right before my eyes. He seemed so lost inside. His grades slipped in school, all while his dad allowed him to be texting until midnight on school nights while in his home.

What in the world can I do to help you before it's too late, before your father totally ruins you emotionally? I wondered. *I'm scared to death you will turn out like him, and as a result end up very much alone, like him.*

But at that moment, my father and my mother needed me, and I did *not* need to be dealing with this BS with Gabriel and his dad again! I left Gabriel at home and went back to the hospital to take care of my parents. While I was gone, Gabe told his dad what I found out, so Colby had Gabriel call Mr. Garrison to tell him what he did, how he and his dad were severely badmouthing me (the "c" word was involved) via text. Just a way to cover their asses. I told Gabriel he was never getting that phone back, and I meant it. I was holding it as evidence for court.

Two days later Colby was coming to pick Gabriel up. I went into Gabriel's bedroom before Colby was to arrive.

"Gabriel," I said, "I'm saying goodbye right now. I am *not* coming to the front door. Your dad is *not* to come into our home, and you are *not* to come back inside to get me and ask me to come out and speak with him."

Despite his urging me to come out anyway, I remained down the hall and told him three times I was not coming out.

Colby arrived, and I heard them at the front door. He leaned inside and yelled for me. "Regina! Give me that [Gabriel's] phone, dammit!"

I Loved You More

I got Rob who came out, carrying a bat by his side and confronted Colby. "Colby," he said, "get out of our house, and get off our property. You're trespassing." Colby had been so unpredictably hostile in the past, Rob didn't know what to expect.

"That phone is my property," Colby shouted in reply, "and I'm calling the police!"

And he did. The police officer did not want the phone from us. He told us Colby had moved his truck down the street as he had his own matters on record to clear up with the police. Later, I found out from Rene that Colby was driving with an expired license, among other things.

Around that time Rene told me she came home from work to find a summons on her front door. They had been divorced about a year at that point. She panicked, worried she had to face Colby in court. Then she realized the summons was for Colby. The Commonwealth of Virginia was taking him to court on Jan. 15 for monies he owed back in 2005.

It never seemed to end. Everyone was after Colby for money or something . . . mostly money.

Chapter 32

PREPARED

January–May 2010

January 26, 2010

You have no idea how much I cry. You don't even realize when I am crying right in front of you. Like tonight on the way home from catechism. It just totally pains my heart what you and I are both going through at the hands of your father. While driving you and JT home, my eyes just filled up, and I got a lump in my throat. It was everything I could do not to let you see me. But you wouldn't; you don't even want to look at me, talk to me. You keep your iPod on all the time. I know that is something you teenagers do, but you are that dark boy again from 2008 . . .

I Loved You More

ON JANUARY 30, 2010, we had a huge snowstorm the previous night and throughout the day. I was so looking forward to a good family day. We had a fire in the fireplace, and I started a crockpot full of lentils, ham, and veggies for dinner. It could have been such a great day, but when I got ready for bed, I broke down and cried again. Gabriel took every opportunity throughout the day to take potshots at me, to argue with me. He was fourteen years old.

Finally, at 9:30 p.m. while the four of us were playing UNO Attack, Rob had enough of Gabriel's mouthing off to me and reprimanded him. After that game, Gabriel left the room to watch TV upstairs. He was not used to Rob stepping in and defending me or correcting him, but Rob had reached his limit with Gabe's attitude and treatment of me. I was thankful he was stepping in for me. I finally went upstairs with bloodshot eyes from crying (and I was still crying). "What in the world have I done to make you hate me so much? I have only tried to be the best mother I can, yet you take every opportunity to treat me horribly. I don't know how much longer I can take this from you." I left the room and went to bed.

There were times I wanted to throw my hands up and surrender, just for my own sanity. But that was not what was best for Gabriel. I started to feel as though he was baiting me, so I would give up.

God help me, I hope I can make it through all of this.

I felt what Colby was doing to Gabriel and to me all those years was robbing us of Gabriel's childhood, robbing us of the relationship we could have had. My heart ached. That dark cloud was still over our lives, so I was not able to really enjoy being a mother in so many ways. This was not what I imagined my life to be. I had always wanted a nuclear family with two to four kids and to be a stay-at-home mother. Unfortunately, that was not meant to be.

One night in February while driving Gabriel home from basketball practice, he had his iPod on, in his own little world. I wondered, as I often did, what our relationship might be like if there was no toxicity from his father influencing his feelings toward me. *Would we be close? Would you open up to me and talk to me about normal things?* I always wanted children, and I was thrilled when I found out I was pregnant with Gabriel. I did not know this journey would be one of so much heartache and pain. *And it is not your fault, son. I do not blame you. My heart cries for both of us.*

THAT MARCH MY SISTER Loretta's cancer was finally diagnosed, after years of a misdiagnosis. They removed the original tumor in her small intestine, and she dropped eighty pounds quickly. So, that weight gain of hers throughout most of her life was due to the fact that she was in stage IV cancer for twenty-five years and never knew it. They never knew about the tumor on her small intestine. They only knew about tumors on her liver in 1995 that didn't change over the course of watching them for a few years, so they assumed they were benign. Unfortunately, they turned out already to be metastasized from the original tumor, which was how they were able to determine she had been in stage IV. Her cancer, carcinoid cancer and carcinoid syndrome was one of the slowest growing. So, both my sister and my dad were battling stage IV cancer simultaneously.

All that criticism and all those insults from my mother about my sister's weight was, as we all suspected, through no fault of Loretta's. It was the cancer. But the pain of those remarks would last a lifetime, not just for my sister, but also for my brother and me.

Loretta and I were very close, mostly as we got older. Can you imagine what she went through when I was three and she was thirteen, and we had to share a bedroom together? Back then I was a pesky little sister, apparently spying on her, though I have no recollection of it. Loretta was the oldest of my four siblings and Gabriel's godmother. She was beautiful, with warm brown eyes and beautiful skin, a great smile, straight brown hair, and an infectiously hilarious laugh. We often told her she could get paid big bucks to be an audience member for sitcoms. She made everyone feel special, as if they were the only person in the room. She was a great listener and giver of advice. We all went to her for that. She was also an advocate, always running interference with our parents on our behalf. Until her cancer diagnosis, she was very overweight, beginning in her late twenties, but she never ate like someone who should be. That's when the cancer began to prey on her body in silence for more than two decades.

I prayed for her a lot.

April 19, 2010

I am so overwhelmed. I am sick of going to court, sick of having to document everything to protect you, not sick of protecting you, sick of having to do so in order to battle your father, so I can make sure you are OK. I have cried several times these past few days. Preparing for battle in court once again. I have so much on my plate right now—going to doctor appointments with your grandfather, grandmother, and now my sister. My dad and Aunt Loretta have terminal cancer. I am the patient advocate for all three of them. That plus always battling to protect you is sometimes more than one person can manage. I try so hard to give it up to God. It is hard. So very hard.

On April 20, 2010, I found Gabriel working on an assignment for school, and I asked him about it. He told me he had to interview the person who had the most significance upon his life. Of course, he was going to interview Colby.

On May 6, 2010, we were in court again. We waited around for three hours because the judge's clerk overbooked her docket. By the time we got inside, we had no time to finish our case. We each had an hour to present, and then it was postponed to June 28. I could not believe it. The only short-term ruling that the judge handed down was that we all enter family counseling with Dr. Kathleen Campos, a forensic psychologist with a law degree. After waiting all those months and preparing, it was put off again. But in the limited amount of time we had, we called Rene to the stand to testify because I was afraid that if she had to wait until a continuance, Colby would get to her and scare her into not testifying. I was so proud of her. She was a nervous wreck because Colby confronted her in the waiting room, and in the courtroom, he tried to make her out to be a liar since he was cross-examining her. But I told her before we went in that all she had to do was tell the truth. If she told the truth, nothing and no one would be able to scare or intimidate her.

Unfortunately, during the three-hour wait, we talked a lot, and she told me something that she did not realize was going to be such a huge deal in the courtroom with the judge, the guardian ad litem, and me. She told me that during the three months that she and Colby had separated but he had not yet moved out, he was sleeping in Gabriel's bedroom with him. There were multiple places he could have slept, including the couch on the second floor or in the weight room on an air mattress. Instead he chose to sleep in Gabriel's room where there was only a twin bed and barely room for much else. It made my stomach sick to think that a grown man had chosen to do this.

ON MAY 12, 2010, AT 9:15 p.m. I was in the hospital with Loretta and my mother while Loretta had her cancer surgery. It was a big surgery, and she was in recovery for four and a half hours, far longer than the one hour we were told. She was in a great amount of pain, so they kept her there longer and had to give her one and a half times the normal pain meds. Then she was sleeping soundly. Nurses came in every hour during the night, and I stayed with her the whole time. They had to take eighteen inches of her small intestine, which had the original tumor in it, and six inches of her colon plus two lymph nodes that had small tumors on them. She still needed to deal with four tumors they'd found on her liver, which had metastasized from the original tumor. One was the size of a small baseball.

The whole experience seemed unreal. Within the span of a year, we had three terminally ill people—my dad, my Uncle Dave, and now Loretta.

> *I have made a huge decision. You and the family need me right now, and I just am unable to handle all of that and my job. Family is first and will always come first. I was originally planning to make this decision based on the court ruling of May 6th. If I won custody, I would definitely take the summer off to be with you and be available for my dad, sister, and mother for their health needs. But there was no ruling. So, after discussing it with Rob, I decided that it did not matter whether or not I got custody. Even if you were only with me half the summer, you needed me there, to be present. So after spending two nights in the hospital with your aunt, I went into corporate to talk to my supervisor and tell her what I needed to do. I was completely in tears, tears of exhaustion, stress, and worry. What you don't know is that I am risking losing my job. I am an independent contractor, and they do not have to hold my job for me. But when you put family first, there are never any regrets.*

Fortunately, when I was about to leave work, Ellen, the owner, came in and asked me how I was. I was visibly upset, so she invited me into her office. I told her about all that was going on with all the health issues but most importantly, with Gabriel and his well-being. I was so blessed. Not only did I keep my job, all the other agents chipped in to work extra days to cover our site. This was really hard on them because my partner was also going away for two months to have a baby. So, we were both taking a leave of absence for our children. One of us was about to birth a new life, and the other was fighting for a life. I was taking off July and August.

I was going to be fully present for my family, and I was going to prepare fully for court, the most important court date of our lives. We were again determining custody. I had my detailed journals that the court always refused to accept, a history of emails and texts, witnesses, and, among other things, I had prepared a thorough list of questions that I suggested my attorney ask various witnesses.

THERE WERE THREE INSTANCES over a two-and-a-half-year period where I had experiences of biblical proportions. I didn't hear voices, but I knew God was speaking to me. It wasn't anything audible. It was all within me.

Between that first court date and the continuation date, I was in the shower one morning when I had tremendous fear that Colby was going to hurt Rene for testifying, that he was going to hurt me, or that he was going to flee the country with Gabriel. The writing started to appear on the wall for Colby when he found out who was testifying and what was coming out as a result. We had shown our hand at court that day before the continuance, through no fault of our own, so I was consumed with dread.

During Catholic Mass, in between the Old and New Testament readings, we have something called the Responsorial Psalm. It's from Psalms and is a sung "respond and acclaim" part of the service music. So, as I was in the shower trying to grapple with this fear of all these things I was afraid might happen, within me I heard, *The Lord is my light and my salvation. Of whom should I be afraid?* It was Psalm 27.

I overanalyze everything so I jumped out of the shower and thought, *I wonder if the verses apply.* I couldn't remember the verses completely, so I threw on a towel and went to get my hymnal.

Now, understand that my hymnal is never in my bedroom. Never. It's always upstairs in my studio or in my huge music bag, but that day it was sitting on my dresser. I didn't think too much about it at the time. I grabbed it and sat down on the bed as I simultaneously opened it and tried to find that psalm. To my shock, it opened to that exact page.

At that moment I had an overwhelming and transformational experience where I literally felt the wind of my breath physically suck out of me. It was life changing, and I wept, deeply. And as I tried to read the verses while my eyes continued to flood with tears, I had a moment where I knew God was speaking to me—not about winning in court but about my relationship with Gabriel being what I wanted it to be. As I began to calm down, and my breathing relaxed, a sense of peace enveloped me like a warm blanket, along with a feeling of security that I was safe, believing that, no matter what happened, Gabriel was going to be OK.

It was the first time in the whole journey that I was able to let go completely. Until that point, even though I prayed about it often, I was still trying to control things, still keeping meticulous notes for court, but that day I was able to let it all go. It was the most freeing feeling. You can't make that choice; it just has to happen. After that I was fine. It was beyond powerful. It was as if the weight of my life was lifted off my shoulders, and I could breathe deeply again.

It was all going to be OK.

Chapter 33

MIRACLES

June 28, 2010

THE BIG DAY ARRIVED, and we were in court for what turned out to be the final ruling on Gabriel's custody. Once again, Colby was seeking full legal and physical custody, to take Gabriel away from me, his mother.

We had been in court on more occasions than I could count throughout Gabriel's early life. It was crushing and terrifying to think my son once again might be lost to me forever.

But I prayed—harder than ever—that the judge would have the wisdom of Solomon, even after so many years of simply giving my ex a minor slap on the hand for the things he had done.

After all the testimony, much of which was beyond disturbing, I finally felt that Gabriel had a fighting chance going forward. His football coach, the coach of the opposing team from the previous fall, and the principal all testified. They talked about how Colby's aggressive and confrontational behavior was so bad that it became a concern for other parents who were around the field that night. The other team's coach said Colby continued to get in their personal space in a threatening way, and he wanted to call the police. Other parents also talked to them about Colby's behavior in the stands and his bad-mouthing the coaches. Also, I presented damning evidence against Colby—the cell phone text messages between Gabriel and his dad with all the profanity and the unspeakable things Gabriel called me, which Colby never corrected or disciplined.

Colby fought to put Gabriel on the witness stand. How cruel, to put a child in that position with both his parents there looking at him and he at them! Both Saul and Mr. Garrison were against it and the judge refused his request.

I had printouts of Colby's Facebook profile where he claimed he was a football coach for Waters Edge High School. When questioned under oath, he admitted he was not a coach there. I also had his Twitter page showing he was following several "escorts" whose profiles were easily accessible to anyone, including Gabriel, and Gabriel had clicked on them. Rene testified to a stack of porn she found the day before court in 2008, with Colby's handwritten notes on them. We were also able to show how Colby would sometimes call our home up to thirteen times a day, often every few minutes, as if he was trying to force us to pick up the phone. He had done this for years and even done it to me at work when I worked at MBNA and when I was Ellen's assistant before becoming a site manager. Such interruptions could have hurt my job.

It was no surprise that Colby wanted Gabriel to testify. He had no other witnesses, just Gabriel. I guessed others had figured Colby out and decided not to get involved, but I didn't know for sure. What I do know is that the judge ultimately ruled far beyond Mr. Garrison's detailed suggestions.

We had been with the same judge for the past eight years, so she was very familiar with our case. What I didn't know until recently was she favored fathers. Had I known, I would have probably requested another judge, if possible. She gave Colby so much latitude and so many opportunities over the years, only to find that things had gotten increasingly worse for Gabriel.

In the report prepared by the guardian ad litem, Mr. Garrison, which I later discovered he had prepared back in May, he said the following.

Dear Judge Wallace:

Please accept this correspondence as the Report of the Guardian Ad Litem in the above-stated matter. As Your Honor is very familiar with both the procedural and the factual aspects of this lengthy and ongoing custody litigation, this report will be rather concise.

Both Mr. Baxter and Mrs. Valentine have filed Petitions for custody and visitation in this matter. Both have asked the Court to grant them legal custody of Gabriel and Mrs. Valentine has filed a Petition limiting Mr. Baxter's parenting time with Gabriel.

During the course of my updated investigation, I have had an opportunity to meet with Gabriel at the Phoenix Gifted School, Mr. and Mrs. Valentine in my office, Mr. Baxter in my office, and I have also discussed this matter with several "team" parents of Gabriel's as well as the head football coach for Townsland Middle School and the principal of Townsland Middle School.

I Loved You More

Basically, the current tenor of this case is the ongoing theme which was presented in the lengthy custody trial held in your Court in October of 2008.

Both Mr. Baxter and Mrs. Valentine claim that the other is poisoning their relationship with Gabriel. Additionally, there was a disturbing incident which occurred over Christmas of this year wherein Gabriel was texting his father and used one of the most derogatory statements a man can ever use in referring to a woman regarding Gabriel's mother. Gabriel referred to his mother as a c***. Mr. Baxter made absolutely no response to this comment being made in a text to him.

In my discussions with Mr. Baxter he alleged that he "skipped" over the text and did not know about it until it was brought to his attention by Mrs. Valentine. Mr. Baxter indicates that he has punished Gabriel by having him do 25 hours of community service.

Additionally, during many of these texts Gabriel refers to his mother in other derogatory ways, and often refers to her by her first name rather than "mom."

In my discussions with the principal of Townsland Middle School and the football coach it was apparent that Mr. Baxter attended virtually every practice that Gabriel had with the football team. Mr. Baxter not only sat in the stands but was seen walking along the sidelines and to "follow" Gabriel as he went through his paces during practice. The football coach indicated that this had a direct impact on Gabriel and made him rather nervous. Additionally, the football coach indicated that Mr. Baxter's presence, he felt, kept Gabriel from interacting as much with the other boys on the team which made building a rapport between Gabriel and these other boys whom he did not go to school with on a daily basis, very difficult. The coach indicated that Mr. Baxter would loudly comment on the coaches' abilities to other parents who may have been at practices.

Most disturbing was an incident that occurred late in the season wherein after a game, Mr. Baxter stomped on the field and began berating the head football coach. This matter was not brought to my attention by Townsland's coach, however, was brought to my attention by the principal. The principal indicated that he received a call from the coach of the opposing middle school team expressing concerns over Mr. Baxter's behavior on the field in front of faculty, parents, and students.

During Gabriel's time at the Gifted School, he has always expressed an interest in science and possibly going to the Math and Science Academy at Ocean Lakes High School. However, over the last year or so, Gabriel indicated he would rather go to Townsland High School and attend the academy there. When I asked Gabriel as to his reasons for going to Townsland, he indicated that he wanted to learn about other cultures because he intended to go to Hawaii once he graduated from high school and that there were other cultures present in Hawaii. This is mirrored by an intention expressed by Mr.

I Loved You More

Baxter that he would be, possibly, moving to Hawaii after Gabriel graduates from high school.

Additionally, I spoke with Mr. Baxter's ex-wife, Rene who expressed grave concerns over Mr. Baxter's attitude toward Gabriel. Mrs. Baxter indicated that Mr. Baxter's relationship with Gabriel was akin to a best friend rather than a father-son relationship. She indicated that Mr. Baxter allowed Gabriel to watch television shows and do things that she felt were above his current age. Mrs. Baxter indicated that Mr. Baxter had no friends, whatsoever, other than Gabriel and that he was fixated on his son.

As the Court is well aware of the facts in this case, I will dispense with applying them to Va. Code Ann. §20-124.3 (Michie, 2009) for this report. However, I have the following recommendations:

1. *Mrs. Valentine be given sole legal and physical custody of Gabriel.*
2. *Mr. Baxter's parenting time with Gabriel be every other weekend from Friday until Sunday evening.*
3. *That Mr. Baxter be barred from attending any of Gabriel's sports practices, whatsoever.*
4. *That Mr. Baxter be barred from approaching any coach of Gabriel's while in the presence of any other students immediately before, during, or after a sporting event.*
5. *Mr. Baxter, Mrs. Valentine, Mr. Valentine and Gabriel be ordered into ongoing family counseling with Dr. Kathleen Campos and*

that they be ordered to cooperate with her fully.

As always, I am available should Your Honor require additional information prior to the hearing in this matter.

In response, the judge awarded me sole legal and physical custody of Gabriel.

I was awestruck.

It meant the truth was clear, and justice had finally prevailed. Not only was Colby stripped of any legal and physical custody of Gabriel (he previously had 50 percent), he was reduced to alternate weekends only, no mid-week visit, and only one phone call and one text message per day. Thank God!

It is important to note that Mr. Garrison did his job by conducting a full investigation, doing interviews, and being deeply involved in Gabriel's case. If your guardian ad litem is not stepping up to do the same, you need to ask why. It's their job, but not all of them take it seriously or are as committed to the role.

When I left the courthouse, you would have thought I'd have jumped for joy and shouted it from the rooftops, but I was numb, totally numb. When I got into my car, I sobbed. I had no plans to call anyone, but I did call Loretta. I was crying the whole time. She thought something was wrong or something bad had happened. But I believe all the stress and worry of the past thirteen-plus years, the battles in and out of court, it all finally came to an end. I finally felt that Gabriel had a fighting chance to heal emotionally and psychologically.

When I got home, I sat down with Gabriel and Rob to tell them the news. I had been crying so much during my two-mile drive home that I had not really prepared myself for what I was going to say. I was emotionally raw and still fighting back tears. I tried to lay some foundation for them both, that there was a lot of testimony and a lot of evidence.

I Loved You More

"Gabriel," I said, "the judge felt she had given us many years to co-parent, and it was obviously unsuccessful. She felt that only one parent should be making the decisions about your life."

I could see it in Gabriel's face, a confident grin was forming, and his eyes started to light up. It was then that I realized he had been misinterpreting my tears. I realized he thought my sadness was because his father won custody, or he got to live with him. Then I dropped the bomb that "that person" was me.

He was enraged. He was angry, crying, yelling—so, so upset. He had a right to be, I guess. I imagine Colby had built things up for him that he was old enough to speak for himself and would get everything he wanted. Gabriel had even told Judge Wallace in chambers privately that he wanted to live with his dad. He told everyone that for a while.

I swear, I thought he was going to run away that night. I had to leave him alone to process his feelings and work through it all. But I also had to tell him that he was going to MFuge, a Christian camp, in a few weeks with his two cousins, Kevin and Max. He did not want to go, but I explained he had no say in the matter. I knew he needed to get away from everything, including both his parents, and just be around kids his own age in a good environment, to have fun and try to forget about stuff at home for a little while. It was a community service-based camp, so he would be working with and interacting with underprivileged kids. Sometimes we need to see what others go through to realize the things we should be thankful for.

Gabriel went to camp. I prayed many times that it would be a positive experience for him, and it was. He loved it and talked about all the kids he worked with and the positive influence he felt he was with them. I believe it was the beginning of healing for Gabriel, a fresh start for our lives at home and the healing of our relationship. Along with counseling and lots of prayer and faith, things started getting better. Gabriel even started talking more in his sessions with Dr. Campos, which was great.

My therapist once told me, "Until you remove the poison, you cannot begin to heal." Colby was the poison. After much of his influence was removed from Gabriel's life, my son began to heal.

Chapter 34

BEGINNINGS

∾

July–December 2010

OUR COURTS ARE EXTREMELY FLAWED. Why are people not allowed to introduce evidence at a hearing that was introduced prior to the last hearing? That makes no sense and prevents victims from showing a pattern of abusive behavior. Why would no one look at my documentation, much of which included emails from Colby spewing his venom and repeated threats? Unfortunately, as previously mentioned, Judge Wallace favored dads. I believe the fact that she and her ex were able to be civil skewed her judgment much of the time, preventing her from seeing Colby for who he really was. When we talk about how "we teach people how to treat us," her repeated rewards of giving Colby "one more day" with Gabriel, despite his despicable behavior, it taught him that it didn't matter. He could continue to do what he wanted, behave badly and even if she admonished him, it would be followed up with a token reward. There were no real consequences for his behavior until the very end. Then again, it is about winning the war, not so much the battles in between.

I have often said that I paid the equivalent of four years of a private college in legal fees, many times just to hold Colby accountable and show him I was not a pushover and that our son came first.

If it were not for Mr. Garrison listening to his conscience and doing what was best for Gabriel, he would have gone to live with his dad at age fourteen. I fear the long-term damage that would have done. I have come to learn that not all guardians ad litem are good ones who take their job seriously. Gabriel got so lucky with Mr. Garrison!

Even though my documents were never seen by the courts, write everything down! One day you will want your children to know the truth—your truth, not distorted memories, which can happen over time. Documenting in real time gives more credibility to your story down the road. Live by example, and teach your children how to be by how you are. They are always watching and listening. Lead with love, kindness, understanding. Also, if you believe negative grooming is going on "over there," do positive reinforcement "grooming," or deprogramming on your end. Let your children know they are loved, not just by you but by the other parent. Even if your ex is the biggest shit around, let your children know that "in their own way" the other parent loves them. As your children get older, change your dialogue to fit their age without slandering the other parent.

When Gabriel was little and would act out after being with his dad, I would let him know I was not upset with him, and these things were not his fault. As a little guy, he didn't yet know all the differences between right and wrong. When he would do something his dad put him up to, how could I blame the toddler? As Gabriel got older, at around age nine or ten, I began to change my script, telling him that no matter who influenced or put him up to something, ultimately the decision to do the right or the wrong thing was his, and only he would have to live with the consequences. That helped a lot.

The seasonally hot, muggy summer flew by, and I never felt like I had the summer off from work. I spent a great deal of time at doctor appointments with Loretta, my dad, and my mother. I also watched my brother Michael's kids any chance I was free. They were stuck in a small apartment while their parents worked and looked for a new home in the area. They moved here in June to be closer to family due to all the illness and older age of our parents. I did not want the kids' memories of their move to Virginia to be boring, miserable days in that apartment. So, they spent a lot of time at our house at the pool, and I took them to putt-putt golf and other places.

Gabriel was so busy with football that he did not have much time with them. I also stayed busy shuttling Gabriel back and forth to football practices. I was exhausted, and six weeks into my "summer off," I had a bit of a meltdown. It was too much for me but it was my own fault for taking on so much. I guess I did not want to disappoint anyone, mostly Gabriel and the kids. I went back to work September 1.

October 30, 2010

. . . For your birthday this year it was the first year we have not done the family dinner with everyone over to celebrate. So we took you (the 5 of us) to Macaroni Grill for dinner, and I brought a Ho Ho Cake! How cool was that? People in the restaurant thought it was the neatest thing, and you have a slight addiction to Swiss Cake Rolls, which are exactly like Ho Ho's.

. . .

Girls — What can I say except I hope you learn how to treat a girl the right way. I worry about what you have seen with your dad over the years with how he has treated me, Rene, and women in general. I pray that Rob and your grandparents and uncles have been what you will use as an example of how to be respectful with girls. It is so important in life, but sometimes we have to learn things the hard way.

Gabriel, things seem to be going so well in our home. We have had some really good talks, and you are so much more respectful and not the "dark" kid you have been in the past that I have talked about in these letters. You are participating in counseling, which is so good. You even came into the kitchen a couple of weeks ago and hugged me—for no reason. You just walked in and hugged me. You have NO IDEA how much that meant to me. Then the next morning (it was a Friday that you would be going to your dad's after school), I was bandaging up your elbow from football and you said, "Mom, right now I am hugging you in my mind." That may sound corny, but it was unsolicited, just like the hug.

. . .

I continue to pray for you every day. I pray that your eyes be opened to the truth, the truth about me and my commitment to you and your well-being, the truth about what your father has done to me and you all these years. I pray that you will accept the truth and live the truth, so that our relationship will heal and prosper. I pray that our Lord and His Mother will protect you from the evils that surround you. I pray that if there is anything inappropriate going on in your life, and you may be afraid to tell anyone, that God will reveal it to me, so I can help you and protect you.

I Loved You More

I love you, son. I know beyond a doubt that I was put on this earth to be your mother. As much as I wanted other children, it is becoming clear to me that you needed me devoted to you alone, so that I could be totally committed to protecting you and doing everything in my power to make sure you are safe and happy and loved. May God continue to bless you, bless our family, and fill our lives with His love and peace.

All my love,

Mom

Chapter 35

MY TURN

2011

AFTER "GABE'S" WIN IN COURT, I was in the shower one morning thinking about how real estate had turned and started to tank. I had been in real estate for years. It provided a good living while Gabriel and I went through our many years of court battles. I thought about how Gabriel's custody was determined for the rest of his first eighteen years and how I wasn't making the money in real estate that I used to. But then, I didn't need that money anymore for legal purposes. I thought about a conversation I had had with my sister several years prior when I was so emotionally shattered. "I would give up my financial success in a heartbeat for a better relationship with my son!" I said.

"Haven't you ever considered the fact that God blessed you with this job so that you could afford all that you have done in order to protect Gabe?" she asked. I pondered all these things.

I Loved You More

Well, what now? I wondered. *Where is my life?* Then I had a realization.

I threw on my towel, ran into the family room, and looked at Rob, who was sitting there watching TV, and I started crying, but this time they were happy tears of excitement.

"What's wrong?" he asked.

"I think God's telling me it's my turn."

"What are you talking about?"

"I think it's time for me to go back to my career that I gave up for Colby and then stayed away from to raise my son as a single parent."

I no longer had any worries. The tables had turned.

Rob and I started talking about how I could make a living in addition to my singing by also doing voiceover work. He even built me a home studio.

That was my second experience of biblical proportion.

I got into voiceover work by accident. When we lived in Delaware, I was doing on-camera auditions in the Philadelphia market for about a year, and I kept hearing "Great read, great read," but I wasn't getting booked. I have a lazy eye, and the camera doesn't lie. Our eyes are the connection to the viewer. I felt like I wasn't getting the jobs because my eye was a distraction. *If they're telling me the truth about it being a great read,* I thought, *then I need to go behind the mic.*

I took three months and wrote all my own copy, bought studio time, and produced my first demo myself (because I didn't know any better). From there my voiceover business took off. I was doing it part time in the Philadelphia market and then in Virginia while doing real estate. In 2011 I started doing it full time, and it was great.

First, nobody sees me if you're working from home, so I can work in my PJs and do a voice job with coffee. The business has evolved over the years from just being the voice to now including the editing and the production, but a lot of my life has been "initiation by fire." I'm self-taught in both voiceover and the engineering ends of the business. I have never taken a class for either. When I go into something new, and I'm driven to do it, I just try to find ways to make it happen.

The coolest voice job I ever did was the that of Eddie, a little boy from the Fisher Price Little People. Back when they were celebrating their fiftieth anniversary of the Little People line, they produced a show that went to all the national zoos around the country. It was a musical revue, and I was the voice of the little blond-haired boy, Eddie. Then they released a new musical toy (Little People Fun Sounds Farm in 2012), and I was Eddie on there as well. I sang all these songs and said lots of phrases about life on the farm as Eddie. It's funny because when they first booked me, they said, "Are you going to be offended that we want you to do one of the little boy characters?"

"Of course not!"

So, I'm on a little Fisher Price Toy. It's probably the most popular work I've done so far. And I bought the toy because they didn't give me one.

I was thrilled to be back in the arts after all those years.

I thought my new voiceover business was going to be a bigger moneymaker than singing, but then I felt God was calling me to focus more on funeral music ministry. I was not at all happy about that. I had out-loud conversations with God: "Really?" I said. "My dad and my sister have stage-four cancer, and you want me to focus on *this*?" But things happened over a period of twenty-four hours that were undeniable as I got a strong impression from God that said, *You're supposed to be doing this.*

It took me three years to land the job that I eventually got because doors kept closing, and I didn't know what else to do. Finally, a job in funeral music ministry came through. I sang for one hundred funerals a year for three and a half years until I finally decided I couldn't do it anymore emotionally.

I struggled deeply with the decision to stop doing the funerals because I knew it was a calling, and I knew it was a healing ministry for families in their darkest time. But when I met with the pastor to speak with him, the human resources manager had a feeling about what I needed to discuss, so she joined us. When I spoke of my struggle, she looked at me and said, "Regina, a calling does not mean it's a life sentence." I love how God works. That was a pivotal moment. It freed me to be OK with my decision to step away from singing for funerals full time.

Later, somebody who sang with me at church, who at the time didn't know the importance of Psalm 27 for me, gave me a card one Sunday. I went home and opened it, and it had Psalm 27 on the cover and on the inside sheet. I still have it on a speaker of my studio. It has this beautiful note written inside, "Your voice is such an inspiration to me musically. Thank you for blessing my life with it."

In the spring and summer of 2011, I wrote Gabriel a new letter and tucked it away to give to him later, as always. He was now sixteen years old.

Spring 2011

The unexpectedly HUGE shift in custody last summer, congruent to your new chapter in life (High School!), was all meant to be. You are at a point in your life of the next level of independence.

...

We ALL can see what a huge change there has been in you. You are so much happier, your spirit is lighter, you have lost that all-consuming need to be argumentative all the time. The boy who would pull away from me when I would go to hug him in the past 2 yrs, or avoid me when he went to bed, now he hugs me back, and he makes a point of saying goodnight and even coming into our bedroom and talking before bed. When Rob is working, you quite often now come in, lie at the foot of the bed, and just talk with me. The boy who used to treat Peyton & Tyson (our dogs) with cruelty, always saying how "stupid" they are, now wants to play with and cuddle with them. Sometimes you ask to take one of them in your room with you when you are studying or reading in bed. My Lord, the changes in you are really extreme. You are more and more the young man I raised you to be. I always knew it was there inside you. He was just dormant for a long time. I have to be honest and say that there were times I worried he was buried so deep inside you that he may never come back out. Most of those fears were founded in the stories I heard from other parents with similar issues with their ex's but their kids, when they became adults, never recovered. Their relationships with the other parent never healed because the damage was done. But honestly, Gabe, I have relied on my faith to get me through all of this. Deep down, I believed and knew you would be OK, and we would be OK—one day. I never knew when that would be. I just always knew it would be one day.

...

Summer 2011

Wow, I can't believe how much you have grown! You are taller than me. My new protector. You are 6' 1," 175 lbs., and growing all the time! You are in the middle of summer football training and doing very well! I can't tell you how happy I am with where you are, where "we" are, etc. You continue to talk to me about girls (I can't believe it!), and it is great! I have learned, and you will too one day if you are blessed enough to be a parent, to just listen. I have learned over the past year not to ask many questions because the less I ask you, the more you seem to talk! It is almost as if all the time you spent shutting me out is now coming out in floods of talking! We laugh so much more now. When you joke with me now, it is funny—no longer that joking that you knew would really piss me off and was not actually funny but annoying, like trying to get under someone's skin.

Just the other day we laughed about Cuddles. Remember him? He was the little chocolate bear you picked out at Hershey Park when you were about 6. We had a LONG standing joke. You named him Cuddles, and I was relentless about calling him Cocoa. OMG, when I think of all the years of laughs we had over that, and just the other day, we laughed about it again. I had asked you where Cocoa was and if you still had him. You were sitting there thinking about where he might be when suddenly you said, "Mom, his name was Cuddles!" And we laughed so hard. I was waiting to see how long it would take you to realize that. So funny! Never fear though, I told you I had him hibernating in my hope chest!

I realized also that it has been over a year since I had any major breakdowns or crying over you or something your dad has done. Wow! Do you know how uplifting that thought was? Yes, I have had some major cries over Grandpa and Aunt Loretta's cancer but none over you because ever since the custody changes, you have just done beautifully! Even when

Uncle Richard came to visit, he said there was such a sense of peace and calmness about you that he had not seen before.

I wrote several letters that year. They seemed to really flow, and I had a lot to say. I think it was part of the healing—Gabriel's and mine. I wrote another in December.

December 29, 2011

The other day something really cool and memorable happened. You came home from school and immediately told me you "had problems." I had just baked chocolate chip cookies that were cooling on the counter. So, there you sat, my "little" boy eating cookies and milk, talking to me about your "big boy" problems with girls. I swear, I will never forget that moment! With all the issues over the years of you not even talking with me about things and being very secretive about EVERYTHING, I loved that you are opening up to me more and more. Because of everything I have been through with you, these small moments mean SO VERY MUCH!

It was a good Christmas this year, busy as always, but I am so thankful that my father is still with us! Today is Dec. 29th, and I have been sitting here in the hospital with him since 9:30 this morning. He is getting another one of his much-needed transfusions, platelets today. I treasure my one-on-one time with him, no matter that we are doing medical things. I really appreciate every moment I have with him. He is the BEST man I have ever known. He has taught me so many wonderful things, loved me no matter what my faults, and he allowed me to follow "my" dreams. They (my parents) opened so many doors for us, whether it was musical, athletic, etc. They taught us good morals, respect, compassion for others, integrity, all things by their own examples, and I am so grateful for that! I can only hope that I am as good a parent to you as they have been to me. I love you, son. I pray for your happiness and your ability to be your own person and follow your dreams. God bless you, son!

All my love,

Mom

It had been quite a ride so far. But between my return to performance and my quality time with Gabriel, I started to think it really was my turn, both as an artist and as a mother.

REGINA ROSSI VALENTINE

PART 6

"The battle of life is, in most cases, fought uphill; and to win it without a struggle were perhaps to win it without honor. If there were no difficulties there would be no success; if there were nothing to struggle for, there would be nothing to be achieved."

—Samuel Smiles

Chapter 36

FANS

∽❦∽

2012–2013

One day when you are married and have a child of your own, if that is the path you choose to take, only then will you fully understand the love of a parent for their child. Of all the accomplishments I have had in my life, both personal and professional, you are my greatest, and I thank God for blessing me with you, Gabriel.

You have grown and matured so much these past couple of years. My once young boy is growing into a man. I never want to wish your life away or the time I have left with you until you journey on to college and your future, your dreams. However, I am excited to see what you choose to do with your life, what you want to do or become, what impact you will have on

> *this world, yourself, and those around you. I believe in my heart it will be wonderful for you, and I pray all the time for you. My prayers encompass many things when it comes to you, son, believe me.*
>
> *. . .*
>
> *Son, I will ALWAYS be here for you no matter what. I know I have shared with you that song called, "Not While I'm Around." And it truly speaks to me, that as long as I have a breath in my body . . .*

Three years after penning this 2012 letter to Gabriel, and less than two short months after my beloved father passed away, I had the privilege and honor of performing this beautiful piece with the Eastern Symphony Orchestra, dedicated, of course, to Gabriel. While the song comes from a dark musical comedy called *Sweeney Todd*, and was initially sung by a young boy, if you take all of that out of it, the gist of the lyrics are what speak to me as a mother. The text of the song talks about how there are many evils lurking in the world that will try to lure you in and charm you, leading you astray. It goes on to say that, no matter what, you can count on me to be there for you, to protect you, that I won't let anyone or anything harm you, not ever. During that performance, it was nothing short of a miracle that, all things considered, I was able to sing it without breaking down. As I believed I was Gabriel's protector, my father was always mine, and he was no longer around for me.

> *Wow! Such powerful lyrics. I know I can't protect you from everything, and I realize that little by little we have to let go, as parents and trust that, with God, we have prepared you well for the future. It's strange, ya know, how all your life I have also prayed for wisdom for myself so that I would and will continue to make*

the best decisions when it comes to you. There is no handbook on how to be a parent. I have also prayed that no matter the outcome of different events in your life that God would do what was best for you because certainly, He knows what is best. Not mine but Thy will be done. I believe that, although there were times I didn't understand His will—at the time—but in time I have come to understand that He was preparing you and me for where we are now. He has not let me or you down, Gabriel, and He never will as long as He is the center of your life.

I have often prayed asking God not to take me out of this world until Gabe no longer needs me. Do I want to dance at his wedding one day? Yes! Do I hope he has grandchildren for me to spoil? Yes! But more important than any of those things has always been to be here for him when it really matters for his well-being.

THE GREATEST GIFT MY PARENTS gave to me was my faith. Certainly, as a young person I did not appreciate it at all. I did not understand why we had to say the family rosary virtually every night, among other things that were important to them but not to me. What I didn't realize then is that they were building a foundation for me. By their example, mostly my dad's quiet walk of faith, humility, and guidance, they gave me what has been the core of my adult life, faith in God. If not for my faith, I would not have survived the gut-wrenching challenges I've experienced. We all have challenges in life; however, when God is the center of your life, you can overcome anything.

I wanted to make sure that Gabriel knew what role faith played in my life and how it contributed to our success in pulling through our ordeal. He also had Rob around during those years as a positive role model, for which I was grateful. Rob, too, had to endure challenges during our time. While he was with the fire department, his struggles basically robbed his soul of his love and passion he had for the job. He desperately wanted to quit and never set foot on a fire truck again, but he made it past all that and retired as a captain after twenty-five years. He will tell you it is all because of his belief that God would get him (us) through it all.

I believed beyond a shadow of a doubt that the gift of time we were enjoying with my dad, who should have died two years earlier, was his reward for an honest life of dedication to God and the Church. One of the most beautiful things I admired in my father was that he was incredibly gifted and kind and giving to others, yet he had the humility of a saint. I am constantly told by others how he impacted their lives and how much they admired him. I see that humility in my brother, Richard, too.

Like them, Gabriel is multi-talented and has a kind heart. He will be a success at anything he wants to do if he works hard and believes in himself.

As always, Gabriel was, and is, the greatest gift God has given me, and it is a privilege and an honor to be his mother.

I was still praying that Gabriel's eyes would be open to the truth about his dad and me and that he would accept and live the truth so that our relationship would continue to heal and prosper. Things did continue to get better. Certainly, we went through all the "normal" growing pains that parents and teenagers endure, but I would happily take that any day over the issues and darkness of earlier years between us.

Gradually, Gabriel came to Rob and me letting us know how unhappy he was at Waters Edge High School, where his dad pushed him to attend and play ball. I was proud because it took courage to be honest about his feelings. He was growing up. Also, I believe it's important to understand that we must live with the outcomes of our decisions, no matter who influences us. That's how we learn that, no matter the influence, we need to make our own decisions and live with them. Gabe was doing that. If we allow others to influence us against what we know to be best for us, then we, not the other person, will suffer the consequences. Now that we knew this, we needed to settle on where he did want to go to school.

One evening I took Gabriel, now sixteen years old, to dinner and presented all of this to him. Imagine my surprise when he asked if he could go to a Christian school. So, the journey began!

We narrowed things down to three schools. After visits, shadowing, and meeting the football team, Gabriel ended up at St. Anthony's Catholic High School. The football team embraced him right away. I could not have been more thrilled, even though he questioned his faith, as we all do at times. Football made his transition as the "new kid" much smoother and easier. Gabriel started every game and played most of every game, if not all of them. It's a long story, but he found a backdoor way to get away from playing quarterback. It was what his dad wanted and expected of him, but it was way too much pressure, and he really shined as an outside linebacker. In one historic game, Gabe made the winning sack on the other team's quarterback to win the game in double overtime. We all went nuts with excitement! To think of how far he had come in every way. Life was good, and another answer to my prayers was playing out—that Gabriel would actually enjoy his last two years of high school before going off on his own to begin college.

God works wonders, that's for sure! I could only imagine how his senior year might go for him next.

That said, he had his share of fender benders (three, to be exact!) and a speeding ticket, which required me to take a court-ordered driving class with him. I did worry about his driving too fast and prayed he steered clear of any serious accidents. He did.

For Christmas we gave Gabe an electric razor. The funny thing was, he started growing a beard after we bought it for him, but he was excited about it. To end 2012 well, we had our annual (my mom's) family reunion party. The family rented the hall at St. Nicholas' Church for it because so many family members were there. We have an amazingly big and wonderful family, and

I Loved You More

because there are so many of us, we had to wear name tags! We are very blessed.

I remained Gabriel's biggest fan.

Chapter 37

CELEBRATIONS

2013–2014

THROUGH HIGH SCHOOL, Gabriel continued to evolve and change, and the things others told me about him made me so proud. He was selected as a peer leader at school, and soon I received an email from one of his teachers, Mr. Miller. He said he wanted to let me know of something Gabriel did that was so kind and would make me proud. While on lunch duty, he saw there was a boy who was "socially awkward." Apparently, he had Asperger's Syndrome. Gabriel invited him to sit at his table, and the boy just lit up. I wondered if Gabe realized how even small, kind gestures like that toward others can change their lives. You never know. There he was, captain of the football team, good looking, with lots of friends, and he had included this kid who had trouble fitting in.

I was so proud.

I Loved You More

Gabriel and I ended up in a very heavy talk one day about his dad and me and how Colby had gotten physical with me in the beginning of our marriage. When I told him how he grabbed me by the shoulders, shook me, and drew back to hit me before I deflected it, he didn't believe me. I was devastated. How could he think I would make something like that up? For years I didn't speak of it to anyone, and the rare times I did, I followed it with the statement that it was the only time Colby touched me, but there was still all the verbal, emotional and psychological abuse he put me through. I did not tell Gabe any of that, not yet.

Over time, as Gabriel grew and matured in his early twenties, I began to tell him about the struggle we had been through with his dad. Ultimately, I would give him the little box of letters I had been writing him all his life, so he could know the whole truth in his own time.

Rob and I knew that Gabriel would move out one day. His dad began pressuring him to move in with him when he was eighteen. There were many indicators that this was going on, including texts Colby would send Gabriel, which included only numbers. I asked Gabe what they meant, and initially he was not forthcoming. When pressed, he admitted that one number was the number of days until he was eighteen. We knew what that meant. The other number was how many days until Gabe, Colby, and Colby's new wife-to-be (number four) took yet another trip to Hawaii. I wondered if and when Gabriel would realize all the luxurious trips he was afforded with his dad were never paid for by him but by the women in his life.

One day, Gabriel finally talked to me about moving out. I'm proud to say I, once again, handled it pretty calmly because I was expecting it. I think Gabriel was shocked I handled it so well. It sounded like he was thinking about living with his dad. After talking to my brother about it, I realized it might be the only time in his life he could experience what living with his dad full-time was like and that maybe he would better appreciate what he had with Rob and me as a result. Once he left for college, coming home would always be like a honeymoon, and he would never know what it was like to live with Colby on a daily basis. And by summer's end, Gabe moved in with Colby.

During Gabriel's senior year, in the fall of 2013, they were undefeated in football, and they won the state championship! We also had a super birthday weekend for Gabriel's eighteenth birthday. We got him a nice leather jacket, and we celebrated with his grandparents, Aunt Loretta, and Uncle Steve, Loretta's husband. I made him a homemade frozen strawberry cheesecake. Gabriel was also given a microwave for college by his grandparents, along with cash, and everyone remarked about how happy and relaxed he seemed and how much more social he was with the family.

We started working on college applications with Gabe. Then things shifted yet again.

We can definitely see a behavior change in you but just with me since you have been living with your dad. I am in the dark on everything going on with college applications. The other night you had one of the football coaches from college over for dinner and never told me that he was coming or was in town. I had to hear it from your coach at St. Anthony's Catholic High. Seems the coach wanted to meet your parents, and I guess you dismissed the fact that I am one. When I asked you about it, you gave me lame excuses saying, "I thought I told you," and it didn't occur to me until now that in the beginning of the conversation when I asked you about it you said, "What, did you see it on my Twitter?" Seems if you had really told me the Twitter thing would not have come up. You continue to lie to me, and I fear you are turning out just like your father who is a habitual liar who wouldn't know the truth if it smacked him in the face.

Meanwhile, I started crying a lot, again, and for a while I could not figure out why. I wondered if maybe I was depressed, but that's not like me, to need to cry all the time for no reason. It dawned on me that it was because of Gabriel and how living with his dad had resurrected his negativity and bad behavior. I made an appointment to see my therapist, who I had not needed to see for almost two years at that point. I could hardly believe what was happening, and I kept wondering when Gabriel was going to wake up and acknowledge the truth about his father and what Colby was doing through his constant control and manipulation.

Meanwhile, I was still dealing with my dad and Loretta's cancer. Sometimes it was so overwhelming for me, too much, in fact.

Gabriel graduated from St. Anthony's Catholic High School with a 3.87 GPA and plans to attend a private college in North Carolina as well as play for their NCAA Division 1 football team. While the college did not award football scholarships, the coaches were so set on Gabe playing for them that they awarded him a $30,000 grant to offset the $45,000 tuition.

I know "God always has a plan," and sometimes "His time" doesn't jive with mine. I can see now that things happened when they were supposed to happen.

We had a big graduation party, and I made all the food, trying to make Gabriel's favorites. I got him a cake with his handsome senior picture on it too. It was a very happy time for me to see him continue to grow and, although sometimes very slowly, become his own person.

Rob and I orchestrated the arrangements for Gabe to go off to college—getting a U-Haul, packing up his stuff with him. I had to make sure he had everything he needed for his dorm room, and shopping for that was fun. Some of his dorm room stuff was given to him the previous Christmas, on his birthday, and at graduation, but there were still so many things to get in the end, not to mention food! We made several trips to BJ's Wholesale Club.

It's funny, once Gabriel left for college, so many of my friends asked how I was doing with him being gone. But I wasn't sad; I was so happy, deep inside, that Gabriel was beginning his life of independence and that he was away from his dad, finally. It was harder for me when he went to live with Colby for his senior year. Now I was so happy for him to have more freedom to discover himself and become his own person. We were also excited to go to his college football games in the fall.

Gabe's journey of true self-discovery was about to begin.

Chapter 38

COLLEGE OR BUST

August 6, 2014

Dear Gabriel,

Well, it's your BIG day, OK, another BIG day. You've had many in your short 18 years—your birth, your 1*st* birthday, your First Holy Communion, your "double-digit" birthday (10), your first day at the Gifted School, and your last day there, your first day of high school, your 18*th* birthday, your football state championship win, your prom, your graduation, not to mention all the other big days of your life—and now your first day of college. Wow, where did all those years go? For me, they blew by, but that comes with being older and the years getting shorter.

First, let me say that we are VERY PROUD of you. You have accomplished so much and have it in *you to be successful at whatever you do. Just always do your best. Give everything 100%, always, all the time. I have said this to you time and again and here it is:*

LISTEN TO YOUR HEART, FIND "<u>YOUR</u>" DREAMS, AND FOLLOW THEM

I know that you have some apprehensions about leaving home and going to college. However, you will be GREAT! You will make new friends, and you will keep those current friendships that are so important to you. It's the best of both worlds! And you guys have it so much easier these days with the Internet. It makes keeping in touch with friends a snap! We only had snail mail and the occasional phone call because long distance calls cost so much "back then." ☺ No kidding!

Just remember that nothing in this world comes easily. Everything worth achieving requires hard work, dedication, and commitment. Make up your mind NOW what you want for your future. Now is when you begin to lay the groundwork for your adult life because you are making your own decisions every day. Choose wisely, thoughtfully, and own those choices. Now that you are 18, there is no falling back on your parents or others. You are responsible for all your choices, so make the best ones you can. You will make mistakes. Own those too. It is freeing for your soul to admit when you falter, and others will have a greater respect for you if you do.

Believe in yourself, Gabriel! *We do! You have it in you to be anything you want to be and do anything*

I Loved You More

you dream! Go for it! We will always support you and be there for you to celebrate the good and to encourage you when the road gets tough. Call us anytime you need us. We love you!

Mom and Rob

Chapter 39

Dad

December 2014

RIGHT BEFORE LORETTA passed away, I spoke with her about our dad. I was with my dad all the time, especially toward the end. I was always taking him to his oncology appointments and his blood and platelet transfusions. We were together a lot, and I took advantage of that time to ask him things about his life, to talk to him, to tell him how I felt, and to tell him how much I loved him and what a great father he was. It was really a beautiful time together. I called them "Tuesdays with Dad" (like *Tuesdays with Morrie*) because it was mostly on Tuesdays. I told Loretta about my conversations with dad because a lot came out of them. We talked about that horrible incident when my dad executed the punishment on me. "You know, none of us ever talked about that again," I said, "and I never cleared the air with Dad because I felt horrible about what happened."

"Regina, Dad never blamed you for any of that," she replied. "He knew it wasn't your fault." Then she surprised me. "You know why Dad did your punishment, right?"

"What do you mean?"

"He was so afraid that mom was going to seriously hurt you because she was so furious and angry with you that he did it to protect you."

I cried. As a mother, I still can't comprehend how parents can inflict abuse like what my mother did to me on a child they are supposed to love. I was fifteen at the time, and I never talked about it with anyone other than Laura. It was so devastating for me because my father never did that to me prior to that day and didn't do it again. He was so good that all he had to do was raise his voice and we were like, "OK, we'll be good." There was never any emotional, psychological, or any other kind of abuse from him. Quite honestly, he was always encouraging and empowering with me.

My siblings and I have said to each other how remarkable it is that all five of us turned out to be such good people. That's a tribute to my dad. He was the balancing factor in our lives. None of us understood how he stayed with my mom, but all of us believe he did it to keep the family together. We all adored him.

When my dad was diagnosed with leukemia and given a year to live, people came out of the woodwork to tell us how he had impacted their lives. He was a remarkable man, and it was such a gift to be able to share with him some of the beautiful things we were being told he had done. It was a wonderful thing to come back to him and say, "Dad, did you know that these people said such nice things about you?" My father was a very humble man; he would just smile with a twinkle in his eye.

He lived five and a half years after his diagnosis—our miracle man, and one for the medical record books according to his oncologist because typically with AML at his age, life expectancy is about a year. His brother up in Canada died after eighteen months with the same leukemia. We were all devastated when my dad died. You're never ready for such a thing. He was such an incredible human being. I had friends who came to his viewing and his funeral who were crying because he had touched their lives. He touched so many lives.

My dad passed away on December 15, 2014.

Chapter 40

Epiphanies

2017

LORETTA LOST HER CANCER BATTLE on January 23, 2017, two years after Dad passed. She was the best godmother to Gabriel. It was just a few short months later that he had his epiphany about his dad. Her death devastated all of us, even more than my dad's because he lived a full life of eighty-four years, but she was only sixty when she passed. So, in the darkness of mourning her death, came this beautiful surprise when Gabe had his realizations.

 After a year at college and suffering another football concussion, Gabe decided in 2015 to go to community college to help bring his grades back up after they dropped due to the injury. He went to college for one year here in Virginia Beach, earning straight A's, only for his dad to pressure him to move to New York and go to another community college there. A week before spring break 2017, Gabriel started sharing with me via texts that he was realizing more and more how right I had been about things, but he didn't give any specifics as to what those things were, and I didn't push.

When he was home for spring break, we got to talk. His long, brown, massively curly hair was halfway down his back—longer than mine! On that visit he was super talkative, probably making up for lost time in his younger years. Gabriel came home kind, considerate, and thoughtful. I looked him over and thought how much he was my "mini-me," given how often people say how much we look alike. Very cool!

After choir practice one night, I went upstairs and sat on the bed to talk and catch up with him.

"Mom," he said, totally unsolicited, "I know I idolized my dad my whole life, but I want you to know I don't idolize him anymore. I know that kids are supposed to grow up and want to be like their parents, but I don't want to be anything like my dad. I still love him; he's my dad, but I know who he is, flaws and all."

I remained completely still until he finished talking, trying to keep from any big expression on my face. I just listened and felt his pain as he spoke. As I laid in bed that night, silent tears streaming down my face, I thanked God for this miracle I had been waiting for so very long.

In that same conversation, we talked about how stressed Gabriel had been about life, moving to New York, and his dad moving there with him with the promise he'd be working. Gabe was bartending while going to school full time and talked about how he would get a paycheck for $800, and suddenly he would only have $150 because his dad would take Gabe's money for bills. His dad was still not working. He was supposed to have started the previous August, but he didn't start a job until January.

"Remember that car my dad promised to buy me this year, the Jeep, if I agreed to take out student loans for his share of my college tuition?" he asked. "Well, I'm sure you realized before me that I'm never going to get that car. When Dad was talking about buying curtains and drapes for our apartment, I told him we first needed to buy new cell phones. Dad didn't pay the bill on the previous cell phones we had, so we got locked out of them being activated by any other carrier. I think I'm more responsible with money than Dad. I know what priorities need to be paid first before luxuries like curtains or drapes. And Dad still owes me the money he has been taking from me."

It was all so much to hear, what Colby was still putting Gabe through. The next morning, I looked at Gabe and said, "Buddy, I have prayed your whole life that you would one day come see to the truth about your dad. While I am relieved it has happened far sooner than I anticipated, I am sad for you, that you know the truth about your dad, because…well, he's your dad."

Gabriel had his epiphany about his dad at age twenty-one, instead of after age twenty-five, when multiple therapists and doctors suggested it would happen—if it ever did—after the frontal lobe was fully developed because that controls our thinking and is our reasoning zone where we problem solve. It came much sooner than expected. It happened for him around the same age I decided to break the cycle of my childhood abuse. This was yet another parallel between our lives.

In May, Gabriel returned my call to touch base and catch up. We talked for an hour and a half, very unusual for us. We had a deep conversation about his future, his current job situation, who he was dating, and his living situation with his dad. He had an offer at the bar where he worked to rent out their basement for $700 a month. As much as he wanted his independence, he was more on a mission to save money, get out from living with his dad, and pursue his own life.

"Mom, in New York, people often give me a hard time about how I say 'Yes, sir' and 'Yes, ma'am' to people. Some people get offended at it, but I tell them, 'That it is the way I am, and I am not going to change.' It has actually become my schtick."

"Tell them, 'You can take the boy out of the South but you can't take the South out of the boy,'" I replied.

We also talked about how we teach people how to treat us by how we treat them, and if we treat people with respect, we will receive respect in return. I went on to say that if we treat people like shit, they will treat us like shit.

"Yes, just like my dad," he said without flinching. "I'm sure you have experienced how he treats people, like customer service people."

"Yes," I said, "I have more than experienced it."

"I often wonder how those encounters affect that other person's life after my dad has done that to someone."

After a moment, Gabriel continued. "Mom, I'm sorry for giving you such a hard time when I was younger. Thank you for raising me with respect and for teaching me how to treat other people with respect."

Validation.

In June, Gabriel was home for two days. We talked for over two hours, half the time out back by the pool.

"I'm not really very close with Dad anymore," he said. "I catch myself sometimes in how I will do or say something, that I'll behave how Dad does. I know I can manipulate people in conversations like my dad does without them knowing it. I don't want to be like that, Mom." I told him the fact that he was even able to identify that behavior and work on correcting it was a huge step. This told me he had insight.

Gabe turned and looked at me. "Dad says he was arrested years ago and that it was you who had him arrested. Is that true?"

"Gabe," I said, "your Mom-Mom thought the same thing. The truth is your dad was arrested for failing to show up to court. It's that simple."

When he had to leave, it was clear he was going to miss me, not just by his words but by his big bear hug and his look of affection for his mother on his face. I could feel us getting closer all the time. Wow, it felt so good to be in this place with him!

In October 2017, Gabriel came home mid-month for a concert festival. We sat downstairs while he had coffee and talked about life. Our conversation moved upstairs to my recording studio where we sat on the floor and talked for an hour and a half. I continued to carefully share things that I had kept from him when he was younger.

He was a bit frustrated. "Mom, I feel like I'm screwed up to a certain degree because one parent shared everything with me, and the other one shared nothing. All I know is what was being told to me, which was by my father. But I'm mature enough now to be told the truth if I wasn't before."

"As screwed up as you feel right now, and as distant as you continue to become from your father for the man you see him to be, can you imagine how royally effed up you would be if I allowed you to live with him before the age of eighteen?" I asked. "I gave in and let you live with him at age eighteen only because I knew it would be your only opportunity to live with your dad full time and see for yourself what he was truly like and the person he was on a daily basis. You can't hide your true self from someone twenty-four/seven, but you can hide it somewhat when you only see each other occasionally."

"Mom, everyone lied to me when they said I would have a choice when I was thirteen or fourteen to go live with Dad."

"Gabriel, that was the truth; however, Mr. Garrison took the stand at 11:45 p.m. in court on one of our last two trial dates, expressed to the judge that he felt like he was about to betray his client and that he was about to do something he had never done in his entire career, which was change his position. He said that all the testimony and witnesses that had been present provided information that he felt would be detrimental to you, and he could not in good conscience suggest you live with your father."

Gabriel was stunned to hear that because up until then he felt like everyone had lied to him. It was also the first time I ever explained to him how often over the years I'd beaten myself up for misjudging his father's character because I felt like I had traveled the world and was a good judge of people. I told him my therapist had to tell me repeatedly that's why narcissists are so good at what they do. I also told him that his dad is a narcissist and what that meant, that a narcissist will say or do anything necessary in any situation to get what they want out of it. I went on to say that my therapist said his dad is such a severe sociopath that he would throw his own mother under the bus to save himself with no remorse. Sadly, he ended up doing that to Gabe repeatedly by taking his money or borrowing it and Gabe having to ask constantly for it back, among other transgressions.

I was worried at one point that I had shared too much with him. He seemed visibly upset. "Now I have a lot of things to think about on my drive back to New York about someone that I already don't like very much," he said.

Later that night when I checked to make sure he got back to New York safely, he texted me the following:

> I love you Mom. And where our relationship is these days. Have a good night!

Epilogue

"That's the funny thing about time. It is only in looking back that it's easy to connect the dots. To see exactly why everything needed to happen the way that it did."

—Rebecca Serle

2019

IT WAS CHRISTMAS 2019, AND GABE was home for the holidays. After retiring from the US Air Force and the Virginia Beach Fire Department, Rob was on to his next venture. He had recently started a new business and asked Gabe if he wanted to take a ride with him to the warehouse to see the operations. Gabe was excited to check things out. On the way to the warehouse, they passed Waters Edge High School, the one Gabe's dad pushed him to attend in his freshman year for football. Just down the street from the school was a McDonald's.

"Man, those were some tough times for me because my dad would drop me every morning at that McDonald's, sometimes before they were even open," Gabe said. "I would have to sit there and spend up to an hour doing my homework and getting breakfast, while Dad drove to his teaching job."

Because Gabe was in the school's Global Studies Academy program, he could have been bussed to school from any place in the city, so leaving him there was totally unnecessary—in fact, the bus even drove right by my house.

"I had to go there after school sometimes too," Gabe continued, "and wait for my dad. These other kids would show up and hang out there, and they were not the crowd I wanted to be around because I hated that."

For Colby it was better to subject his son to that than allow him more time with me. We were never aware this was going on.

I DON'T SEE Colby anymore. I have no reason to. He texted recently, but I didn't know who it was at first because he has had more phone number changes than anyone on earth due to non-payment to the carriers. One of the things I learned is to remove the poison and to disconnect, if and as soon as you can, when you detect personality traits like Colby's, like those of a narcissist and sociopath. If you can't, sometimes all you can do is keep notes, insist on written communication, journal, and refuse personal contact or live phone calls. These things come in handy, even if not accepted by a court. One of the things that helped me along the way was that Colby knew I was keeping a record of everything. When narcissists know this, their attitude might change, or not.

I did catch a quick glimpse of him online not too long ago. It seemed like the years and the stress had caught up to him at last. No longer the preppy law student I married, he was disheveled, worn out, and weathered but not in a good way like Harrison Ford. He looked pudgy, out of shape, stodgy, and I believe from what Gabe and others have told me, he has no real friends to speak of. No one sticks around once they figure him out. That internet search also yielded a discovery that he has misrepresented himself on a website called, "Together We Serve", listing his former rank in the Navy as a Lieutenant Commander, when in fact, he was just a Lieutenant when he got out.

Before sending my book off to a copy editor, I decided to give Colby a call. We had not spoken in almost four years, and I was extremely anxious and fearful over making the call. I considered taking a Xanax to calm my racing heart. I knew he was aware I was writing a book, and I assumed he was not too happy about it. He said I caught him off guard by calling and thought for sure I had butt dialed him by accident.

Colby was very emotional, disclosing his remorse for the pain he caused me and his regrets over the loss of our marriage, and he said he did not want to cause me further pain. I was in shock and didn't know how to respond because history has taught me not to trust him. I had to remind myself that he had used tears to manipulate me many times before. But he said he had been working on himself over the past few years, trying to be a better person, and that his life was in a better place. It was a surprisingly good conversation, and my heart rate eased. I really wanted to believe him, but I'm at a point in my life where it doesn't affect me anymore, and quite honestly, I just don't care. It's on him and him alone. Having said that, Gabriel means everything to me, and having the best version of his dad in his life is what's most important. I hope, for Gabe's sake, that any positive changes his dad has made are sincere, genuine, and lasting.

That night I was the cantor at mass. When I walked up to receive Communion, the organist began playing an instrumental arrangement of Psalm 27. He had no knowledge of the history of Psalm 27 for me. My breathing hitched, and tears betrayed my eyes as I tried to maintain my composure because I had to sing a hymn once I returned to the microphone. I flashed back eleven years to 2010 and that first feeling when I knew God was speaking to me, when He assured me that, no matter what, Gabe would be OK. At mass, in that moment, I felt God was telling me to breathe deeply and keep the faith, because once again, everything was going to be OK.

Back when Gabriel was in high school, around 2013, Colby was able to secure another woman in pursuit of the good life, I suppose. Wife-to-be number four was Jane. She was a pretty, blue-eyed blonde, tall, average build, nice smile, sweet, with a somewhat quiet demeanor. She financially supported Colby when he went through school to become a physician's assistant (he has been calling himself a "doctor," since he got his *juris doctorate* from law school, which is a doctorate degree but in no way justifies calling oneself "doctor," if it means one is presumed to be a medical doctor). In one of his online profiles as a physician' assistant, he still misrepresents himself as "Dr." I was also told he convinced her to rent out the townhome she owned, so they (she) could rent a beach house. Apparently, he had promised to pay half of the cost to live there, which, of course, he has yet to do.

I ran into Jane recently. I recalled she had told me something a while back, and I didn't have the facts straight, so I asked her, again. She told me that at some point when they were together, their cell phones synced, merging their contact lists. There were a lot of names and numbers of women she didn't recognize. So, she decided to create a fake account to be able to research the numbers through a website called Backpage. She discovered that many of Colby's contact numbers matched up on this site and appeared to be escorts. I believed his behavior in this arena had greatly escalated from that day long ago when I first caught him on the porn website and a few years later Renee discovered those pages of escort profiles in his office.

Healing is a process. Often we compartmentalize and want to shut away the darkness of painful experiences. We realized that Loretta had blocked out a lot of her abuse when Richard and I told her, the year before she passed, about how we hid in our rooms and cried when Mom criticized her about her weight.

She looked at us, hesitating at first, with sadness in her eyes as if searching inside. "Wow," she said. "I had forgotten about all of that."

Self-preservation.

In the conversations a few years ago that ensued with my siblings about what Mom had said and done to all of us, we were all now on the same page. She abused all of us, but she abused Loretta and me the worst—and I got it the worst of all. In our new and vulnerable transparency, this was confirmed by all four of my siblings. While unsavory, finding out that I was not crazy and that the abuse was as bad as it seemed helped to confirm my own sense of reality as reliable. Progress.

A couple of years ago, before Loretta passed, my brother, Richard, also said something to me that I never said out loud to anybody, not even my husband. "I think Mom's jealous of you." I couldn't believe he said that because I never articulated it to anyone before. I started feeling that way because I resurrected my career in 2011. Yet, she had been on Broadway, and I was never on Broadway. Huh.

In the last five years of my father's illness, I did so much for my parents, and I was at their place all the time. Even before I could get up the stairs at their condo, my mom would be at the top of the stairs insulting or criticizing me, speaking negatively about something. Later, my dad would say to me in private, "Oh, just be like a duck. Just let it roll off your back."

"Dad, every time I walk in this door, I start with a clean slate, and she just goes after me," I replied. My brothers couldn't believe it because I was doing a lot for her, for them. Why would you be so mean to the person who was helping her out so much, more than anyone else?

But you can't change the past, and as a child of a narcissist, you can't change them or their behavior. All you can do once you are older is choose to navigate forward, learn from all the bad, and commit to breaking the cycle, which involves identifying the abuse.

I worry that Gabe will always have to deal with the fallout of his narcissist father's behavior, just like I have had to continue to work through it with my mother. Even as she is nearing the end of her life, she regularly uses emotional blackmail on me with her constant claims of, "I will most likely die before you get around to calling me back," gaslighting me by saying, "I'm embarrassed to tell my brother and sisters how horribly my daughter treats me," and "I forgive you" when I'd done nothing wrong, and she was the one emotionally wounding me. It continues to be very painful for me despite how much I try and tell myself that it no longer affects me. That's why ongoing therapy is important because the journey never truly ends. However, once the person is no longer physically present, it becomes easier to place the painful memories in the rearview mirror.

Gabriel amazes me all the time. The fact that he had his epiphanies about his dad at the young age of twenty-one with no information or solicitation from me is nothing short of a miracle. He is very smart, aware, and sensitive. Imagine my shock when he came to me, unsolicited, and said he no longer idolized his dad, that he wanted to be nothing like him, that from his dad he has learned "how not to be". In time and with reflection, I have learned the very same thing about my mother. And I learned it from Gabriel. I believe God was always guiding both of us on this journey. During that time when Gabriel was a teen, hated me, and treated me horribly because of the grooming from his dad, I looked at him one day in the hallway and said, "My God is bigger than your dad!" I meant it because I knew at some point God was going to get us out of this mess.

Ever since the first "reveal" by Gabriel, he continues to talk with me a lot, and I cherish those sometimes-lengthy conversations. Many times I feel as though we are both making up for all the years we didn't really have that gift because of his inner turmoil and conflict of loyalty to Colby. He has told me about things he has come to realize about his dad—how Colby treats people, disrespects them, and uses them. It's clear Gabriel is the antithesis of all of that, and I could not be more relieved! Because of the many years of being controlled by his dad, he does continue to struggle with what his future holds. It deeply saddens me when he says he has no dreams, but that's because his dad mapped out his whole life and future for him and never allowed Gabe to dream beyond what Colby dictated for him. Now my prayers for wisdom are for Gabe, that he will be able to discern the path that will make him happy and bring joy to his life both personally and professionally. I believe that because of all he has and continues to learn from his life experiences, he is going to make some lucky woman a wonderful husband one day, if that is what he chooses for himself.

It's an ongoing recovery. While I don't think I'll ever get to a place of forgiveness because of how deeply he hurt my child, I feel nothing for Colby now. How did I recover? I went to therapy, but most of that was trying to deal with how to handle him relative to what he was doing to my son and how to navigate it. I'm still in therapy. Sometimes I'll go a year and not see my therapist. Then I'll need to check in for a tune-up because something will happen. I've been seeing him a lot lately because of things that I've realized about my childhood abuse that relate back to marrying somebody like Colby. So, therapy has played a positive role, as has having a great support network of friends who I can just dump on. They don't necessarily always know what to say, but by listening, they help me get it out. In the end, it was always more about protecting Gabriel than anything that I needed personally.

Do whatever you want to me. Just don't touch my freaking child.

Seriously, I was always laser-focused on protecting Gabe, and it was always about that, but recovery and healing is an ongoing journey. Back then we didn't have the broad use of the terms, "narcissist" and "sociopath," like we do today. Today, we have so much more access to research, to information at our fingertips at all hours of the day. We can find out about this behavior, this personality type, and we can identify it. Heck, I didn't even know what it was called back then. I just knew it was abusive. Now I feel like I could spot a narcissist a mile away.

Gabriel can too, I believe.

"Mom, I'm scared to death that my dad has burned every bridge in his life, and he's going to die, and I'm going to get stuck with $100,000 of his debt," Gabriel said to me one day.

"First of all," I replied, "you are not responsible for his debt. It's his estate, and he will probably die penniless because he most likely won't have any money. You won't be responsible. There'll be a funeral, but your uncles will probably have to step up and help with that because they're his brothers, and you don't have that kind of money."

We sat quietly for a bit after that. Gabriel had ridden his motorcycle down from New York City to see me and Rob for a visit at our home in Virginia Beach.

"Hey, Mom, do you have that first electric guitar of mine?" he asked.

When he was little, I had gotten Gabriel a Baby Taylor guitar when he started guitar lessons. His dad always had to one-up me, so he went and bought a used electric guitar at a garage sale that supposedly was played by Frank Zappa.

"When you got my stuff from Jane's house last year, did she have my Frank Zappa electric guitar?"

"Oh my gosh!" I said, "I didn't know she had your guitar!"

"Well, it's probably gone forever then because that means it was in a storage unit that my dad lost."

"What do you mean *lost*? You mean lost because of non-payment, so they confiscated everything?"

"Yes."

"Oh, wow! What else was in there of yours?"

"I don't want to tell you. It'll just upset you."

I paused before speaking. "I won't verbalize what I want to say about your dad because that's the one thing I have never done is said those things to you, but you can only imagine my sentiments right now. It totally sucks that he did that to you."

"It's all good, Mom," he said. "They're just things. They tend to be lost with time anyway, and I see it as an opportunity to rid myself of a little more attachment, which is a healthy practice. It's a central tenet of Buddhism and in meditation, but that's a whole other thing."

As Gabriel explained that, I thought, *This goes to his maturity.*

Then he went on a long tangent about Buddhism. "It's mislabeled as a religion. It's really more of a philosophical practice rooted in spirituality. But there is an initial Buddha who is credited with starting the movement and attaining Buddhahood, synonymous with enlightenment. It's something everyone can achieve and should strive for, but on paper and in practice, it more resembles a philosophy class at the local college than it does a church service. Nothing and no one is worshiped is the main point I'm driving at. And with that in mind, it's entirely compatible with Christianity and almost all other monotheistic or polytheistic religions." This was my brainchild kid. "Prayer equals meditation, except that prayer is often directed outwards while meditation is often reflected inwards."

Boom! Telling your Catholic parent that you're into Buddhism! But it did make sense. I told him I meditated, and I believed in letting things go. "That's a healthy perspective on losing a lot of your life mementos because your dad's an ass and can't pay his bills—letting it go. Gabe, you can't change the past. You can only navigate through it and choose better for yourself. You know I've said your whole life to follow *your* dreams, not the ones dictated to you by your dad. Wherever your life takes you, and whatever you do, make a difference in the world and do good." ,

We smiled at each other. I felt like we were really in tune and that it was time. I decided there and then to give Gabriel the letters I'd been writing, sealing, and decorating since he was a one-year-old. I decided to give him the letters because he'd had his epiphany about his dad and because he was going to be twenty-five in October. I believed he was finally ready to receive them, but I couldn't wait a few more months for that birthday. *I'm going to give him all the letters now as an early birthday present.* He didn't know I'd been writing and saving these letters for him. He knew I had documents, but he had never seen them.

At the time, Gabe was visiting us in Virginia with plans to move here very soon. He'd been living in New York because his dad dragged him there three years earlier. He manipulated Gabe to move with him to New York the same way he had with me all those years earlier.

Giving him those letters came far sooner than I expected, but things between us were already so much better than I could have hoped. When you've lived in such a darkness with your child, and you stay the course and you're still disciplining, you're still the bad guy, it freaking sucks. But I'd been looking forward to the day Gabe could handle all of this and could understand why I did the things I'd done.

I thought about Saul, my attorney, who handled my custody battle and how he said something to me that was so important: "Have faith in the foundation you have built for him because the time you have with your child *after* they turn eighteen is much longer than before they turn eighteen."

Gabriel was thinking for himself now. He had made the decision in early January, and by late February he told me, "I still haven't told my dad I'm moving back to Virginia. It's not going to be a fun conversation, and I'm not looking forward to it. I still haven't even given him his Christmas gift, Mom." He hadn't seen his dad, and they lived right down the street from each other because Gabe had finally moved out on his own.

My kid and I went through all this shit. He hated me at one point, and now we are so close. On this recent visit home for a weekend, his motorcycle broke down, and he ended up staying for a week. Then he told me, "Well, I'm not going to leave the day before Mother's Day," and he left the following Monday.

While he was here, we talked so much. I overheard him on the phone calling about a clutch or some part he needed for his motorcycle. I was touched by it. I didn't say anything right away, but Rob came in the room, and when Gabriel made his next call, I told him he needed to listen to how Gabe was speaking to people. "He's so polite and respectful."

I know I shouldn't sound shocked at that because I certainly taught him to be that way, but when you know that the other parent is the antithesis of what you're trying to teach, you always wonder what gets through and what sticks.

The following night we were having dinner. "Gabriel, I have to tell you, you were so polite on the phone and so respectful," I said. "And I'm sorry I sound shocked . . ."

"No, I know, Mom," he said. "My dad is an asshole to everybody. He's an asshole to the Burger King clerk, and he's an asshole to people in general. I mean, he's just like that."

So, Gabriel had identified that.

"I think I learned a lot of how *not to be* by watching his horrible treatment of people," he continued.

"Well," I said, "I'd like to think that you learned *how to be* because that's how I taught you, and that's the example Rob and I have given you."

After all we'd been through together, it was so satisfying, so gratifying, and so reassuring.

Recently, I was telling my hairdresser about it.

"How old is your son?" he asked.

"He's twenty-four, almost twenty-five."

"That's still pretty young in today's day and age to conduct himself that way."

"I know, but he's always been so mature for his age. That's why he dates older women." We both laughed!

This journey has been about being a parent and making tougher choices because I love my child more. In the end I could only hope it all played out, and he became a better person.

When I started writing him those letters when he was just a year old, they were milestones and cute little things he did or said. In time, they became communications of my heart to him about all that his dad was putting us through, all the things I kept from him to protect him, all the hateful ugliness we were living with. I knew I could not give them to him until he was "ready." What *ready* meant, I didn't know. I didn't know if it would be when he got married one day, when he had his first child, or after I died.

Initially, I gave my sister the instructions on how and when to give them to him if I passed away early and to be sure he was ready to read the truths in those letters. But Loretta passed away, so Rob was the next one tasked to do so in the event of my death. Thankfully, I was able to give him the gift of letters this year. It was a beautiful privilege I had hoped to have. I felt he was mature enough and enlightened enough to "all things Colby" to get more truths and hidden secrets from me. He had a cross-country trip planned on his motorcycle before he officially moved back to Virginia Beach and began to work his way up the ladder for Rob's company. It was the perfect time to give them to him because he would have lots of quiet time on each of his travel stops to read them.

It was time, and it was very cool to give him the letters.

I handed him the beautifully gift-wrapped box with the following note inside on top of the stack of letters.

Gabriel Anthony Baxter

1995 - 2014

Your Life...

...from my  to yours

Love, Mom

"Mom, I think this is the most thoughtful gift I, in my whole life, will ever get," he said as he hugged me tight, as if he didn't want to let go.

He was very excited to read them as soon as he was alone.

"Gabe," I said, feeling like I should forewarn him, "I just recently read one paragraph from a letter I wrote in 2008, and it wasn't very radiant of you and your behavior. I think you have to understand it's part of the journey of life. Sometimes your kids are little shits."

"No, Mom, I get it. I understand, and that's OK."

"And they really are from my heart to yours."

As he smiled at me, his beautiful blue eyes expressed genuine, total love for me, his mother. My heart felt a comforting warmth I don't think I had ever felt before. We all walked outside into the miraculously bright sunshine and cloudless blue sky. There was a slight breeze that made Gabe's long curly locks flutter in the wind, just like mine. Gabe tied the treasured box of letters to the back of his motorcycle on the passenger seat with his luggage. Precious cargo. After another prolonged hug in the driveway, Rob and I stood arm in arm as we watched him ride away to continue his journey of life and self-discovery.

~ The End ~

Acknowledgements

MY TREASURED GIFT FROM GOD, my son, who has grown into a man who I am beyond proud of, you continue to impress me every day. Thank you. Your kind heart, empathy, and compassion for others and your ownership of your place and choices in this world are something to behold (not to mention your handsome looks!). I appreciate your love and support on this journey we survived and for selflessly giving me your blessing to move forward with this book because you respected my calling to help others. I love you to the moon and back—and then some!

Seth, the MBNA colleague of mine who stood in my cubicle that day and changed my and my son's life forever for the better by simply saying, "You may want to write that down," thank you.

Thanks also to my son's guardian ad litem, former president of the Virginia Bar Association, for literally saving my son's life by speaking the truth. As his attorney, you made it clear at the onset that Gabe was your top priority. You lived by that, especially on that fateful day when you changed your legal position about what was best for Gabriel. That courage, insight, and wisdom changed his life for the better going forward. I will be forever grateful to you for your sincere commitment to my son.

Thanks to my attorney and friend for your legal counsel in all my custody battles, which ultimately led to our friendship of more than two decades. Thank you for always reminding me to have faith in the foundation I gave Gabriel and to see "the bigger picture."

Thanks to my therapist who started out as a co-parenting counselor/therapist and ended up being my personal therapist for the past fifteen years. Just when I thought I no longer needed you regularly, I disclosed my childhood abuse to you for the first time while writing this book. Now you have more work to do with me. You were monumentally instrumental in helping me navigate not only dealing with my ex, protecting my son, and preserving our relationship, but in all the growing pains of a blended family when I remarried!

To my beautiful sister and three handsome brothers for your love and unending support through this journey of life, thank you. You have no idea how important it was for me that you confirmed my deeply painful memories of childhood abuse and for stating that you each endured much of the same. While it is not a badge of honor that I wish to wear, thank you for validating that, of the five of us, Loretta and I got it the worst and that I, by far, got *the* worst of it and still do. I know it sounds nuts, but that acknowledgement helps me deal with the abuse a little better and know that I am not crazy.

My husband, Rob, the love of my life! You have been my rock through so many difficult times on this journey. You have been my biggest cheerleader and the driving force that led me to get back up on stage and perform again. You were and still are the best role model for my son to see how a woman should be treated with respect, love, compassion, and as an equal partner. Your example showed him the meaning of hard, honest work. Most importantly, you and Gabriel have built a beautiful relationship that continues to evolve into something I always dreamed of for him in a father figure. Thank you for that, for being you, and for loving us.

John, the cruise ship passenger turned friend (you know who you are!) who helped me realize that being "sensitive" is a gift, not a curse, forever changed my life and helped me see that I was not damaged goods, thank you. You are a beautiful human being!

I Loved You More

Rodney, my editor, who took over after I penned the first ninety pages through countless tears and without whom this book may never have come to complete fruition. Thank you for collaborating with me to convert my life's work of journals, emails, letters, and legal documents into a thought-provoking story that I know will help so many others who are trying to navigate the difficult road of dealing with a narcissistic ex and choosing to love their children more.

Last, and certainly not least, it's probably clear through this book, that my faith is literally what got me through these twenty plus years of trials. From the depths of my heart, I thank my dad for his humble and quiet walk of faith, which was the truest and most sincere example of how to live. I never doubted his love for me, ever. His ability to make me believe in myself, even when I didn't, was beyond any gift I could ever have imagined! I conquered so many of life's challenges because of his unending support and encouragement! I can still hear his words today, even on my journey with this book. "You can do anything you set your mind to!" I hope that, despite revealing raw truths in this book, *my* truths, that he is looking down on me and still proud of his baby girl.

About the Author

Author Photo © Stacey Pryce, Cute E's Photography

REGINA ROSSI VALENTINE made her singing debut at the tender age of five in a church talent show and has been entertaining audiences ever since. In addition to her college accolades at UNC Chapel Hill, she went on to perform at Opryland USA and on several cruise lines and scored many leading roles in regional theaters, where she ultimately earned her Actor's Equity Status. After walking away from a successful career for marriage (the one that didn't work out) and family, it was twenty years before she resurrected her performance and voiceover career full-time in 2011 to a degree that she did not think possible at that point in her life. She has been thrilled to perform with multiple Broadway stars over the past few years.

You can learn more about Regina's life on the stage and see some live performances at www.ReginaRossi.com.

www.ingramcontent.com/pod-product-compliance
Lightning Source LLC
Chambersburg PA
CBHW050311120526
44592CB00014B/1859